D0970288

Christopher Isherwood

MYTH AND ANTI-MYTH

Columbia University Press    New York
1978

# Paul Piazza

# Christopher Isherwood:

# MYTH

# AND

# ANTI-MYTH

823
I79 gp

**Library of Congress Cataloging in Publication Data**

Piazza, Paul, 1941–

Christopher Isherwood: myth and anti-myth.

Bibliography: p.

Includes index.

1. Isherwood, Christopher, 1904–

Criticism and interpretation.

PR6017.S5Z8    823'.9'12    77-14271

ISBN 0-231-04118-7

Columbia University Press

New York    Guildford, Surrey

Copyright © 1978 Columbia University Press

All rights reserved

Printed in the United States of America

Acknowledgment is made to the following for permission to quote from copyrighted material: to David Higham Associates Limited and to Little, Brown and Co. in association with the Atlantic Monthly Press, for extracts from John Lehmann's *In My Own Time: Memoirs of a Literary Life,* copyright © 1955, 1960, 1966, 1969 by John Lehmann; to The Marvell Press, England, for the quotation from "Poetry of Departures" by Philip Larkin, reprinted from *The Less Deceived;* to Harcourt Brace Jovanovich, Inc., for an extract from T. S. Eliot's "The Waste Land," reprinted from *Collected Poems 1909–1962;* to Random House, Inc., and Faber and Faber Ltd., for extracts from W. H. Auden's "The Model" and "Another Time," from *The Collected Poetry of W. H. Auden,* "Address for a Prize Day," from *The Orators: An English Study,* and "Atlantis," "Lullaby," and "A New Age," from *Selected Poetry of W. H. Auden;* to Random House, Inc., for extracts from *The Ascent of F-6,* by W. H. Auden and Christopher Isherwood, and *Journey to a War,* by W. H. Auden and Christopher Isherwood; to Farrar, Straus & Giroux, Inc., for extracts from Christopher Isherwood's *Chrisopher and His Kind,* copyright © 1976 by Christopher Isherwood; to Simon and Schuster, Inc., for extracts from Christopher Isherwood's *Down There on a Visit,* copyright © 1959, 1961 by Christopher Isherwood, *A Meeting by the River,* copyright © 1967 by Christopher Isherwood, and *Kathleen and Frank,* copyright © 1971 by Christopher Isherwood.

To Louise

University Libraries
Carnegie Mellon University
Pittsburgh PA 15213-3890

# CONTENTS

# A NOTE ON THE TEXTS

The following abbreviations are used in the text when I am quoting from Isherwood's works. When the first edition is not used, the date of the original publication is given in parentheses. In all cases, I refer to Isherwood's American publishers.

### I. NOVELS

AC  *All the Conspirators.* New York: New Directions, 1958 (1928).

M   *The Memorial.* Norfolk, Connecticut: New Directions, 1946 (1932).

N   *The Last of Mr. Norris.* In *The Berlin Stories.* New York: New Directions, 1954 (1935).

GB  *Goodbye to Berlin.* In *The Berlin Stories.* New York: New Directions, 1954 (1939).

PV  *Prater Violet.* New York: Random House, 1945.

WE  *The World in the Evening.* New York: Random House, 1954.

V   *Down There on a Visit.* New York: Simon and Schuster, 1962.

SM  *A Single Man.* New York: Simon and Schuster, 1964.

R   *A Meeting by the River.* New York: Simon and Schuster, 1967.

### II. AUTOBIOGRAPHY

LS  *Lions and Shadows.* Norfolk, Connecticut: New Directions, 1947 (1938).

KF  *Kathleen and Frank*. New York: Simon and Schuster, 1971.

CK  *Christopher and His Kind 1929–1939*. New York: Farrar, Straus and Giroux, 1976.

### *III*. BIOGRAPHY

RD  *Ramakrishna and His Disciples*. New York: Simon and Schuster, 1965.

### *IV*. PLAYS (with W. H. Auden)

D  *The Dog Beneath the Skin*. In *Two Great Plays by W. H. Auden and Christopher Isherwood*. New York: Random House, 1959 (1935).

F6  *The Ascent of F 6*. In *Two Great Plays by W. H. Auden and Christopher Isherwood*. New York: Random House, 1959 (1936).

F  *On the Frontier*. New York: Random House, 1939 (1938).

### *V*. TRAVEL

J  *Journey to a War* (with W. H. Auden). New York: Random House, 1939.

CC  *The Condor and the Cows*. New York: Random House, 1948.

### *VI*. COLLECTIONS

E  *Exhumations*. New York: Simon and Schuster, 1966.

# ACKNOWLEDGMENTS

I wish to thank the following for their significant contributions to this book:

John D. Russell, of the University of Maryland, for first suggesting Isherwood as a subject and for his dogged insistence on clarity and correctness in the writing of this book

The Reverend Edward J. Romagosa, S. J., for being, to use Isherwood's description of E. M. Forster, "my absolute guru"

J. F. Gammell, Headmaster of Repton, Isherwood's public school, for giving me access to early issues of *The Reptonian*

Doris and Leslie Hider, of St. Albans, England, for their friendship and hospitality

William F. Bernhardt, Assistant Executive Editor of Columbia University Press, for accepting the manuscript; Carolyn G. Heilbrun, for recommending its publication; and David Diefendorf, for his expert editing

Canon Charles Martin, Headmaster of St. Albans School for Boys, Washington, D. C., and my colleagues and students there, for their encouragement and interest

Molly Emler and Roylene Sims, for their fast, flawless typing of the manuscript

My parents, family, and my wife's mother, for cheering me on

My wife, Louise, for her encouragement, criticism, corrections, and countless readings and rereadings of the manuscript.

*Washington, D.C.*                                        PAUL PIAZZA
*July 1977*

Christopher Isherwood

MYTH AND ANTI-MYTH

# Chiefly about
# ~ Christopher ~

*Kathleen and Frank,* Christopher Isherwood's biography of his parents, and his more recent autobiography, *Christopher and His Kind, 1929–1939,* do not resemble the valedictions one might expect from a writer in his late sixties and early seventies. Rather, autobiography as Isherwood writes it—diffuse, candid, and as complex in its point of view as a Conrad or a James novel—is not an end, but an exuberant, sometimes playful, and altogether unexpected beginning.

For the first time in a literary career that reaches back more than half a century, Isherwood conceals himself neither behind his impassive camera nor behind the subtle blanket of his lucid yet evasive prose. The "Christopher" in these later works is not at all the earlier fancied projection of self; he is, in fact, "himself" perceived in the present. Isherwood's statement at the beginning of *Christopher and His Kind* pertains equally to *Kathleen and Frank*: "The book I am now going to write will be as frank and factual as I can make it, especially as far as I myself am concerned" (CK 1). When one contrasts this declaration of intent with his prefatory caution in *Lions and Shadows,* an earlier autobiography (1938), one can measure the length of the inner journey Isherwood has traveled.

> I had better start by saying what this book is not: it is not . . . an autobiography; it contains no "revelations"; it is never "indiscrete"; it is not even entirely "true."
> . . . Read it as a novel.                                                    (LS)

The paradox of this inner journey is that by trying to escape from the past, Isherwood only became more enmeshed in it. That journey Isherwood now retraces in the two books he has written in this decade.

Both recent books are part of an extensive autobiographical project, yet the tone of each differs markedly. *Kathleen and Frank* is a book of discovery, an exploration into the unknown. Through the diary of his mother, Kathleen, and through the letters and reminiscences of family and friends, Isherwood relentlessly reconstructs his family history. Always on stage or in the wings, he unravels ancestral tales and legends, oversees the troubled courtship of his parents, pauses thoughtfully before each portrait in the family gallery, hoping to find some early version of himself. His intent is always to come to terms with his birth, growth, and rebellion in the family and the England that hurt him into writing.

Like *The Tempest, Kathleen and Frank* is unexpectedly a benediction. Isherwood, at peace finally with his own personal history, his *karma,* pierces through "this unsubstantial pageant" of Bradshaw-Isherwood[1] history to glimpse what Isherwood, as a child playing with a toy theatre given him by Frank, called "a back-of-backstage" (KF 308):

> Impossible to say exactly where Kathleen and Frank end and Richard [Isherwood's young brother] and Christopher begin;

they merge into each other. It is easy to dismiss this as a commonplace literary metaphor; hard to accept it as literal truth in relation to oneself. Christopher has found that he is far more closely interwoven with Kathleen and Frank than he had supposed, or liked to believe. (KF 509)

Isherwood then asserts that he, the anti-son, after years of resistance and rebellion, has reached a kind of perfect harmony with his parents, for he is finally able to say, "Our will be done!" (KF 510).

This Vedantist serenity, this redemptive dimension is scarcely evident, however, in *Christopher and His Kind;* in this work the older Isherwood remains in the wings, yielding center stage to the young writer. His revels are not ended, for this young-old Isherwood is still questing—for an end to restlessness, for pattern, for "the ideal companion to whom you can reveal yourself totally and yet be loved for what you are, not what you pretend to be" (CK 339), for a coherent self. Isherwood's goal here is not to discover the truth—as it is in *Kathleen and Frank.* Not a benediction, this book has a more compelling purpose: to reveal the central truth about Isherwood's life—his homosexuality. Determined to present himself as he is, Isherwood writes:

> At school, Christopher had fallen in love with many boys and been yearningly romantic about them. At college he had at last managed to get into bed with one. This was due entirely to the initiative of his partner, who, when Christopher became scared and started to raise objections, locked the door, and sat down firmly on Christopher's lap. (CK 3)

Reenacting his life, Isherwood, now in his seventies, unmasks. And, because he can finally be candid with no fears, he is immensely thankful. Recalling his first love partner, he concludes: "I am still grateful to him. I hope he is alive and may happen to read these lines" (CK 3).

As a child and young man, Isherwood feared the past because it signified the domain of his mother, Kathleen; and, as she extended its boundaries, the past threatened to swallow the young Isherwood's future. The arch-symbol of the past is Marple Hall, ancestral home of the Bradshaw-Isherwoods; indeed, Marple Hall dominates *Kathleen and Frank* in the same way that *Howards End* dominates E. M. Forster's novel of the same name. Kathleen's past is Edwardian England, what Isherwood in *The Memorial* calls "the old safe, happy, beautiful world" (M 88). The principal inhabitant of this world is Isherwood's father, killed in the Great War. From his letters in *Kathleen and Frank*, he emerges as a sensitive, artistic, conscientious husband and father. Isherwood fondly recalls his father illustrating a daily cartoon paper for him, "The Toy Drawer Times" (KF 349), on the back of military communiqués.

After Frank is killed, however, Kathleen apotheosizes him into a cult hero: he becomes not a person but a power. With his death, time stops for Kathleen. Because the present is intolerable, she constructs her own private world, peopling it with her own creations, shading events with her own prejudices. She transforms her senile father-in-law into the Squire of Marple Hall (KF 259), the villagers into quaint "retainers of the Feudal type" (KF 25). The past is happier by definition while the present is the "domain of the independent, the ungracious and the downright rude" (KF 25). Her own role is that of holy widow-mother; Isherwood's is expected to be that of sacred orphan. Their lives are to be war memorials to Frank who, as hero husband, assumes the compelling power of Agamemnon.

But Isherwood, smoldering with guilt and resentment, eager for independence, rejects the role of Orestes and instead embraces the role of the anti-son. Faced with the myth of the past, compounded principally by Kathleen, "schoolmasters and other busybodies" (KF 10) who want him to live in honor of Frank, Isherwood retaliates "early and passionately" (KF 10) with his own anti-myth. For a precocious adolescent, the construction of a counter-myth is a ready-to-hand escape from the constricted existence authority presents. In Isherwood's case, such fantasizing is a family trait, for he inherits Kathleen's myth-making capacity. Like her, he becomes a celebrant of the past, keeping a diary, composing the autobiography *Lions and Shadows* at the age of thirty-three, writing autobiographical novels in which many of the protagonists bear the name Christopher Isherwood, and now, in the seventies, revisiting his past in *Kathleen and Frank* and *Christopher and His Kind*.

Like Kathleen, Isherwood also views his life as history and invests "minor domestic events with an epic quality" (KF 10). Throughout *Kathleen and Frank* and *Christopher and His Kind,* Isherwood speaks mythically. He proclaims a Beatrix Potter tale one of his "great early myth books" (KF 307); he names his postadolescence a period of Freudian myth-making (KF 191); he superimposes the Brontë myth upon Wyberslegh, the home in which he grew up.[2] When he returns home, he imagines himself as Heathcliff:

> It was as Heathcliff that he rode his bicycle uphill and down, through the familiar but transformed landscape, dreaming of death and despair and hopeless love. As Heathcliff he imagined himself standing all night in a storm outside Catherine Linton's window; Catherine being for the moment a blond boy with a charming grin and long legs, who played hockey.    (KF 255)

Even the older Isherwood relishes the part of Heathcliff "the traveller who returns after mysterious wandering to the scene of his youth" (KF 255). Visiting Auden in a small German village, Isherwood writes, "It was easy to pretend to yourself that they [the villagers] were human beings bewitched, for the whole place could have been a setting for one of Grimm's fairy tales, except that it had a railway station" (CK 8). Even his homosexuality is mythic. He describes his introduction to the boy bars in Berlin as an initiation rite. His first boy-love in Berlin claims "the leading role in Christopher's love-myth" (CK 4). This boy had to be blond because "Christopher chose to identify himself with a black-haired British ancestor and to see the Blond as the invader who comes from another land to conquer and rape him" (CK 4). Later in America, Isherwood discovers "The American Boy . . . The Walt Whitman Boy" (CK 315).

Further, Isherwood imitates Kathleen's penchant for renaming characters in her diary. She calls her mother Baby Mama; her father, the Ignorer; herself, Elizabeth (after Elizabeth Barrett Browning); a suitor, the Child; a woman infatuated with Frank, Venus. Likewise, in his novels, Isherwood gives other names to friends and family. Edward Upward he calls Allen Chalmers; W. H. Auden, Hugh Weston; Stephen Spender, Stephen Savage; Kathleen, holy widow-mother; Frank, the anti-heroic hero; himself, the anti-son; his life and work, the anti-myth.

We can see the beginnings of this escape into a world of personal fiction in Isherwood even as a child when he delighted in disguising himself in elaborate costumes and staging and starring in melodramatic plays for his toy theater.[3] The love of disguise is a life-long trait. He recalls that later, as a young man in Berlin, he masked for a Christmas ball as a "common street hustler" (CK 33). In China he wore a "beret, a turtleneck sweater, and oversized riding boots," his war correspondent's costume (CK 301). He admits, "My 'character' is simply a repertoire of acquired tricks, my conversation a repertoire of adaptation and echoes . . ." (CK 305).

Isherwood's anti-myth is complete in every detail. In place of Kathleen's Frank, Isherwood substitutes another, "the anti-Heroic Hero" (KF 503), whose military uniform is only a disguise. Isherwood converts him into "an artist who renounced his painting, music and writing in order to dedicate his life to an anti-military masquerade" (KF 503). Frank plays the masquerade to the end and even gets killed in battle, thus duping everybody, Isherwood continues, except his son, into believing that he is a military hero. But Isherwood knows that Frank's life and death, in reality, demonstrate "the absurdity of the military mystique and its solemn cult of War and death" (KF 503). Because "ancestor worship was vile" (KF 304), Isherwood focuses on Judge Bradshaw, who presided over the trial of Charles I and refused him an opportunity to speak in his defense. Boasting that he is descended from this Regicide and various family eccentrics, Isherwood distorts his family history in accordance with a statement from Baudelaire's *Intimate Journals*, which he translated in 1930: "'My ancestors, idiots or maniacs, in their solemn dwellings, all victims of terrible passions'" (KF 305). Thus, Isherwood concludes, he is "obviously the offspring of a doomed line and must expect to be dragged off, some day soon, screaming in a strait-jacket" (KF 305).

The role of shattering creeds and demolishing idols becomes a lifestyle, so that homosexuality is not merely his nature; much more, it is Isherwood's own particular form of rebellion:

> Girls are what the state and the church and the law and the press and the medical profession endorse, and command me to desire. My mother endorses them, too. She is silently brutishly willing me to get married and breed grandchildren for her. Her will is the will of Nearly Everybody, and in their will is my death. *My* will is to live according to my nature, and to find a place where I can be what I am ... But I'll admit this—even if my nature were like theirs, I should still have to fight them, in one way or another. If boys didn't exist, I should have to invent them.     (CK 12)

Homosexuality is anti-sex, anti-marriage, anti-family.

Isherwood was also anti-education. At Cambridge, abetted by his lifelong friend, Edward Upward, Isherwood reacted against the strict academicism of the university by fabricating a private world, "an anarchist paradise in which all accepted moral and social values were turned upside down and inside out,"[4] a grotesque region of ghouls and gothic monsters called "Mortmere."

The anti-myth, begun as a revolt in the nursery, or anti-nursery, materialized at Repton, and was expanded at Cambridge with Upward and after Cambridge with Auden. It forms the foundation of Isherwood's fictional output and instills pattern into works which might otherwise appear distinct and unconnected, a mere farrago. Isherwood's anti-myth splits the world into two camps: the Enemy, or the Others, and the conspiratorial clique of the writer and his friends. The Enemy is Kathleen or anyone else who narrow-mindedly demands that Isherwood be like Frank and live up to Frank's supposed expectations. Isherwood's antagonism is translated into the novels in terms of the alienated protagonist at odds with society. Whether the protagonist is Philip Lindsay or Eric Vernon or the Bradshaw-Christopher narrator of the Berlin books or, in the later novels, Stephen Monk or George, the hero is the outsider, uprooted and dislocated, the single man agonizingly conscious of the gulf between himself and humanity. Homosexuality widens the gulf and increases the estrangement. Not until Isherwood's conversion to Vedanta is the Enemy seen not as other people but as one's self, one's own lack of love.

To be a young man of Isherwood's generation also meant that one's formative and most impressionable years were passed in the wasteland between two world wars. War had robbed Isherwood of a father, of a mother (for Kathleen's affection was monopolized by the dead Frank), and, most important, of a chance to prove his manhood. Too young to enlist, he could never test his bravery under fire. As he tells us in *Lions and Shadows,* he was, like most of his generation, obsessed by the idea of war, terrified by it, guiltily ashamed that he had not been a combatant. C. Day Lewis, a contemporary of

Isherwood, speaks for his entire generation in his "Letter to a Young Revolutionary," printed in 1933 in Michael Roberts' *New Country*:

> ... I was old enough to feel the later war atmosphere and at my most sensitive during the early post-war years. The one gave me a perhaps exaggerated horror of bloodshed and destruction, which rather queers my pitch as a practical revolutionary. The other has left in my system germs of "acedia" and mental *sauve qui peut.* . . .[5]

In his autobiography, *The Buried Day*, Lewis proposes that because he was distanced but not isolated from the war, the war was transmitted from history into myth: "the terrible names— Ypres, Loos, Hill 60, Passchendaele, the Somme—sounded in my ears like Troy, Ilion, Scamander, legendary and time-less. . . ."[6] Isherwood shrilly strains to ignore this Homeric glorification of war: war is "obscene, not even thrilling, a nuisance, a bore" (LS 76), the game of the Others. Still he cannot escape its baleful influence. In his anti-myth, Isherwood substitutes in place of war what he labels the Test, which G. H. Bantock rightly sees as a "masochistic substitute for the trenches."[7]

Isherwood identifies the Test as any hopelessly perilous situation. In his fiction, the Test exists only for what Isherwood considers the Truly Weak Man, a neurotic whose fear reck-lessly impels him to hurl himself into the most extreme acts of daring. Yet, the Truly Weak Man can never pass the Test. Even if he could, it would make no difference, for, like the Hemingway hero, he is irrevocably wounded, so insecure that he must continually prove himself in pointlessly arduous risk-taking. He is immersed in the destructive element without any chance of rescue. The antithesis of the Truly Weak Man is the Truly Strong Man who, in his tranquility and even-tempered reasonableness, is confident of success and feels no spur to indulge in daredevil antics. In the early books, the heroes may be categorized neatly under these two character types; but in the later books, particularly in his last novel, *A Meeting by the River,* these two concepts are seen not as mutually exclusive qualities but as potentialities existing simultaneously in the same person. Of course Isherwood is then interpreting his anti-myth according to the wisdom found in Vedanta.

This recasting of the anti-myth underlies an essential aspect of Isherwood's fiction. Though not as localized as William Faulkner's Yoknapatawpha County, Isherwood's world, whether its action takes place in London or in Berlin or in Hollywood, is the same everywhere. As David Pryce-Jones states, "His writing is concerned with himself and his own development, and not with abstractions or ideologies."[8] What Isherwood writes of Upward may be said of himself: wherever he is, all places are the same, because all places become part of himself (LS 236).

Just how consistent Isherwood's fictional preoccupations are may be seen by comparing two autobiographical passages, the first from *Christopher and His Kind* and the second from *Lions and Shadows,* written almost forty years earlier.

The selection from *Christopher and His Kind* concludes the book. Christopher and Auden are looking over the rail of the *Champlain.* Isherwood writes: "This is where I leave Christopher . . . looking eagerly, nervously, hopefully toward the land where he will spend more than half of his life." At present, he continues, "he can see almost nothing of what lies ahead. In the absence of the fortune-telling lady from Brussels, I will allow him and Wystan to ask one question—I can already guess what it is—and I will answer it . . ." (CK 339).

"Yes, my dears, each of you will find the person you came here to look for—the ideal companion to whom you can reveal yourself totally and yet be loved for what you are, not what you pretend to be." Wystan, Isherwood continues, will find his love very soon, within three months. And Christopher? "You Christopher will have to wait much longer." Thus far Isherwood has built a tender, high seriousness in the passage, raised nearly to mythic proportions by the apostrophe, the epic motif of the search, the archetypal quality of alighting in a new world. But counter to this solemnity runs a comic element. Isherwood concludes the book with this humorous anticlimax.

> He [the ideal companion] is already living in the city where you will settle. He will be near you for many years without your meeting. But it would be no good if you did meet him now. At present, he is only four years old.        (CK 339)

This ironic, self-mocking tone, a unique component of the Isherwood anti-myth, also marks the earlier passage from *Lions and Shadows*. In another moment of reflection, Christopher is walking along the edge of a beach. He is alone; the moment promises to be Joycean. Christopher is glad Weston is not with him, glad that Philip or the Cheurets or Chalmers are away. "And so, finding that, for once, I was not sorry to be alone, I said to myself: I am happy" (LS 237). He then restates his joy: "Perfectly happy, I repeated, as my eyes roamed wide over the brilliant desolate sea and the empty contours of the land" (LS 237). The reader begins to wonder. Is Isherwood mocking this moment of self-realization? The repetition and the stark landscape, contrasting with Isherwood's professed happiness, puzzle the reader. Isherwood continues:

> Were they [his absent friends], after all, searching for something that was lacking? I hardly knew. A tiny obstinate figure by the dwarf obelisk under an enormous sky, I declared for the third time: I am absolutely happy, absolutely content. And, increasingly overcome by a profound melancholy which I interpreted simply as an appetite for supper I began to walk downhill, towards my sitting-room, my holiday task and my lonely bed.        (LS 237)

The contrast between Isherwood's thrice-expressed joy and the connotation of the sterile images which rapidly descend from melancholy to isolated despair ("holiday task" and "my lonely bed") creates a tension which mocks his epiphany of joy. By the time of *Christopher and His Kind,* Isherwood's philosophical outlook has obviously deepened; but in both passages he is still recording himself, still viewing himself and the world in terms of his own personality. Like his mother, he is investing the events of life with epic proportions. Even after his adoption of Vedanta, his concerns are the same: he merely reinterprets them.

It is surprising that scant attention has been paid to this aspect of Isherwood's *oeuvre.* The first major assessments of Isherwood's work were not written until the end of the thirties. Cyril Connolly, an early admirer of Isherwood, in his introduction to the 1939 Traveller's Library edition of *All the Conspirators,* glimpses the beginnings of a recurrent motif when he points out the dominant role played by the fiercely possessive mother in Isherwood's work.[9] In *Enemies of Promise,* published a year earlier, Connolly is highly laudatory of Isherwood, but warns him about the fatal readability of his vernacular style, which may lose its edge because of its simple diction and syntax.[10] Yet that Connolly highly regarded the Isherwood of the thirties is shown by his selection of *Goodbye to Berlin* as one of the hundred most important modern books (1880–1950) published in England, France, and America.[11] John Lehmann, who published many of Isherwood's stories in his magazine *New Writing,* and who has been throughout the years an intimate friend and colleague of Isherwood, tries to present an overview of Isherwood's work. Lehmann interprets *The Berlin Stories* as the epic Isherwood intended and stresses Isherwood's flair for fantasy and the grotesque.[12] In a review of Isherwood's Berlin works for *The New Statesman and Nation* in 1939, David

Garnett underlines Isherwood's mythopoetic powers. Garnett pays Isherwood the supreme compliment by comparing the impact of his Berlin novels to that of Blake's *The Marriage of Heaven and Hell*. Like Blake, Isherwood has "the distinguishing mark of original writers and painters, the mark of imaginative greatness"; that is, he is able "to impose a personal vision."[13]

When Isherwood left with Auden for America, just before England's entry into World War II, British reactions were startled, strident, and almost universally bitter. Their move was seen as an act of treason and cowardice. Connolly, echoing Somerset Maugham's remark to Virginia Woolf,[14] wrote that with Isherwood left the hope of English fiction.[15] Hugh Walpole, as Lehmann reports in his autobiography, could not comprehend their going.[16] Even Stephen Spender, one of Isherwood's closest friends, "in an unguarded moment at lunch in the Athenaeum," grinningly referred to "'Christopher and Stalin, those great neutrals.'"[17] Spender, however, in his autobiography published nine years later, does gain perspective on what came to be called the "Auden-Isherwood affair": "The only important question was whether they could produce better work in the United States than in England."[18] In the same paragraph, however, he shows his true feelings by regretting, as Lehmann also does, "the unwritten stories of Isherwood about London and Manchester in the Blitz, or about the Occupation of Germany, and the poems of Auden from wartime England." Isherwood and Auden's departure pulled down the curtain on an era, an era which, as Lehmann writes, was fragmentary, a "period where promising beginnings had failed again and again, among all the distractions of political causes and the continual earthquake tremors that had been shaking the old established ways of life." Isherwood's case, Lehmann continues, is the most spectacular example of blighted promise: "*Mr. Norris Changes Trains* and . . . *Goodbye to*

*Berlin* seemed to me far too inadequate an *oeuvre* for someone who had been tipped, for every kind of good reason, as the most promising novelist of his generation."[19]

To most critics and reviewers, however, the question was not whether Isherwood could write better fiction in America, but whether he could write any fiction at all. Although Isherwood was intensely busy in America—he wrote scripts for Metro-Goldwyn-Mayer, edited *Vedanta and the West* for two years, translated two Hindu classics with his friend and guru, Swami Prabhavananda, revised his translation of Baudelaire's *Journaux Intimes,* visited South America and wrote a travel book, *The Condor and the Cows*—he published only one novel, *Prater Violet,* a short work about his film experiences with Berthold Viertel in England in 1934. Hollywood materialism and Indian mysticism seemed to sap his creative energies. G. H. Bantock's review in 1947 sums up much of the hostile criticism against Isherwood at this time. Bantock begins with the provocative query, "Why should such a comparatively negligible figure— negligible that is to say, by any reasonably mature standards— have achieved the reputation he has?"[20] He then goes on to note that Isherwood's characterization is shoddy and superficial, his technique worn and trite, his theme limited and immature, and ends by patronizingly declaring that his books are only good to while away a leisurely hour.

In the early fifties Isherwood's name was conspicuously before the public. John van Druten's *I am a Camera,* an adaptation for the stage of Isherwood's Berlin works, featuring "Sally Bowles," opened at the Empire Theater in New York in November 1951 and won the Critics' Award. A West Berlin production, starring a favorite actress of pre-Hitler days, Grete Mosheim, was well received. The British even made a film of *I am a Camera* starring Julie Harris and Laurence Harvey. Yet all this was familiar territory, and most people felt inclined to agree with Jacob Isaacs, who announced on BBC that Isherwood's talent had probably burned itself out in the thirties.[21] With the publication in 1954 of *The World in the Evening*, the death knell was sounded. The book is certainly inferior to Isherwood's other works, and most critics lost no time pointing out that fact. V. S. Pritchett saw the book as "simply the Berlin stories, resown in America and coming up as a poor thin crop of lowered vitality."[22] Kingsley Amis's review for *Twentieth Century* was unkind, even crude.[23] Thom Gunn seemed nearer the truth when he agreed that the book had faults, but suggested that perhaps Isherwood was trying something new and excitingly different.[24] But most critics rephrased what a writer for the *Times Literary Supplement* had said in a 1946 review of *Prater Violet*, that Isherwood's promise "may not be fulfilled within the field of fiction."[25]

In spite of this critical disappointment with Isherwood, three very good analyses of his work were written in the fifties. In 1953, Richard Mayne concluded that Isherwood's talents were well suited for comic novels such as *The Last of Mr. Norris*, but that he had not yet been able to combine his filmic conception of the novel with his desire to write serious fiction.[26] Jean Weisgerber, noting Isherwood's kinship to Auden, took up where Connolly, Lehmann, and Garnett left off by tracing the Isherwood anti-myth (Weisgerber doesn't use this term) which always centers on "des problèmes individuels."[27] Hena Maes-Jelinek (taking advantage of Weisgerber's important article, of Lehmann's *I Am My Brother*, the first of an autobiographical trilogy, and of Spender's autobiography, *World Within World*) wrote a complete interpretation of Isherwood's books, up to the publication of "Mr. Lancaster," the first part of *Down There on a Visit*. Maes-Jelinek interpreted the Isherwood anti-myth as a progressive attempt to gain a knowledge of man; unfortunately, he said, echoing Richard Mayne, Isherwood has not yet found the "adequate form to express his deeper insights into man."[28]

Between 1962 and 1967, Isherwood published three novels, one-third of his fictional output, and once again conclusively demonstrated that if there is anything we can expect from him, it is not a fulfillment of our expectations but a shattering of them. With the success of these novels, and of *Cabaret*, both the Broadway musical and the Hollywood movie, and of his numerous lectures, television appearances, and interviews, Isherwood was once again before the critical eye. Hena Maes-Jelinek dedicated a long chapter to Isherwood in his book, *Criticism of Society in the English Novel Between the Wars;* Maes-Jelinek continued the thread of his earlier article, but saw the Isherwood anti-myth as essentially the same as in the beginning.[29] Carolyn G. Heilbrun contributed a very readable summary of Isherwood's work in the Columbia Essays on Modern Writers series in 1970. And in 1971, Alan Wilde published the first book-length study of Isherwood in Twayne's United States Authors series. Considering Isherwood one of the great ironists of modern times, Wilde focused on Isherwood's ironic consciousness and his deep moral impulse.

With the publication in this decade of *Kathleen and Frank* and *Christopher and His Kind*, Isherwood has begun to receive the study he rightly deserves. Carolyn G. Heilbrun has edited a special number of *Twentieth Century Literature* (October 1976) dedicated to Isherwood, with contributions by John Lehmann, Edward Mendelson, and Colin Wilson. Unpublished Mortmere stories have been released by Edward Upward. Brian Finney is writing a definitive biography of Isherwood, and Stathis Orphanos, Alan Clodd, and John Byrne are preparing a bibliography to be published this year by Black Sparrow Press.

In *Kathleen and Frank* and *Christopher and His Kind*, Isherwood himself calls attention to what he has been doing throughout his career: revolting against Kathleen, the holy widow-mother; against Frank, the hero-father; against the romantic conception of war; against the romantic conception of the hero; and against the heterosexual dictatorship of the establishment. By that revolt, in his fiction and nonfiction, he inevitably built his anti-myth. It is easy to overlook when reading his work, for his books are readily understood without the suspicion that the anti-myth is present and determinative. For instance, although Julian Symons complains that the Auden group as a whole indulged in the private language of a literary clique,[30] and Justin Replogle, who echoes Dilys Powell's evaluation in 1934,[32] claims that Auden, Spender, and MacNeice cannot be understood without referring to their private myth, such complaints cannot be leveled at Isherwood himself. He is too much the novelist, the master builder. He never presents the myth itself; rather he uses the myth as a foundation and, as in all well-made structures, the foundation is unseen. Nor is Isherwood's fantasy so exorbitant that it invites the eccentric interpretations, for example, of Upward's "The Railway Accident." Isherwood rejects Mortmere, the surrealist world he and Upward created as an escape from Cambridge, precisely because it had no connection with the real world. Although his imagination constantly verges on fantasy, even on nightmare— the references to *Alice in Wonderland* throughout his work are innumerable—mere Arabian Nights fantasy does not satisfy him.

This gradual fashioning of a personal world, rendered in a "superlatively readable"[33] style and with remarkable irony, rescues Isherwood's books from the excesses of mere reportage and political extremism which vitiate much of the writing of the thirties. Like Elizabeth Rydal, novelist and mystic in *The World in the Evening*, Isherwood never deals "directly with world situations or big scale tragedies. That wasn't her way. But she tried to reproduce them in miniature, the essence of them" (WE 110). Isherwood's books are mirrors with which he paints self-portraits, as well as looking glasses through which the reader enters a distinctly different and private landscape.

In the fifties, Isherwood edited a book for Dell entitled *Great English Short Stories*. In his introduction, he says that he chose these thirteen stories because they represent thirteen worlds: "by 'world' I mean not only the rest of his [an author's] works but also the kind of people and places he may be expected to write about in the future or about which he might have written if he had lived longer: his entire artistic potentiality."[34] Isherwood's nine novels, taken together, are broader and deeper than the confines of each read individually; they represent an intensely personal world, which, as Kathleen ironically remarked about *The Adventures of Mummy and Daddy,* the lost work of Isherwood's childhood, is "chiefly about Christopher" (KF 510).

# CHAPTER

# 1

# ◟Mothers and Sons◞

In *The Ascent of F 6,* Michael Ransom, freelance adventurer and mountain climber, is manipulated by his corrupt twin brother and his pleading mother into scaling the haunted mountain, F 6, which loftily fringes the borders of British Sudoland and Ostnian Sudoland. The legend is that the "white man who first reaches the summit of F 6 will be lord over *both* the Sudolands, with his descendants, for a thousand years" (F6 125). After losing his crew and, more important, his idealism, Michael succeeds, only to find, perched on F 6's peak and veiled in ghostly white, the real object of his quest, his mother. He promptly kneels and lays his head on her lap. Such contrived and blatantly Freudian symbolism (critics wince at this undergraduate prank)[1] accentuates the dominant role of the mother in the fictional world of Christopher Isherwood.

With matriarchal arrogance, the mother rules Isherwood's first two novels, *All the Conspirators* and *The Memorial,* written just before his Berlin books. Like Kathleen, she has lost her husband in the Great War; and, like Kathleen, she affects her favorite role, that of holy widow, with flawless mastery. A representative of constricting authority, she is Isherwood's first enemy, but a necessary one. Later in life, Isherwood confesses that he desperately needed Kathleen, for his own work has been a rebellion against her. Paradoxically, Kathleen is both Muse and Medusa, her opposition "a counterforce which gave him strength" (KF 507) prodding him "continually into revolt" (KF 506). In the later novels, after his conversion to Vedanta, mother figures become kind, even saintly, as Isherwood no longer postures as the young man "angry with the family and its official representatives" (AC "Foreword").

Although Isherwood chafed against all authority, particularly its initial manifestation in his mother, his first novel cannot be classed either as a manifesto of independence or as a polemic in the same way that D. H. Lawrence's *Sons and Lovers* and James Joyce's *A Portrait of the Artist as a Young Man* can. *All the Conspirators* is a portrait of the artist as a hapless mother's boy unable to sever his ties to mother and to home. Isherwood exposes not only the Edwardian manners of the older generation but also the postwar sensibility of the younger generation as bogus and smug. His targets are pretentiousness and Prufrockian escapism, neither trait exclusively possessed by either generation. Rather than "a call to sound the cry to the barricades,"[2] *All the Conspirators* is an autopsy of a malignant family with Isherwood a coroner dissecting "the great malady, horror of one's home"[3] and "Acedia, 'the malady of monks,' that deadly weakness of the will . . . the root of all evil"[4] that sickens unto death.

As Cyril Connolly points out in what Isherwood calls a "brilliant but too generous introduction" (AC "Foreword"), the novel is a study in weakness;[5] but, as Connolly fails to recognize, it is also a study of strength in weakness, for both Mrs. Lindsay and Philip acquire power by feigning helplessness.

Drawing-room Fascists whose domestic tyranny matches that of any character in a Compton-Burnett novel, mother and son possess a complete repertoire of rehearsed responses and stage ploys: they weep, fast, fret, scold, and scheme as occasion demands, masochistically relishing their roles as martyrs.

Isherwood assembles his book as if he were editing a film, juxtaposing snips of action and dialogue with sparse descriptive passages. Though early reviewers key on the book's "modern cleverness,"[6] its indebtedness to E. M. Forster and to James Joyce,[7] the writer for the *Times Literary Supplement* strikes the most characteristic criticism of the book: "It is a first sketch of a novel rather than the complete and rounded novel itself."[8] This charge of sketchiness stems from the novel's jerky, cinematic technique and Hemingwayesque dialogue,[9] which needlessly obfuscate. What, for example, is a reader to make of the following conversation:

> "Well, then, what earthly difference can it make?"
> "None."
> "Then you'll come?"
> "No."
> "But, if it doesn't, why don't you?" (AC 12)

As the story clips by, however, pronouns find antecedents, early ambiguity yields to clarity, blurry scenes come into focus. Even the obscurity of the last few pages, called by an older Isherwood "repressed aggression" (AC "Foreword"), can be understood if seen in the light of the entire novel.

When the book begins, Philip Lindsay, a mock Stephen Dedalus, has made the first of two grand operatic gestures: he has quit his office job and, with his cynical friend Allen Chalmers, has fled to a remote island. There he fancies himself an artist in exile. Philip's conversation and mannerisms, however, expose him as an impostor and a fool. Ineffectual and boorish, he is interested only in dashing off saleable paintings and books, concerned only with pleasing his mother, his sole audience. On the island, Philip dabbles on various canvases, pontificates about the nature of art, and squabbles with Allen. Because he finds Allen unsympathetic and critical, Philip gravitates toward Victor Page and his uncle, Colonel Page, who are holidaying in the same hotel. Both Victor and his uncle are stock Edwardian types, members of what Isherwood and Upward in their Cambridge days castigated as the "poshocracy" (LS 55). Philip has every reason to avoid their company: Allen despises Victor, his former schoolmate now attending Cambridge; and the Pages represent all that Philip has just renounced by leaving home. Yet, in a conversation, Philip casually invites Victor to visit him at home to meet his family— the home and family Philip has forsaken for art's sake.

Philip displays all the tics of a genius, but none of the aptitude. For example, his conversations are often interrupted by flashes of vision; talking with Allen, Philip suddenly drifts off, having "as it happened, at that moment seen a picture. . . . A few hours' work; bold, attractive, easy" (AC 16). Observing a slab of rock on the beach, he remarks: "I say, Allen, isn't that absolutely Epstein?" (AC 20). Later he censures Allen for avoiding the common man's viewpoint. All Philip's fradulent sensibility Isherwood mercilessly exposes, featuring Philip as a pseudomartyr of the arts: "Philip rose to his feet, stretching himself wearily: posture of bored crucifixion, against the sea" (AC 23). Even Philip's "audacious, purifying,/ Elemental move"[10] is half-hearted and futile, for without his mother he merely hangs about—impotent, even paralyzed. So intensely does he crave her presence that he unconsciously forces Allen to take her place. After a day of quarreling, Allen realizes what his relationship with Philip has become, as Isherwood gives the reader a glimpse into Allen's mind: "How strange. I said that in the sort of tone one used to a child" (AC 26). Almost overnight, Philip's vague gesture of rebellion founders. Outraged when Allen appears drunk in the presence of women, Philip cancels his holiday-rebellion and returns, in a huff, to London. There, met by his sister Joan, he continues to whine, complaining to Joan that his life does not foster great art. His querulous tone causes her to reflect that "as so often, he was addressing not her but their mother" (AC 77).

On the home front, Mrs. Lindsay, disapproving of Philip's attempt to break free of his home, his office job, and the life she has mapped out for him, rallies with her own tactics of "domestic guerilla warfare" (AC 127): she simply refuses to see Philip. Stymied, Philip drags himself to his room, miserable and disappointed. Until he can impress her and make her adopt his point of view, he has no peace. He forgets his easel and paints, destroys his manuscripts, and wastes his days and nights. His mother straitjackets his consciousness—he dare not play a record in his study because she'll assume he's not work-ing; leaving the house, he senses her face at the window, watching. He lives in her presence, yet dreads a direct encoun-ter because before her he is powerless. When he does meet her accidentally on the stairs, he is "bored, shamed, wishing only to get away" (AC 68), stricken with a "queer atrophy of the will" (AC 66), as she storms his feeble defense with her telepathic questions.

The relationship between Mrs. Lindsay and Philip, however, is more complex than that of a termagant mother and a disturbed, naughty child, for both are locked in a symbiotic union. Without him, Mrs. Lindsay is grim and morose; without her, Philip cannot even begin a painting or a book. These early lines by W. H. Auden diagnose Philip's sickness:

> Yours you say were parents to avoid, avoid them
>   if you please
> Do the reverse on all occasions till you catch the
>   same disease.[11]

Philip has caught "the same disease": though he professes rebellion, he acts, on every occasion, like his mother. After

Allen's drunken scene on the island, Philip refuses to breakfast with him (AC 47)—just as Mrs. Lindsay declines to take tea with Philip when he returns from his defiant holiday (AC 64). Only when directly addressed does Mrs. Lindsay speak to Philip (AC 74); when angry, Philip will not utter a friendly word to Allen (AC 42). At times even their conversations follow the same pattern: exasperated with Allen, Philip closes a discussion by exclaiming, "Oh, Allen, you are utterly impossible sometimes, you know" (AC 13); discussing Philip's future, Mrs. Lindsay concludes, "Oh, you're impossible" (AC 69). Isherwood calls attention to their similarity by observing in another place that "Mrs. Lindsay, with pursed lips, strikingly resembled her son" (AC 129).

For a while, Philip fecklessly pursues the romantic life of a misunderstood artist; but, unable to endure his mother's abrasive seclusion and silence, he surrenders and childishly asks (metaphorically laying his head on her lap), "What do you want me to do?"(AC 78). Because mother wants him to and because he must comply, he returns, emasculated, to his loathed office job.

When chapter seven begins, Joan returns from a tennis match with Victor. Isherwood's method, as so often in this first novel, is to start in the middle of a scene and then, as the chapter proceeds, fill in the missing information. The reader must gather that Victor has accepted Philip's invitation to visit and has even fallen in love with Joan. Now, with Philip tucked away in an office, Mrs. Lindsay trains her psychological weapons on Joan and Victor. Because Victor's social status makes him an enviable catch, she contrives an invitation to Cambridge for a weekend (AC 122). By masterful stage-blocking, she manages to overhear Victor's proposal. In Victor and Joan's first scene of intimacy, "Mother, outside, could hear every word" (AC 147). Mrs. Lindsay pulls the strings of their relationship. When Victor presents Joan with an engagement ring, he confesses, "I hope it'll fit all right. Your mother lent me a

ring she was wearing, which she said you'd tried on once" (AC
162). Joan's quip portends the ensuing collapse of their courtship: "You and Mother seem to have thought of everything,
between you" (AC 162). Indeed, Mrs. Lindsay thinks of everything as she cunningly frames scene after scene. Just before
Victor's arrival for tea, she arranges for two friends to drop by
so that she may exhibit Victor to them and announce Joan's
engagement (AC 158). During this triumph at tea, "Mrs. Lindsay smiled like a revolving lighthouse" (AC 159). Admiring her
stratagems, Philip later tells Allen, "All that was lacking was a
concealed orchestra to burst into the finale of '1812'" (AC 160).

But Philip is too much his mother's son to be inactive. With
Victor a potential member of the family, Philip vies against his
mother to clinch him as an ally in his struggle for artistic
independence. In a scene worthy of his mother, a scene in
which even Philip muses, "this was playing to the gallery with a
vengeance" (AC 170), Philip struts and frets before Victor,
bemoaning his sterile life and middle-class job, and thus extorts
Victor's sympathy. But Mrs. Lindsay is not to be outflanked.
Sensing that Victor has joined with Philip in the war at home,
she skillfully connives to remove Victor from the scene by
playing on his jealousy. She suggests—ever so quietly—that
there is a subtle attraction between Joan and Allen:

> "There's just one thing, Victor dear, about Allen Chalmers. I
> wouldn't, if I were you, mention the subject to Joan."
> "Why not?" He was startled.
> "Well, I've done so already. And she simply won't hear a word
> against him. It's such a pity to make unpleasantness over a thing
> like that. Much better just to ignore it. The darling child's so
> generous towards everyone. Though I'm afraid, in this case,
> that her generosity is rather misplaced."          (AC 190)

Victor, who has never forgotten Allen's debauch on the island,
cannot abide Allen—nor any woman even slightly attracted to
him. Moreover, since Philip is the family's chief concern, Victor

is understandably rankled because his engagement slides to
secondary importance. Even Joan begins to slight Victor. The
extent of her identification with Philip may be gauged in the
following dialogue between Joan and Victor. Joan asks:

> "Victor, what *are* we to do for Philip?"
> " ... It's Philip every time I come into this house."
> To his discomfiture, she flashed into anger: "I'm sorry. I
> ought to have known our affairs would bore you, sooner or
> later."                                                    (AC 191)

Unlike the Lindsays, Victor is weak and diffident. He fears
sexuality, recoils from Joan's affection and from declaring his
own feelings; nor does he share their penchant for fatuous
play-acting. He eventually seals his own doom by obtaining,
through his uncle, a position for Philip in Kenya, which Philip
accepts. Outraged and horrified, Joan suddenly fills her
mother's place and plays the dominant female until the end of
the novel. She flares at Victor for getting Philip the post; she
visits Allen and writes him several desperate letters pleading
for him to dissuade Philip. She is tearful and terrible in her
determination to block Philip's departure. Ostensibly her reasons are that the climate and the job "will kill him [Philip]
inside a year" (AC 192). Yet her real reasons are deeper and
darker: like her mother, Joan needs to cosset Philip; and, at
this point in the novel, having recognized that she can never
marry Victor, she, like her mother, also needs Philip as the
man in her life.

Here Isherwood's portrait of Mrs. Lindsay sags. Earlier he
had charged her with the ruthlessness of Lady Macbeth; now
Joan usurps her place as family head while Mrs. Lindsay
placidly accepts Joan's rule and Philip's job in Kenya. Isherwood does not suggest that Mrs. Lindsay's resignation is a ploy
to prevent Philip's migration—she merely accepts, completely
out of character.

Once Philip plans to emigrate to Kenya, however, the novel totters from a lack of purpose. Isherwood implies incest between Joan and Philip (AC 207) and an affair between Joan and Allen (AC 251), but carries nothing through. Philip desperately makes his second grand operatic gesture: he decamps in a scene that parodies the decadent romanticism of Poe or Baudelaire. Philip, sick with brain fever, flees through thick fog, down sombre, dirty streets, among crowds of malevolent people. The following passage, in which Philip rents a room, burlesques the conventions of outrageous melodrama:

> A fat woman, with a prospect of gas-lit hall and staircase behind her, eyed his bedraggled figure coldly, but admitted that she had a bed to spare. She called shrilly for a consumptive-looking manservant, whom Philip followed thankfully up flights of rickety stairs to a bedroom, a tiny garret under the roof.    (AC 235)

When Philip's absence is discovered, Joan excoriates her mother in a convulsive argument which Isherwood, in his worst tea-tabling manner, chooses not to dramatize. He shows us only the outcome of this mother-daughter fray: in a house still tense with the electric shock of argument, Joan reigns supreme. Philip is found, of course, having collapsed in the street, and Joan preempts her mother's place: no one can nurse Philip but Joan, because of "the special things to do with the nursing" (AC 246). But Mrs. Lindsay has also changed: "She was radiant. She looked years younger. She no longer seemed slightly timid, slightly apprehensive of something unpleasant about to happen. She was confidently gay" (AC 240). Is it that with a convalescent at home, she is content? Or that with Philip home she has married off Joan, not to Victor, but to Philip? Again, Isherwood's extremely sparse method forces the reader to supply the motivation. With mother hovering in the background, and with Joan ministering to his every need, Philip has established his own island—a safe, compact, middle-class kingdom, with regular meals and constant ego-reinforcement. During his convalescence, he sells a poem and has several paintings commissioned. This commercial success is the standard by which he and his family judge his artistic genius. It is significant that he is working on a portrait of Joan. Visiting Philip, Allen finds the room "was like a greenhouse." Philip is enthroned in a wheelchair, his legs muffled by a plaid-rug, his hands warmed by mittens (AC 244). This closing shot of Philip as convalescent tyrant of a "suffocatingly dull and respectable" family seems to deny strongly Colin Wilson's recent judgment that Philip's next "attempt to escape his home will be more successful."[12] Philip cannot escape and does not want to escape.

Who is the victor in this melodrama of pseudoangst and convenient neurosis? Not Joan, for although she writes Victor asking him to marry her, she is rent by the guilt of having betrayed the family. Not Mrs. Lindsay who, described as hap-pier, has nonetheless relinquished her motherhood to Joan. Not the deluded Philip, who concludes the book with a formu-lated phrase whose irony pins him to the wall:

> "You see, Allen, what I really dislike about your attitude is
> that it gets you nowhere. You refuse to venture, that's what it is.
> You're timid. Oh, I grant you one's got to have the nerve. . . ."
>
> (AC 255)

Allen's early judgment of Philip still holds true: "Philip, your imagination wants lancing. It's swollen with pus" (AC 202). Perhaps not an individual, but the family has won, with Mrs. Lindsay's and Joan's and Philip's separate conspiracies uniting them into a family—the kind of family Louis MacNeice por-trays in his ironic poem, "Happy Families":

> The room is all a stupid quietness,
> Cajoled only by the fire's caress
> We loll severally about and sit
> Severally and do our business severally,

> For there's a little bit for everybody;
> But that's not all there is to it.[13]

"Not the sort of book with which a writer goes straight to the heart of the public,"[14] *All the Conspirators* is important, nonetheless, in the Isherwood canon; as an early reviewer surmises, "I guess the author to be a young man. If he is, he will do very good work (for he has plenty of ability). . . ."[15] Horace Walpole thinks that it is one of the eight or nine "unjustly neglected books of the twenties."[16] Cyril Connolly values the book because it

> reveals the nature and peculiarities of the author, and the nature and peculiarities of his time. Like Prufrock, which was a key to T. S. Eliot and to the Teens, this first novel is a key to Isherwood, and the Twenties. . . . [It] introduces a dominant theme of his work, the Evil Mother, fierce, obstinate, tearful, and conventional, who destroys her son in *All the Conspirators* as ingeniously as in *The Memorial* and *The Ascent of F 6*. It is a novel . . . of atrocities witnessed at tea in the drawing room, or over Sunday night supper . . . horrible and barbaric . . . like a Sunday film about scorpions.[17]

Perhaps the final judgment of *All the Conspirators* can be gleaned from a review Isherwood wrote in 1935 of a novel entitled *Perilous Privilege*.[18] The situation in both books is analogous: in *Perilous Privilege,* an overbearing mother, Mrs. Fergus, victimizes her daughter, Janet, "an artist, a painter of genius." Isherwood's criticism is strikingly apposite. For example, he asks,

> Why are these people so unhappy? Because they are living under the tyranny of an efficient, ambitious, discontented woman.

Everywhere there is covert violence that never erupts:

> All through the story we are expecting an act of violence. . . .
> But no, this tragedy is even more terrible: there is no release.

Mrs. Fergus sets her lips and dusts and sweeps and polishes, in mute outrage against her fate. And Janet submits dully to her nagging with a hardening heart.

The truth would free these people: "Those pure, fearless words of hatred, which alone could break down the barriers between them now, are never uttered. Mother and daughter draw further and further apart." In his indictment of Janet the artist, Isherwood also condemns Philip:

> The "perilous privilege" (surely it is most unjust to father this ugly alliteration on Thomas Mann) is the privilege of exceptional talent, of being able to see and feel more than other people. The title makes a claim which this book fails to justify. "Janet Fergus," as the author presents her, is sensitive and precocious, no doubt, but she has none of the authority, none of the ruthlessness of genius in its adolescence. She is an underling. . . .

Both the Lindsays and the Ferguses are trapped in a "sad suburb, where the lace curtains are changed twice a month, but never the heart."

*All the Conspirators* ultimately fails because Mrs. Lindsay looms too large for the young Isherwood: at the end, Isherwood either retires her in the wings or renders her bland and inept. In his second published work, *The Memorial,* Isherwood is competent and versatile enough to create a world with the ambience and time not only for a character like Mrs. Lindsay to flourish, but also for her opposite. In Lily Vernon, Isherwood presents a masterful portrait of the "Evil Mother, fierce, obstinate, tearful and conventional." Lily's antithesis, Mary Scrivens, is a dilettantish, exuberant mother who lives only in the present; nevertheless, like Lily, she too destroys her children. Both women bequeath unrest and death to their families.

Isherwood's method is a sophisticated refinement of the jerky, stop-go cuts in *All the Conspirators.* Isherwood still composes like a film editor, but in *The Memorial* he lengthens his vignettes, clarifies his dialogues, varies and develops his characters. If *All the Conspirators* is his short feature, *The Memorial* is his attempt at an epic film—or, as he describes the book in *Lions and Shadows*, "an epic disguised as a drawing-room comedy." To avoid the dull chronological approach of most epic novels, Isherwood decides

> to start in the middle and go backwards, then forwards—so that the reader comes upon the dullness half-way through, when he is more interested in the characters; the fish holds its tail in its mouth, and time is circular, which sounds Einstein-ish and brilliantly modern.                                    (LS 297)

To avoid an "I remember" digression, he does not construct a continuous narrative but arranges his story "in self-contained scenes, like a play: an epic in an album of snapshots" (LS 297):

> First snapshot: a group of men and women drinking cocktails in nearly modern dress, the fashions of the year before last. Second snapshot: an Edwardian tea-party. What charming, funny costumes! But, hullo—wait a minute! We seem to recognize some of the figures . . . And now, here's the third snapshot: the dresses still look queer, it's immediately post-war. Looking at it carefully, you can see what ten years have done to these men and women.                                    (LS 297–98)

*The Memorial* is divided into four snapshots: in the first, Isherwood presents his characters in 1928, a year earlier than the book's present; with this image frozen in our minds, he turns back the picture album eight years, three years, then forward to 1929. We see the characters at four critical periods through the subjective eyes of other characters and through the writer's own descriptions. What emerges is a chilling, prescient portrait of a family dominated and damned by its women.

We first approach Lily Vernon, mother of Eric, the young protagonist, through the infatuated eyes of Major Ronald

Charlesworth, a retired army officer who with Lily belongs to a quaint society that visits historic sites. Lily emerges as a curiously contradictory figure. Although she appears to be "no more than thirty," she is surrounded by a "curiously mature air of sadness and quietness" (M 23). Dressed in black for mourning, she has "absolutely the look of a child," smiling sadly and yet gaily (M 23).

The formalism of Isherwood's style bears this same ambiguity. In fact, with its balanced sentence structure, its numerous dependent clauses, its unusually long sentences, Isherwood's style in this section is aptly described by Cyril Connolly's term, "Mandarin."[19] The style is artificial, shaped by a writer who assumes his reader is unhurried. But the style's very artificiality contradicts its meaning: the words carry one meaning which the sentence structure mocks. In each of the following sentences, the left-branching construction with the personal intensifier seems a trifle too dramatic to be taken at face value. The first sentence describes Ronald Charlesworth's pain on asking Lily about her dead husband; the second, his empathy for Lily's solitude:

> Himself so sensitive, he recoiled immediately, blamed himself for his clumsiness in paining her with his questions.   (M 24–25)

> Lonely himself, having few friends even at his club, suffering often from the after-effects of enteric fever, which he had developed during the Boer War, Ronald yet thought of Mrs. Vernon's life as being lonelier still.                    (M 25)

Similarly, the antithesis in the next two sentences ridicules Ronald's self-importance: the first sketches Ronald's surprise at how much history Lily knows; the second, his outrage at the way her son, Eric, ignores her:

> Ronald was surprised at her knowledge. It was not great, but it was much greater than he would have expected from a woman.
>                                                                         (M 24)

Ronald was a mild man, but he felt himself utterly without
mercy in his judgment of that young bounder, who'd behaved
so vilely to her.                                             (M 26)

Charlesworth plays Major Dobbin to Lily's Amelia. Charlesworth's doting on Lily and Lily's cloying sweetness that smoth-
ers life in memory of her dead husband recall Thackeray's
sentimental lovers. However, Dobbin does win Amelia; and
Amelia, though also described in ambivalent terms ("The very
joy of the woman was a kind of grief" and "her weakness was
her principal charm"),[20] is merely tiresome. But Lily, as domi-
nating as Becky Sharp and as weak as Amelia, is the classic
example of the helpless shrew. Any doubts the reader might
have about Lily, Isherwood banishes very early in the novel,
when Lily has dinner with her son, Eric.

For Major Charlesworth, Lily is martyr, widow, and siren;
for her son, she is all of these as well as the perfect mother. She
serves Eric his favorite pudding, offers him his favorite cigarettes, inquires about his recent trip to Wales. She deftly manages Eric into playing the perfect son; he enjoys the pudding,
accepts the pack of cigarettes, dutifully answers her questions,
all the time wondering, "Why need we go through this? Which
of us wishes it?" (M 45).

Lily moves cautiously, correctly; Eric answers her moves. As
a result, the dinner scene comprises a series of short question-
answer dialogues that lead to impasses:

"You see I've got some new cups?"
"Yes."
"How do you like them?"
He looked at them dully. Cups, he though. Cups.
"They're very nice."
She seemed pleased.
"I got them at that new shop just opposite the Bank. I don't
know whether you noticed it as you came past to-day?"
"No, I didn't."
Lily sipped her coffee.                                   (M 47–48)

When she offers him cigarettes, the conversational pattern is the same: Lily's move, Eric's countermove—stalemate.

> "Those are the sort you like, aren't they?"
> "Yes, thank you. They are."
> He broke open the packet, lit a cigarette. He didn't want it. She said:
> "Why not take the whole packet?" She smiled sadly. "They'll only get stale."
> "Thank you very much."
> Obediently, he put them into his pocket. She watched him smoke.    (M 48)

When Eric leaves, he castigates himself for his anger, yet despairs of a solution:

> Darling Mother. Can't I help you? Must we go on like this? It seems so miserable and senseless. His mind ranged for solutions, followed the old circle. No, there's nothing.    (M 51)

The question Isherwood raises is, how has Lily achieved such demonic power over her son? Is she really the ogress Eric believes her to be? Is Eric the persecuted son he imagines? To answer these questions, Isherwood shunts us back to the beginning, the year 1920: the day of the War Memorial dedication. Lily has lost her husband, and Eric is a stuttering seventeen-year-old, deprived of a father. On this day, Lily opts to die. Isherwood's first description here of Lily echoes Joyce's portrait of Eveline: both women are passive, locked out from the living:

> [EVELINE]
> She sat at the window watching the evening invade the avenue. Her head was leaned against the window curtains and in her nostrils was the odour of dusty cretonne. She was tired.[21]

[LILY]

> Lily, with her feet up on the chintz window-seat, her cheek
> resting against the oak shutter, thought: How tired I am. How
> terribly tired.                                              (M 65)

Death images pervade this section, attesting to Lily's slow
dying. Unlike the speaker in Emily Dickinson's poem "Because
I could not stop for death,"[22] Lily does stop, as Isherwood's
images echo those in the Dickinson poem: Kent, the chauffeur,
drives Lily's father-in-law, old, paralyzed Mr. Vernon, "round
and round the sundial like a clock" (M 65); a "thin wild
mournful" train whistle shrills through the drowsy atmosphere
(M 65). Lily, tired and beaten, feels she has arrived at the end
of her life as she faces "the silver-framed photograph" of her
dead husband on the mantle (M 68). Isherwood discloses Lily's
feelings in monstrous fusings: she forces herself to "be glad to
think of dying" (M 65); the war gave purpose to her life
because "there was patriotism and hatred" (M 66); still young,
she thinks "she was old, finished with" (M 66).

These strained, unnatural feelings climax in Lily's narciss-
ism. In the following scene, Lily scrutinizes her grief-ravaged
features in a mirror:

> Her lips trembled; she was frog-faced, half-smiling. Some-
> body knocked at the door. She sighed deeply. Her face drew
> down at the mouth and eyes. She looked five years older. "Come
> in," she sighed aloud.                                       (M 71)

There is another knock at the door. Like an actress preparing
for a tragic role, Lily answers her curtain call:

> She picked up her hat from the dressing table and put it on,
> arranging the little veil. The hat made her eyes look extraordi-
> narily lost and tragic. She could still occasionally feel the pathos
> of the sight of herself in black—a small restrained figure beside
> which always stood, in her imagination, the charming fresh

> image of a girl in spreading cream skirts and a large hat with
> flowers, puffy-sleeved . . .                               (M 71)

She repeats her invitation to enter and catches a last look at
herself in the mirror. Speaking to Mrs. Beddoes, the house
servant, she says:

> "I've been ready for the last half hour," and she too smiled—a
> smile, as she suddenly felt—catching a glimpse of it in the
> mirror—of the most extraordinary pathos and sweetness. She
> saw the effect of the quick sad smile together with her slightly
> inflamed eyes on Mrs. Beddoes. . . .            (M 71–72)

As she descends the stairs, Lily enchants Eric: she is like a
goddess from a fairy tale. For dramatic effect, Lily stands in the
sunlight, dazzling, "her face lit pure gold, like an angel . . ." (M
73). The irony is damning: surrounded by signs of life, Lily has
anesthetized her emotions and thoughts, yet she still dazzles.

Her life is in the past: by closing her eyes, Lily carries herself
back to the day of her arrival at the Hall. Her remembrance of
that fragile, perfect world "where nothing will ever happen"
(M 87) is rendered in participial phrases. The absence of verbs
stresses the stagnation of that life:

> Mamma under the tree, exclaiming, as visitors were announced:
> "The philistines are upon us!" Papa telling how an Italian
> coachman had jumped off the box and snapped Papa's walking-
> stick across his knee in a fit of temper: "And, if you'll believe me,
> he said neither Dog nor Cat—simply got back into his seat and
> drove as hard as he could go. . . ." Richard's voice from the
> tennis court, calling the score.                 (M 87)

Our last glimpse of Lily is in 1929, once again refracted
through the gulled eyes of Major Charlesworth. He leaves her
apartment from an afternoon of tea, thinking, "She is a
saint. . . . I have known a saint" (M 261). Isherwood wants us to
think otherwise as he presents Lily, in this, her finale, with

chilling discernment. She is the bewitching seductress, preparing her *mise en scène*: opening the door, she greets the purblind Charlesworth, "I've been waiting for you . . . I've let the maid go out with her young man. We can make tea ourselves" (M 254). She lures him with her demure flirtation:

> "Shall you be going to the meeting on Sunday?"
> "I'm not quite certain."
> "I shan't go, unless you'll be coming."        (M 255)

She entices him to the brink of familiarity: "I should very much like it if you would call me Lily" (M 256). Then she coquettishly reverts to the martyr-widow role: "I wish you and Richard could have known each other. I think you would have had a great deal in common . . . I've sometimes felt that he is pleased we are friends" (M 260).

Ironically, Isherwood describes Lily's chaste deception in religious imagery. Ronald holds a tea cup as if it were "a sacred vessel in a religious mystery. She smiled, pouring in the hot water . . ." (M 255). Her room is "as quiet and isolated as a shrine" (M 257), cloistered from "the intense crawling movement of the far-away traffic" (M 257). Having entered Lily's apartment with the intention of proposing marriage, Major Charlesworth departs, grateful that "she had beautifully . . . indicated what their relation must be . . . had saved him . . . from the misery of her refusal" (M 261).

Isherwood depicts Lily with flensing irony. She is indisputably villainous, though her villainy is swathed in velvet. His portrait, however, of Mary Scrivens, Eric's aunt, is equivocal: many critics eulogize Mary as the young Isherwood's most positive portrait, and indeed her vitality, in contrast to Lily's necrophilia, is certainly winning.[23] But the reader usually sees Mary reflected through Eric's eyes, and Eric, particularly when young, is as infatuated with Mary as Charlesworth is with Lily. Repulsed by his mother's constricting grief, he naturally responds to the élan of Mary and her children. With Mary's family he seems more confident and stammers less. But he doesn't recognize that just as Lily revels in her emptiness, Mary resorts to the opposite extreme, crowding her life with noisy excitement. Lily denies life; Mary impersonates it.

Mary is first presented through the eyes of her daughter, Anne. As in our introduction to Lily, we are at once puzzled. Is Anne trying to persuade herself that her mother is as wonderful as everyone says? The repetition arouses suspicion:

> Your mother's wonderful, they said. Anne had heard it all her life. Your mother's wonderful. It was quite true.      (M 13)

But Anne is disturbed by the convictionless atmosphere of Mary's hurried household:

> If one had to criticize Mary, one could say nothing, absolutely nothing. She was above criticism. But must you always—Anne could sometimes have yelled out—must you always be so tolerant? Had Mary ever, during her whole life, had any really absurd, old-fashioned, stupid prejudice? Had she ever hated anybody? Had she ever really felt anything at all?      (M 15)

Meeting Mary herself a few pages later, we see that she is fond of her life:

> Coming down the gas-lit mews with three beer bottles under her arm, Mary experienced, as often before, a pang of love for her home. My dear little house, she thought.      (M 31)

Engrossed in the present, however, she fails to acknowledge the past. Unlike Margaret Schlegel in *Howards End,* she cannot connect.[24] To her, life is merely restless movement. Mary cannot connect activity with passivity or the present with the past. She is too busy "unsticking" parties by her mime of Queen Victoria, excluding grief by a false bravado—in short, shutting out what E. M. Forster refers to as "goblin footfalls."

Mary's goblin footfalls are revealed in her interior monologue during the Memorial Dedication. Isherwood skillfully
juxtaposes Mary's reflections with the pietistic platitudes of the
Bishop. While the Bishop drones about the common sorrow
that draws all to the foot of the Cross, Mary considers her
antipathy toward Lily. As the Bishop asks, "What did the War
mean to you?" (M 106), Mary recalls ration cards, visits to the
hospital, the infidelities of her husband, Desmond. When the
Bishop suggests that the Cross stands for Freedom, Remembrance, and Inspiration (M 109), Mary is riddled by her own
bitter remembrances—Desmond's last night, asking to be
taken back; her own freedom—her refusal to accept Desmond; her own inspiration—a cunning and cautious love. She
resolves these reflections with her own truism: "Living people
are better than dead ones. And we've got to get on with life" (M
113).

Though vigorous and captivating, Mary leads a truncated
life. She has chosen to disregard any memory, emotion, or
person that would trench upon her false tranquility. She has
sold her soul to the present. So have her children: Anne and
Maurice are both entangled in the moral laissez-faire atmosphere Mary engenders. Anne is disturbed by her own loss of
conscience, but nonetheless marries Ramsbotham for his
money. Maurice is more like his mother, clowning and caper-
ing through life, borrowing money from Eric, involving himself in both homosexual and heterosexual liaisons.

Eric, however, has lost his soul neither to Lily's past nor to
Mary's present: the contrary forces of Lily and Mary that had
split him as a child continue their destructive work in his
adulthood. Attempting to involve himself in the present, he
abandons a promising career at Cambridge to serve in the
General Strike. He temporarily embraces Marxism and tours
the slums of Wales; but always he is haunted by his mother's
ghoulish grief and the guilt it has planted in him. Unlike

Caddy Compson in *The Sound and the Fury*, Eric cannot repu-
diate the past, cannot heed the advice of an early Auden poem
in which the very act of breaking free heals all grief:

> To throw away the key or walk away
> . . . makes us well
> without confession of the ill.[25]

Instead, the past that began with his father's death and his
mother's mourning clings to Eric. Eric cannot forget Lily "hideous with grief. Her eyes swollen into slits . . . her face blotched
. . ." (M 151–52). Nor can he forget his own incapacity to
comprehend or allay her agony. He tries desperately: in one
dialogue, he vows never to marry, to live forever with her. But
Richard exacts Lily's complete devotion, and Lily only despises
Eric for his clumsiness, his stammer, his failure to replace
Richard. Thus, scorned by his mother, Eric scorns himself as
every "kind of cheat, deceiver. . . vile" (M 161).

Eric's buoyant Aunt Mary, however, represents freedom and
vitality. One morning, merely riding his bike in the direction of
Gately, her home, Eric feels his chronic distress lifted. But his
elation is short-lived, for Eric is the outsider, the spectator: he
watches Mary and her children playing hockey; he does not
join them. The scene is emblematic of Eric's state: he burns to
join the living, but cannot, because he is too much like his
mother. Again, Isherwood brings home the resemblance
between mother and son, as he had with Mrs. Lindsay and
Philip. This description of Eric recalls Isherwood's earlier portrait of Lily on the eve of her courtship: "Eric turned away
from the window, deeply sighed. He was weary—weary to the
bone" (M 208). Isherwood even repeats the image of the circle.
At a party Eric is presented as "turning round and round lest
some kind of area of danger should form behind his back" (M
39).

Eric is always the tense, befuddled adolescent. In awkward
circumstances, his stammer returns. Persuading Edward

Blake, his father's best friend and the prototype of the Truly Weak Man, to break off his homosexual relation with Maurice, Eric's cousin, he can scarcely articulate:

> "There's s-something"—Eric made a desperate effort to control his voice, but it was loud, hoarse, abrupt, and the stammer seized him—"s-something I must t-talk to you about." (M 219)

His confused motives still rattle him: after the meeting with Blake, Eric recognizes his overweening jealousy and flagellates himself:

> Liar! he thought. Hypocrite! Liar! Cheat! He stared furiously at the dark ceiling. I was jealous. The whole thing was nothing but jealousy. (M 227)

Eric's conversion to Catholicism, announced by letter to Blake a few pages before the book's conclusion, is the last we hear of Eric. Like his socialism, his Marxism, indeed, like his good intentions to treat his mother kindly, Eric's Catholicism can only be a temporary escape, another fadish attempt to exorcise his devils. The *mysterium tremens* of Catholicism in the thirties, its ritualized piety, its categorical assumptions about life doubtlessly attract a person like Eric. More important, Eric substitutes one mother figure for another—Mother Church, with her infallible authority, her cult of the Virgin, her celibate clergy. Having escaped from one mother, he is now tragically immured with another more tyrannical one.[26]

After *The Memorial*, the figure of the despotic mother disappears. In *The Berlin Stories*, the narrator is distant and dry, with few commitments to the human family. Even though Isherwood wrote the autobiographical *Lions and Shadows* to elucidate his career to Kathleen, he does not overtly reckon with her own presence in his life, but, as he confesses in *Kathleen and Frank*, he makes veiled references to her in innocuous phrases such as "my female relative" or "my relatives or my family" (KF 488).

After Isherwood's acceptance of Vedanta, however, mother figures reappear, at first limp and discreetly submissive. In *Prater Violet* and *A Meeting by the River*, the mother, unobtrusive and ineffectual, has lost her sting. Mrs. Isherwood of *Prater Violet* is a pleasant, sympathetic woman who keenly anticipates her son's needs and admires his talents. After a phone call from Imperial Bulldog Pictures, a self-important Christopher casually enters the kitchen. Asked by his mother, "Was that Stephen?" he comments, "She generally knew when I needed a cue line" (PV 5). Bergmann's analysis of the Englishman's Oedipal complex, which he calls the English tragedy, describes the plight of Philip Lindsay and Eric Vernon, but not that of the later Isherwood heroes:

> "You are a typical mother's son. It is the English tragedy."
> I laughed. "Quite a lot of Englishmen do get married, you know."
> "They marry their mothers. It is a disaster. It will lead to the destruction of Europe."
> "I must say, I don't quite see . . ."
> "It will lead definitely to the destruction of Europe. I have written the first chapter of a novel about this. It is called *The Diary of an Etonian Oedipus.*"                    (PV 29–30)

Bergmann's rhetorical generalization is, as always, dogmatic, but this time misleading, for by the time of *Prater Violet* Isherwood's heroes are beginning to shake free of their mothers to discover their own independence. In *A Meeting by the River*, the mother is smug and suffocatingly provincial. Though she recalls Mrs. Lindsay and Lily Vernon (she is a widow, paints watercolors, plans her children's lives), she is powerless over her younger son, Oliver, preparing to become a Hindu monk. Asking Patrick, his older brother, to unravel his actions for their mother, Oliver says to tell her "that I'm in perfect health . . . and getting enough to eat. . . . Those are the only two things she really cares about" (R 11).

*Prater Violet,* however, as we shall see in the next chapter, centers on Christopher's successful search for a father; *A Meeting by the River,* on Oliver's and Patrick's disparate strivings for truth. In both novels, the mother is peripheral. It is in *The World in the Evening* that Isherwood limns with depth and detail the mother figure as inspirational and wise, a Beatrice who steadies Stephen Monk, the protagonist, through his dark night of the soul.

Actually, two mothers impinge on Stephen's world: Sarah Pennington, a Quakeress, replaces his dead mother by rearing Stephen with simplicity and affection. She substantiates her role as surrogate mother at the novel's end when she reveals that Stephen's father was the only man she ever loved. Stephen's second "mother," his first wife, the novelist Elizabeth Rydal, ten years older, abides his bluster and egotism. Only after death do the lessons she embodied, recorded in her numerous letters, spur Stephen to a change of heart.

Though bloated and overwritten, Isherwood's novel does have some structure, revealed by the titles of its three sections. In section one, "An End," Stephen Monk, a middle-aged adolescent, is rudely blasted out of his abulia. At a dreary Hollywood cocktail party, Stephen discovers his second wife, Jane, making love with a screen star. Disgusted and jealous, he bolts home, wrecks her bedroom, and flees to Aunt Sarah and the family mansion, Twelfan, in Dolgelly, Pennsylvania. It is significant that, for the first time, an Isherwood hero's initial impulse is not to run from home to solve his problems, but rather to seek home as a place to thrash them out. There, sensing that he still can't face his failures, he deliberately steps in front of a speeding truck. He does not kill himself, however, and the major portion of the novel treats Stephen's physical and psychological recovery as he recalls and relives his past.

At Twelfan, Sarah is the first to greet Stephen. Isherwood's portrait of her is disappointingly wooden. Her peculiar idiom and assorted eccentricities compose not a person but an idealized type. "Being constantly anxious not to waste anything" (WE 29), she writes letters "in a microscopic hand on various odd scraps of paper, such as grocery bills and the covers of Quaker pamphlets about peace" (WE 29), and she stores dead mice "in the icebox to keep fresh until the kitten got hungry again" (WE 51). She is drawn instinctively to problem animals (WE 51) and has a "passion for criminals" (WE 29). She gleefully splutters at such banalities as "I'm counting on you to help me wrestle with the Demon Nicotine" (WE 27). In short, she is "poor as a mouse, eager, busy, happy" (WE 41). The following dialogue about "clips" epitomizes the halo of unreality with which Isherwood crowns Sarah. Asking Stephen's permission to turn Twelfan into a community center, Aunt Sarah prefaces her request by assuring Stephen that, of course, what she wants to do is not for herself. Stephen replies,

> "Not for *you*, Aunt Sarah?" I pretended utter amazement. "I thought you needed another pair of diamond clips. You mean, you haven't lost the ones I gave you last year?"
> "Why, Stephen, I declare—you're teasing me again! Not that I don't know you'd give me anything for myself I cared to ask for . . . I must admit, I don't quite understand you, though. Do you mean clips for holding papers together? Why in the world would anyone want them made of diamonds?"
> "No, Aunt Sarah—they're to wear."
> "Oh, how stupid of me . . . I might have guessed that, might-n't I?"                                                        (WE 288)

Stephen's reflections that the foreign language he and Sarah converse in has its limits and that the phrases sound like quotations from a phrase book (WE 24) are undeniably true, but these admissions do not salvage Isherwood's rendering of Sarah. Imbued with impeccable honesty and a staunch contempt for worldly things as so much twaddle, Sarah is cumbersome and unconvincing, her innocence overwrought. Thom

Gunn sums up Isherwood's problem with Aunt Sarah: "The author states the strength or wisdom without completely conveying it to us."[27]

It is not Sarah's Quakerism that accounts for her lack of vital elasticity. Gerda, a German refugee whose husband is incarcerated in a Nazi concentration camp, is a figure from Isherwood's Berlin past. Yet she also labors under a ponderous beatitude. Thom Gunn senses uneasiness and unsureness in Isherwood's treatment of Gerda;[28] Kingsley Amis sees her as "nothing more than a generic refugee."[29] Many of her scenes are irreclaimable, blunted by self-conscious banter and shallow humor. Dr. Charles, Stephen's physician, pays a visit to the sick room:

> There was a very gentle tap on the door; so gentle that it was obviously meant to be comic. Then the door opened a little, and Charles Kennedy's head appeared, thrust forward into the room and peeking around cautiously, like a conspirator.
>
> "Hello," he said to Gerda, in a hoarse stage whisper. "Is he still breathing?"
>
> "Oh, very much!"
>
> "You're quite certain?"
>
> "But of course I am certain!" Gerda started to giggle. She loved being teased by Kennedy. (WE 53)

Gerda's giggles at Kennedy's archness and pedestrian humor seem out of proportion to the "awkward jocularity" in the scene. In this next dialogue, Isherwood strains again for a facetious response. Dr. Kennedy asks,

> "How are the bowels?"
>
> "Ask Gerda. That's her department."
>
> "They are excellent," Gerda told him. She went out of the room with the bedpan, laughing. (WE 54)

Gerda laughs while the reader grimaces at such heavy-handed episodes. This awkward angling for comedy is particularly fatal in the conversation between Bob Wood, homosexual lover of Charles Kennedy, and Stephen:

> "I paint with my paw," said Bob, "in various styles. I'm the canine Cézanne, the pooch Picasso, the mongrel Matisse. . . ."
>
> "Sure you are." Charles patted Bob's shoulder, as though he were trying to soothe an hysterical patient. "*And* the tyke Toulouse-Lautrec. Don't be scared of him. . . . He gets these attacks quite often, especially when he's in company. I see I shall have to take him home now and muzzle him. Then he'll sleep it off in his kennel. He's really perfectly harmless." (WE 59)

Angus Wilson discusses this very dialogue as an example of "embarrassing facetious 'goodness' . . . an extraordinary lapse of judgment" on Isherwood's part, which reveals the "curious confusion in Isherwood's mind between 'goodness' and 'cosiness.'" This cosiness "throws out of balance *The World in the Evening*—at its worst in Aunt Sarah, the true vessel of spiritual light."[30] Nevertheless, Isherwood sees these people as singularly good: Sarah Pennington's fidelity hounds Stephen to the very end. His last sensation before his accident is "a whiff of Sarah's dinner, a concentration of all the dinners she had ever cooked for me. It was an intolerable smell. It was the smell of Sarah's love" (WE 48).

Unlike Sarah, Elizabeth Rydal, modeled on the Katherine Mansfield of the journals, strikes a happy balance of basic humanity and clairvoyance. Isherwood lends shape to Elizabeth by a favorite device: the confessional letter. In the second part of the novel, "Letters and Life," Stephen, while recuperating, reads Elizabeth's letters, which he hopes to edit for a book in the same way J. Middleton Murry edited Katherine Mansfield's letters and journals. While reading these frank, inspirational letters, Stephen vicariously relives the struggle of this perceptive, sensitive woman seeking to comprehend her work, her inner life, and her life with Stephen. The letters reveal a career of rare courage and expansiveness. The hours Stephen spends with her letters are transformed into moments of high truth during which he reexperiences his own past.

> When Elizabeth mentioned the Schwarzsee, I could literally smell the wet lilac bushes; when she described our trip to Khalkis, I felt a sudden intense hunger for fried squid. Now and then, these sense-impressions were so vivid that I wondered if this wasn't something more than memory: if I wasn't, in some way, actually reliving the original event. (WE 101)

Isherwood intends Stephen's letter-reading to be more akin to prayer than to nostalgic recall of a former lover's words and actions:

> First, I had to get into the right mood. Sometimes I'd lie quite still with my eyes closed for as much as half an hour, letting myself sink slowly into a state of reverie that was almost a trance. (WE 100)

In her *Journal,* Katherine Mansfield records this same reliving of the past:

> It often happens to me now that when I lie down to sleep at night, instead of getting drowsy, I feel more wakeful and, lying here in bed, I begin to *live* over either scenes from real life or imaginary scenes. It's not too much to say they are almost hallucinations: they are marvellously vivid. I lie on my right side and put my left hand up to my forehead as though I were praying. This seems to induce the state.

She even experiences the same vivid sense-impressions Stephen does:

> Then, for instance, it is 10:30 p.m. on a big liner in mid ocean. People are beginning to leave the Ladies' Cabin. . . . I am *there*. Details: Father rubbing his gloves, the cold air—the *night* air, the pattern of everything, the feel of the brass stair-rail and the rubber stairs. Then the deck. . . . All these things are far realer, more in detail, *richer* than life. . . . [31]

Two themes reverberate in Elizabeth's letters: her honesty as a writer and her heroism. As Stephen affirms, "She never made any compromises, and she never stopped trying. She may not have been first-class, but she was a real writer: a serious writer. It's something to know you're that" (WE 280). When Gerda denounces Elizabeth's novels as irrelevant to politics, Stephen's counter is also an appraisal of Isherwood's own work:

> "She never dealt directly with world situations or big-scale tragedies. That wasn't her way. But she tried to reproduce them in miniature, the essence of them."            (WE 119)

Articulated with Elizabeth's ruminations on the novel are her reflections on life:

> . . . he [Stephen] hasn't been *out in the great woods,* as I have. Do you know what I mean by that? Once you've been out there, once you've been truly and utterly alone—oh, it's so hard to come back. Not that you pine for freedom.            (WE 126)

Dying, she wrings from her wasted frame the resolve to persist in writing her novel. This commitment to her craft is tantamount to a decision to live on:

> . . . and I'm still not more than three-quarters through the wood. I feel absolutely no interest, no enthusiasm. I only know that I have to go on. I drag myself to my desk. Opening my notebook is like forcing the door of a safe—a safe which turns out to be empty, anyhow!—and psychologically speaking, my pen weighs at least a hundred pounds; I have to use all the muscles of my will to pick it up.            (WE 170)

The dread of death threatens to cave in whatever defenses she might erect. Worse than the awful fact of death is the almost unbearable "fear of death" (WE 255). This fear she personifies as a baby whom she gathers into her arms, nursing and soothing it (WE 235). Stephen lives in the giant shadow of his dead wife, who is more present to him than anyone else. Her memory, however, does not eclipse, but floods the present with life. His dependence on Elizabeth, his egotistical cruelty to Michael, a homosexual lover, and to Jane—all the ugliness in his life—he finally faces. He even finds the resources to counsel Charles Kennedy and Bob Wood, who, beginning to get on each other's nerves, are verging on a separation. Stephen finally grows up, still loving Elizabeth, but needing her less (WE 214). He has toiled through the Dantesque woods mentioned in Elizabeth's letters; and, as in Isherwood's Vedantist books, Stephen's experiences are mystical. Though he doesn't know it, his description of his spiritual illumination is invested with Vedantist terminology:

> I didn't dare to admit that I had seen what I'd seen. That would be getting in too deep. The whatever-it-was was so vast that I daren't let myself go toward it. (WE 293)

Here Stephen echoes Elizabeth, who had been far more explicit. She had viewed death not, in actual fact, as severing her from Stephen, because

> I know that Stephen is essentially in It. But what really hurts me, in my ignorance, is my attachment to Stephen as an individual, and the thought that I must leave him. I keep telling myself that we shall still be together as part of It. (WE 236)

Renewed, stripped of his egoism, Stephen discloses his new life to his second wife, whom he has granted a divorce. He has enlisted in World War II in the civilian ambulance service. Even more important, he declares, "I'll even forgive myself. As a matter of fact, I just have. Do you know something, Jane . . . I really do forgive myself, from the bottom of my heart?" (WE 301) This third and final part of the novel is fittingly entitled "A Beginning."

And though sentimental, at times flabby, the novel nonetheless augurs a fresh start for Isherwood. The book does not simply repeat "*The Berlin Stories,* resown in America and coming up as a poor thin crop of lowered vitality,"[32] but, as Thom Gunn perceives, it is "something far more serious, far more complex"[33] than Isherwood had previously ventured. This significant new note can be garnered from a provocative article written by Edwin Muir in 1940, "The Natural Man and the Political Man."[34] John Lehmann calls Muir's article "One of the most remarkable articles I ever published—in fact, I believe one of the most important published anywhere during the war."[35] Though Muir does not explicitly refer to Isherwood, in reviewing the novels of the past twenty years and in observing the switched viewpoints of a novelist such as Aldous Huxley, Muir's interpretation prophetically graphs the drastically altered lines of Isherwood's artistic concerns. Muir contends that with the disappearance of man as religion and traditional humanism conceived him, "There . . . emerged a new species of the natural man firmly dovetailed into a biological sequence and a social structure."[36] This new natural man is capable of improvement, but "unlike the natural man of religion had no need of regeneration. He is simply a human model capable of indefinite improvement on the natural plane, the improvement depending on the progress of society, and of things in general."[37] Hence a Hemingway fathers forth the natural men, Jake Barnes and Frederic Henry, who grow into the political man, Robert Jordan, the natural man with a social consciousness. Life is development and "that development is simple and inevitable."[38] But, because this development leads only to the bankruptcy of communism and fascism, many novelists, "Mr. Aldous Huxley, for example," have turned "elsewhere for a more adequate conception of man." Whether they turn to Vedanta, as Huxley and Heard and Isherwood did, or Catholicism, as Waugh eventually did, these authors view life as a conflict, and "conflict implies a choice, and the choice complexity, the existence of more in human life than can be compressed into a formula."[39] In *The World in the Evening,* then,

Isherwood strives mightily to chart the spiritual awakening and growth of Stephen Monk, who, under the tutelage of Aunt Sarah and Elizabeth, his mothers in the spirit, learns how to live. What they teach him is succinctly recapitulated by an entry in Katherine Mansfield's diary:

> September 30. "Do you know what individuality is?"
> "No."
> "Consciousness of will. To be conscious that you have a will and can act."
> "Yes, it is. It's a glorious saying."[40]

Stephen Monk's journey from anger to appeasement mirrors Isherwood's own change of attitude toward himself and his life. As a young man, fatherless and raised by a widow, he was appalled by Kathleen's obstinate reliving of the past, her outmoded opinions, her antique, prewar style of life. In *Kathleen and Frank*, he recollects:

> It was wonderful how naturally they disagreed. Christopher used to say that if Kathleen and he had landed on an alien planet where there were two political parties about which they knew nothing, the Uggs and the Oggs, she would have instantly chosen one of them and he the other, simply by reacting to the sound of their names. (KF 507)

Like Hamlet, before Isherwood could accept his mother and his mother-ridden life, he needed first to discover the truth about his father's ghost, and not Kathleen's version of the truth. In desperately trying to unclench Kathleen's grip on his life—by refusing an academic career; by expatriating himself; by emigrating to Germany (a country Kathleen's generation detested); by becoming an American citizen, thus "separating himself from Mother and Motherland at one stroke" (KF 508)—Isherwood was all the time casting about for a solution to his personal conflicts. As we shall see in "Fathers and Sons," his attraction to Vedanta is based on his need for a father figure—a need fulfilled in the guru-disciple relationship. Only after discovering a surrogate father can Isherwood look back on his life with Kathleen not with rancor, but with tranquility and gratitude. Writing from a Vedantist viewpoint, he can, like his protagonist Stephen Monk, vaunt his heart-felt forgiveness:

> It was Kathleen, more than anybody else, who saved him from becoming a mother's boy, a churchgoer, an academic, a conservative, a patriot and a respectable citizen.          (KF 507)

The irony with which he decks his novels he begins to glimpse in his own life as a saving grace. His expatriation in the United States did not sever his ties to Kathleen, but actually strengthened them, for in the end he had fulfilled her wishes. By teaching "in colleges he had become an academic"; by "embracing Vedanta he had joined the ranks of the religious"; by opposing "those fellow citizens whom he regarded as a menace to his adopted country he had turned into a patriot" (KF 508–9). To paraphrase assorted Auden fragments, Isherwood had thrown away the key, crossed the frontier, toiled up F 6, only to find perched on its peak, but filled with blessings and not recriminations, Kathleen, his mother.

CHAPTER

# 2

# ⚲Fathers and Sons⚲

By the time of *The World in the Evening,* Isherwood comes round to recognizing that much of his work was provoked by Kathleen's dogged opposition to anything that smacked of the twentieth century. He is, in turn, appeased, reconciled to her, and abundantly grateful. He even pardons what is perhaps her greatest treason: her mythologizing Frank into a heroic husband and father. But, for his own survival, he cannot accept her version of Frank.

Only eleven when Frank was reported missing, Isherwood hardly knew him, yet knew enough to realize that Kathleen's version was her private fiction. Isherwood retaliated by creating his own father. Jacob Isaacs sums up Isherwood's predicament, as well as that of many other young men who grew up during and after the Great War:

> The psychological situation was particularly interesting. There were, as they confessed frequently, men like Christopher Isher-

wood particularly involved in a struggle against "the Father" as
an authority from which an escape must be made, and against
"the Mother" from whose entanglements and clutches it was
equally necessary to emerge. The novels of Christopher Isherwood, and Auden and Isherwood's play *The Ascent of F 6* show
this with great clarity.[1]

Fashioning a father, and thereby slipping free of the clutches
of both mother and father, was not difficult, Isherwood tells
us:

> Nothing had to be invented. Christopher had only to select
> certain of Frank's characteristics, doings and sayings (which
> meant censoring the rest) and make a person out of them,
> giving it Frank's body and voice.                    (KF 503)

The precise opposite of Kathleen's version, this Frank aptly
embodies Isherwood's resentment of Kathleen and the English
middle class. Thus, Frank's behavior, as Christopher construes
it, is always subversive: "He shows his contempt for army
documents by doing comic sketches on them, and for his
dignity as an officer by knitting in the midst of a bombard-
ment" (KF 503–4). In *An Approach to Vedanta,* Isherwood
recalls what his version of Frank meant to him:

> My father had taught me, by his life and death, to hate the
> profession of soldiering. I remember his telling me, before he
> left for France, that an officer's sword is useless except for
> toasting his bread, and that he never fired his revolver because
> he couldn't hit anything with it and hated the bang. He was
> killed while leading an attack, carrying only a swagger stick, with
> which he was signaling directions to his men. I adored my
> father's memory, dwelling always on his civilian virtues: his
> gentleness, his humor, his musical and artistic talent.[2]

Hence, Isherwood's Frank is courageous and inspiring, pos-
sessing the qualities of E. M. Forster, whom Isherwood refers

to as "my absolute guru."[3] Isherwood's description of Forster in
*Down There on a Visit* defines the anti-heroic father:

> . . . he's far saner than anyone else I know. And immensely,
> superhumanly strong. He's strong because he doesn't try to be a
> stiff-lipped stoic like the rest of us, and so he'll never crack. He's
> absolutely flexible. He lives by love, not by will.         (V 175)

> We need E. M.'s silliness more than ever now. It gives courage.
> The other kind depresses and weakens me more than the worst
> prophecies of disaster.                                     (V 176)

Flexibility, a quiet courage, love, an inward radiance, humor,
even silliness—these are the functions, according to Isherwood, of Frank's fatherhood.

Opposed to Isherwood's portrayal of his father stands the
father of the Others: A Kiplingesque force, representing duty
and obligation, personifying "the Empire, the Flag, the Old
School Tie and the Stiff Upper Lip . . . what life was really
like. . . ."[4] Isherwood's Repton Headmaster discourses on the
qualities of this man in his oration following the dedication of
the Repton War Memorial, quoted in the chapter entitled
"War." Henry Green, exiled to an English boarding school
because, like Isherwood, he was too young to enlist, recalls the
invidious authority this impersonal father wielded: "If we mis-
behaved, we were told that they were out there fighting for
us."[5] In *All the Conspirators,* Mrs. Lindsay, trying to cajole Philip
into returning to his office job, evokes Philip's dead father in
the same way by dropping this reminder of his father's wishes:
"Your father always hoped that you would make a position for
yourself in the world" (AC 79).

Two father types appear in Isherwood's fiction: in the early
novels, the forbidding ghost whose legend, kept alive by Kathleen, emasculates his son; and in the later books, after Isherwood's settling in America and adoption of Vedanta, the sympathetic, broadly human, anti-heroic father.

The father of the Others is fully fleshed in *The Memorial.*
There, seen through the admiring eyes of Edward Blake or the
love-beclouded eyes of Lily, Richard Vernon (Eric's father) is a
cynosure of classical manhood, "a hero and a great man . . .
sure of himself . . . brave" (M 133). Eric shudders when he
remembers his father, has nightmares that "Father would
come back from the grave" (M 205), prefers death to incurring
his displeasure. Isherwood's brother, Richard, reveals a similar
nightmare in *Kathleen and Frank:*

> I did so hate being everlastingly reminded of him, when I was
> young. Everybody kept saying how perfect he was, such a hero
> and so good at everything. He was always held up as someone
> you could never hope to be worthy of, and whenever I did
> anything wrong I was told I was a disgrace to him. You know, I
> used to have a recurring nightmare that he wasn't dead after all
> and that he was coming back to live with us! And then I was
> horrified, and I wanted to run away from home and hide
> somewhere before he arrived. I used to simply loathe him.[6] (KF
> 502)

It is this loathed father, cold and forbidding, who stalks the
pages of *The Memorial.* The nearest an Isherwood hero comes
to accepting the father of the Others is in *The World in the
Evening.* After years of despising his father, reformed Stephen
Monk, gazing at his father's portrait, discovers that

> . . . something very strange was happening to me . . . a kind of
> hypnotic effect. For the first time, I seemed to be seeing it
> through Sarah's eyes. Was she willing this? The face on the
> canvas didn't exactly change, but it presented a different
> expression. As I examined it, feature by feature, the mouth
> looked to me more flexible, the eyes deepened. Wasn't there,
> after all, a certain humor in them, as Sarah had claimed? (WE
> 290)

Here, however, Stephen is not seeing with his own eyes but
with Sarah's.

For his own sanity, Isherwood had to cut himself free from the father of the Others. Hence he plays so often and so well the role of Heathcliff, the fatherless child, the mysterious outsider without home and country. Only in *Prater Violet* does Isherwood, still without father and country, transcend these losses and convert them into spiritual gains. *Prater Violet* is significant because it bears witness to Isherwood's reinterpretation of reality in terms of Vedantist philosophy and because, for perhaps the first time, his hero establishes intimate contact with another human being whom he fittingly calls "father." But this is not the father of the Others.

Vedanta presented a religious version of Isherwood's antiheroic hero. And for this reason—as much as for any other—Isherwood converted to Vedanta. In an article explaining this conversion in the collection *What Vedanta Means to Me,* Isherwood clearly shows that the search for a father and the search for a religion had become inextricably interwoven in his consciousness.[7] Unlike the lucubrations of Huxley and Heard, which appear in the same volume, Isherwood's article is unforbidding, humorous, completely personal.[8]

He begins by discussing his hatred of Christianity's dualism because of his "father-complex" and because of "certain experiences in early childhood [with] authority." He could not abide Christianity's God, who presided over sinful subjects on earth: "We were bad. We were so bad that, when he sent his Son down . . . we promptly crucified him" (46). Christianity seemed to consist "almost entirely of don'ts; everything you could possibly want to do was forbidden as a sin" and Christians were "a collection of dreary, canting hypocrites; missionaries of ignorance and reactions," stiffly pious, sickeningly humble, and selfishly devout in their prayers for "rain, health and national victory in war" (47). Just how extravagant Isherwood's utter scorn for Christianity became can be judged in an anecdote recorded in "Waldemar," the third section of *Down There on a Visit.* In China, Isherwood writes, he and Weston

(Auden) idled away their leisure time by arguing about anything they could think of. "But whenever we started on God and the soul, I would find myself getting passionately angry—as always in recent years":

> "I don't give a shit," I'd tell Hugh, "what anybody else says: I know *I* haven't got a soul. And I'm willing to bet that no one else has, either. All that talk makes me sick. I can't just be neutral about it. I think it's obscene and evil. When I hear the word 'God' I want to vomit; it's the dirtiest word in the language. It describes everything that's filthy—Franco, Hitler, the Fascists—everything!"

Weston would of course take it all good-humoredly:

> "Careful! Careful! If you keep going on like that, my dear, you'll have *such* a conversion, one of these days! Oh dear, I can just *picture* you being received into the bosom of Mother Church, with all those masses and candles!"        (V 142)

In spite of his banner-waving atheism, Isherwood adds, he was not without a religion, for in place of Christianity he had substituted a belief in art. But he was too much of a "hard-boiled operator in the fashionable literary racket" (48) to emulate the great masters of literature who had not feared "poverty, ill-health, public ridicule, even imprisonment and death in their struggle to express their inspiration" (48). Moreover he knew that he would be doomed as a writer if he were to abandon "my own kind of writing and devote myself to political journalism and propaganda" (49).

Isherwood's other religion substitute, pacifism, was "too limited and negative to form a basis for living; it didn't go beyond the decision to refuse to fight, if there was a war" (5).

Therefore "in a very disturbed and confused state of mind" (50) Isherwood first came into contact with the teachings of Vedanta.[9] In California, Isherwood was introduced by Heard and Huxley to their friend Swami Prabhavananda, a Hindu monk of the Ramakrishna Order who had founded a small Vedanta society in Hollywood. Prabhavananda was the right man at the right time to comfort and cheer Isherwood, whose last strands of manhood, in the words of Hopkins' most famous terrible sonnet, were beginning to slacken and "untwist."[10] "After I got to know Prabhavananda, I gradually ceased to be an atheist; because I found myself unable to disbelieve in his belief in God" (E 97).

Vedanta answered Isherwood's every need. It is nondualistic: God is not above and beyond man, but the Atman is within man. Unlike Christianity, Vedanta is not narrowly moralistic:

> Vedanta does not emphasize the vileness of man's mortal nature or the enormity of sin. It dwells, rather, on the greatness of man's eternal nature, and refuses to dignify sin by allowing it too much dramatic value. . . . (54)

To be more precise, unlike Christianity, Vedanta does not condemn homosexuality but views it as "merely another form of attachment, neither worse nor better"[11] than heterosexuality.

This, Isherwood writes, is "the message of Vedanta as Vivekananda preaches it" (55). Vivekananda was the most influential missionary of Vedanta to the West, and his example and interpretation of the Vedas have inspired, and continue to inspire, the many Vedantist societies in America. In extolling Vivekananda, who took up "the spiritual heritage of Ramakrishna and disseminated the grains of his thought throughout the world,"[12] Isherwood arrays Vivekananda with all the excellencies of the anti-heroic father, thus contrasting his ideal with that of the Others:

> Here, at last, was a man [Vivekananda] who believed in God and yet dared to condemn the indecent grovelings of the sin-obsessed Puritans I had so much despised in my youth. I loved him at once, for his bracing self-reliance, his humor, and his

courage. He appealed to me as the perfect anti-Puritan hero: the enemy of Sunday religion, the destroyer of Sunday gloom, the shocker of prudes, the breaker of traditions, the outrager of conventions, the comedian who taught the deepest truths in idiotic jokes and frightful puns.

At the end of his fifteen-page essay, Isherwood nonetheless despairs: "I have written all this; and yet I have said really nothing" (57). Consequently he turns once again to the foundation of his belief:

> I only know that, as far as I am concerned, the guru-disciple relationship is at the center of everything that religion means to me. . . . If . . . I could in some terrible way be deprived of it again, then my life would become a nightmare of guilt, boredom and self-disgust.[13]

In fiction, as has been said, Isherwood first attests to these religious preoccupations in *Prater Violet*. The novelette's plot is slight, based on Isherwood's collaboration with Berthold Viertel in London in 1934 on the film *Little Friend*.[14] The narrator, Christopher Isherwood, is hired to compose a script for the movie *Prater Violet,* to be directed by the extraordinary Viennese genius, Friedrich Bergmann. As a portrait of Bergmann, of the rapacious motion picture world, and of Christopher's relationship with Bergmann, the novel is a *tour de force*. Diana Trilling's sensitive reading of the novel suggests that the "deceptively slight" story is merely "the pebble in the lake, from which [Isherwood's] novel ripples out in ever-widening circles of implications."[15] Mrs. Trilling traces several circles, construing *Prater Violet* as a novel of narrative and social observation; as a study in sensitivities; as a presentation of the relation of the individual to society and to himself; and as an examination of heroic dedication to work. As perceptive as her essay is, it nonetheless sees only a segment of the curve and fails to follow the complete circumferences of the circles she scans. In contrasting Isherwood's seasoned humanity with the mysticism of Heard and Huxley, she neglects the book's own mystical ramifications—or, to continue her image, fails to recognize that Isherwood's pebble is cast into an Indian lake. Similarly, James T. Farrell interprets the book as defining the "position of the artist in the period of monopoly capitalism" by a "contrapuntal structure . . . which . . . shows how shabby motion picture art presents counterfeit images of life."[16] But Farrell also fails to complete his thesis: the novel's counterfeit images are, in a spiritual sense, truthful reflections of life, for according to Vedantist belief, reality resides behind the visible world. The visible world is mere illusion. Hence, "from one point of view," as Richard Mayne writes, *Prater Violet* is "an amusing account of some hopeless film making": but "seen from another point of view, it might also rank as a mystical tract."[17] Read as such, *Prater Violet* is clearly inspired by the *Bhagavad-Gita,* the greatest of Hindu epics, translated by Isherwood with Swami Prabhavananda a year before the publication of *Prater Violet.*

In his synopsis of the *Gita,* Isherwood stresses what is a major theme of the novel: the illusory nature of appearances. In the *Gita,* Arjuna, a leading general, has Krishna for his charioteer, a fellow mortal, "personal friend and his illumined teacher" as well as a god (E 106). Before the battle begins, Arjuna asks Krishna to drive his chariot into the no-man's land between the two armies. Krishna complies, and Arjuna, thunder-struck by the thought of all the men he will slay, refuses combat. Krishna's reply, occupying the rest of the epic, untangles Arjuna's personal problems and crystallizes the whole meaning of action and of life.

Krishna commences by addressing himself to Arjuna's feelings of revulsion. Krishna reminds Arjuna that he should not shrink from the act of killing, because "in the absolute sense, there is no such act" (E 107); because "the Atman, the indwelling Godhead is the only reality . . . he only seems to kill" (E 107). In his recapitulation, Isherwood then quotes the *Gita:*

> Some say this Atman
> Is slain, and others
> Call It the slayer:
> They know nothing.
> How can It slay
> Or who shall slay It?

"Therefore, if Arjuna is objecting to the act of killing, as such, he need have no scruples. For he only seems to kill" (E 107).

Then, as a fellow mortal, Krishna addresses Arjuna: it is Arjuna's caste-duty to fight. Hence he must wage war, without fear and desire, in a spirit of detachment. "For Arjuna, a member of the warrior caste, the fighting of this battle, in defence of his family and property, is undoubtedly 'righteous.' It is his duty" (E 108). Illuminated, Arjuna confidently and joyously obeys.

Arjuna's education consists in distinguishing appearance from reality. Vedantists call this journey toward light the "path of analysis or knowledge, or the path of discrimination." It consists essentially in purifying the vision, training the eyes to distinguish between the genuine and the counterfeit.

In *Prater Violet,* Christopher takes a few tentative steps on the path towards illumination. He progresses from bewilderment to the beginning of spiritual intuition—only the beginning, for, even at the novel's poetic finale, Christopher still shrinks from complete commitment. Bergmann, the analogon of Krishna, is Christopher's friend, teacher, and ghostly father. In his first meeting with Bergmann, Christopher is at once captivated:

> I couldn't help smiling as we shook hands, because our introduction seemed so superfluous. There are meetings which are like recognitions—this was one of them.          (PV 16)

Bergmann's later remark to Christopher brings to mind the brothel scene of Joyce's *Ulysses,* in which Stephen discovers a father in Bloom: "We are like two married men who meet in a whorehouse" (PV 23). The next day in his apartment, Bergmann, discoursing on the Englishman's predilection for living with his mother, on the film *Prater Violet,* on life in general, prophetically promises Christopher: "I shall teach you everything from the very beginning" (PV 30).

Bergmann keeps his promise. He is the Vergilian guide, the Jewish Socrates, a friend and teacher to Christopher—the disciple, the learner, Aloysha Karamazov—even, as Bergmann dubs him, "Balaam's ass, 'who *once* said a marvelous line '" (PV 37).[18] Like a teacher of the Vedas, Bergmann always stresses the truth behind appearances. He bludgeons Christopher with the reality of imminent war: "We are dying with our heads . . . in the oven" (PV 41). He expatiates on the manageress of a restaurant they frequent: "I have only to look at her to know that she is satisfied. . . . She understands all of us. . . . She understands Michelangelo, Beethoven, Christ, Lenin—even Hitler. And she is afraid of nothing, nothing. . . . Such a woman is my religion" (PV 43–44). He continually throttles Christopher's sensibilities, forcing him to fathom all of life. When Dorothy, their secretary, despairs, "Those Nazis aren't human," Bergmann wisely corrects her: "You are wrong, darling. . . . We must not fear them. We must understand them. . . . It is absolutely necessary to understand them, or we are all lost" (PV 47). He derides Christopher's British isolationism.

> "You see, this umbrella . . . I find extremely symbolic. It is the British respectability which thinks: 'I have my traditions, and they will protect me. Nothing unpleasant, nothing ungentlemanly can possibly happen within my private park.' This respectable umbrella is the Englishman's magic wand, with which he will try to wave Hitler out of existence." (PV 31)

Even the treacly plot of the movie *Prater Violet* Bergmann embroiders into a symbolic fable: The dilemma of Rudolph, the protagonist who, because he loses his comfortable security, must join the proletariat, Bergmann inflates into the dilemma of the declassed intellectual. "His [Rudolph's and the intellectual's] relation to the proletariat is romantic no longer. He now must make a choice" (PV 50). Did Rudolph really love Toni, the impoverished violet vendor? Now is his chance to prove it. Is the intellectual serious about his socialism? Soon he will have the opportunity to prove it. Bergmann's moral sounds as if it were lifted right out of Virginia Woolf's essay on young writers of the thirties, "The Leaning Tower":[19] "This symbolic fable . . . is particularly disagreeable to you [Christopher and his generation] because it represents your deepest fear, the nightmare of your own class" (PV 50).

Friend, teacher, and, above all, creative father, Bergmann brings extension and excitement to everything he encounters. When Christopher is unable to write a satisfactory line of dialogue, Bergmann at once takes command:

> It was astounding. Everything came to life. The trees began to tremble in the evening breeze, the music was heard, the roundabouts were set in motion. And the people talked. Bergmann improvised their conversation, partly in German, partly in ridiculous English; and it was vivid and real.          (PV 36)

Enthroned in a director's chair, Bergmann assumes the Olympian power of a deity, his creative touch quickening the actors who wait like puppets.

> I watch him [Bergmann], throughout the take. It isn't necessary to look at the set; the whole scene is reflected in his face. He never shifts his eyes from the actors for an instant. He seems to control every gesture, every intonation, by a sheer effort of hypnotic power.          (PV 79)

Christopher marvels at Bergmann's dynamism. The spate of verbs and predicate adjectives in the following passage, along with the rise and fall of the cadence caused by the repetition of predicate adjectives and of the adverb "now," communicates the mercurial activity, the storm and stress of Bergmann's genius:

> His lips move, his face relaxes and contracts, his body is thrust forward or drawn back in its seat, his hands rise and fall to mark the phases of the action. Now he is coaxing Toni from the window, now warning against too much haste, now calling for more expression, now afraid the pause will be missed, now delighted with the tempo, now anxious again, now really alarmed, now reassured, now touched, now pleased, now very pleased, now cautious, now disturbed, now amused.

Christopher concludes: "Bergmann's concentration is marvelous in its singleness of purpose. It is the act of creation" (PV 79).

Bergmann's greatest creation is Christopher. In the book's penultimate scene—after a party celebrating the completion of the movie—Christopher and Bergmann are walking home. Bergmann has been a success at the party, and naturally Christopher is happy—"the way you feel when your father is a success with your friends" (PV 121–22). During the walk, Christopher suddenly sees, with new fire and energy, Bergmann, Europe, his own life, all of life, from a radically changed perspective. For the first time, the inner life of Christopher unfolds. The scene is lucid and low pitched, rendered in a style which approximates free verse. The opening inversion ("It is . . .") repeated thrice slows the sentences and releases Christopher to ponder, to spin out his reflections which amplify like concentric circles from the penumbral street scene to the world and to man's consciousness of himself and of others, widening to grasp knowledge of a Greater Consciousness. Because the lines are enriched with poetic techniques (similes, metaphors, incremental repetition, assonance, consonance, rhythm, symbolism), I have arranged the lines in Whitmanesque free verse. Isherwood's first paragraph, sketching the late night–early morning street scene, sets the quiet mood of the entire passage.

> IT WAS that hour of the night when the street lamps seem to shine with an unnatural, remote brilliance,
> Like planets on which there is no life.
> The King's Road was wet-black, and deserted as the moon.
> It did not belong to the King, or to any human being.
> The little houses had shut their doors against all strangers and were still,
> Waiting for dawn, bad news and the milk.
> There was nobody about. Not even a policeman. Not even a cat.

The diction: "unnatural, remote brilliance"; the cosmic generalizations: "life," "human being," "all strangers"; the unearthly similes: "like planets . . ." and " . . . deserted as the moon . . ."; the sibilants: "street lamps seem to shine" and "shut their doors against all strangers and were still"; the repetition of key words and grammatical constructions—all achieve a lyrical, mystical effect.

In the next paragraph, the repetition of the opening lines heightens the solemnity as Christopher moves into the personal sphere:

> It was that hour of the night at which man's ego almost sleeps.
> The sense of identity, of possession, of name and address and telephone number grows very faint.

Again Isherwood repeats the opening inversion:

> It was the hour at which man shivers, pulls up his coat collar, and thinks,
> "I am a traveler. I have no home."

He mulls over the last two words, repeating them like a mantra, holding them up for scrutiny:

"A traveler, a wanderer."

For a book that begins with persistent self-confirmation (the book opens: "Mr. Isherwood?" "Speaking." "Mr. Christopher Isherwood?" "That's me."), *Prater Violet* is Isherwood's longest journey, from inveterate ego reinforcement to a loss of name and identity. Christopher's self-divesting elicits the following perceptive comment from Mrs. Trilling: "It is a book written in the author's own person, yet utterly without ego. . . ."[20] Here Isherwood asks fundamental religious questions: "Who am I? Where do I come from? What is my destiny?"—perplexing riddles, to which answers "cannot be found as long as we remain clogged within the bounds of the plodding intellect."[21] In the next paragraph, Christopher relinquishes all names, alluding to himself and to Bergmann as fellow travelers. Again the echoing questions, the repetition of salient words and phrases, sustain the metaphysical tone. The question is "too brutal," yet the only question "worth asking our fellow travelers":

> What makes you go on living? Why don't you kill yourself?
> Why is all this bearable? What makes you bear it?

Isherwood's reply approximates the Vedantist doctrine of non-attached work, the advice Krishna gave to Arjuna:

> I supposed, vaguely, that it was a kind of balance, a complex of tensions.
> You did whatever was next on the list.
> A meal to be eaten. Chapter eleven to be written. . . .

His answer hardly approaches the grandeur of Krishna's, for Christopher acts not from duty and conviction but from a vague need for harmony. His love affairs Christopher inter-

prets as a hunger for a deeper relationship. Possibly this reflection inspired one critic to call Christopher not only Ishmael
"but Ahab himself . . . a different sort of Ahab but the chase is
the same whether it is after a white whale or the top of F 6 or,
as in *Prater Violet*, a purity of relationship that will transcend"
his phobias and complexes.[22] Thoughts of love and the sleep
following love lead Christopher to broach the subjects of death
and war. With what D. H. Lawrence calls "stark directness" and
T. S. Eliot, elaborating on Lawrence, calls "essentially poetry,
with nothing poetic about it, poetry standing naked in its bare
bones,"[23] Christopher looks towards personal and universal
nightmare. Again the style is meditative; the words and
phrases, sparse and controlled, slow the pace for reflection.

> Death, the desired, the feared. The longed-for sleep. The
> terror of the coming of sleep. Death. War. The vast sleeping
> city, doomed for the bombs. The roar of oncoming engines.
> The gunfire. The screams. The houses shattered.
> Death universal. My own death. Death of the seen and known
> and tasted and tangible world.
> Death with its army of fears.

In exploring his fears, Christopher moves into specifics and
varies the rhythm of his sentences. This rhythm crescendoes
into what he calls the arch-fear:

> Not the acknowledged fears, the fears that are advertised.
> More dreadful than those: the private fears of childhood.
> Fear of the height of the high-dive,
> Fear of the farmer's dog and the vicar's pony,
> Fear of cupboards, fear of the dark passage,
> Fear of splitting your finger nail with a chisel.
> And behind them, most unspeakably terrible of all, the arch-
> fear:
> The fear of being afraid.

With triple insistence, Christopher reconciles himself to his arch-fear:

> It can never be escaped—never, never.
> Not if you ran away to the ends of the earth
> (We had turned into Sloane Street),
> Not if you yell for Mummy, or keep a stiff upper lip, or take
> to drink or to dope
> That fear sits throned in my heart.
> I carry it about with me, always.

But the movement of the meditation is not downward; for the moment, Christopher glimpses an alternative. The long left-branching sentence conveys Christopher's difficulty in grasping the solution in a way that approaches T. S. Eliot's "auditory imagination":[24]

> And, at this moment, but how infinitely faint, how distant.
> Like the high far glimpse of a goat track through the mountains between clouds,
> I see something else: the way that leads to safety.
> To where there is no fear, no loneliness,
> No need of J., K., L., or M.
> For a second, I glimpse it.
> For an instant, it is even quite clear.

Isherwood's imagery suggests these lines from the *Bhagavad-Gita:*

> Let him who would climb
> In meditation
> To heights of the highest
> Union with Brahman
> Take for his path
> The yoga of action. . . .[25]

But F 6 is too threatening, its air too rarified—at least for the time being. The four heavy stresses of the ensuing transitional clause convey the abrupt blockage experienced by the speaker:

> Then the clouds shut down, and a breath off the glacier, icy
> with the inhuman coldness of the peaks, touches my cheek.
> "No," I think, "I could never do it.
> Rather the fear I know, the loneliness I know . . .
> For to take that other way would mean that I should lose
> myself.
> I should no longer be a person.
> I should no longer be Christopher Isherwood.
> No, no. That's more terrible than the bombs. . . .
> That I can never face."

Although Christopher cannot yet surrender his ego, I interpret the movement of the scene as forward and upward; for to know the path one must travel in life is a step on that path and certainly a prerequisite for salvation. Christopher is not lost, but, like most novices, cowed by the pangs the goat track into the clouds holds in store. I further ground my hopeful, even optimistic reading of the passage on the concluding epiphany. Turning toward Bergmann, Christopher resorts to theatre imagery, or more accurately, Vedantist imagery, for reality here resides "back of backstage":

> We had written each other's parts,
> Christopher's Friedrich, Friedrich's Christopher,
> And we had to go on playing them,
> As long as we were together.
> The dialogue was crude, the costumes and make-up were
> absurd, more of a caricature, than anything in *Prater Violet:*
> Mother's Boy, the comic Foreigner with the funny accent. . . .
> (We had reached Bergmann's door, now.)
> For, beneath our disguises. . . . We knew.
> Beneath outer consciousness, two other beings,

Anonymous, impersonal, without labels,
Had met and recognized each other. . . .
He was my father. I was his son.
And I loved him very much.

This scene finishes with a theophany:

Bergmann held out his hand.
"Good night, my child," he said.
He went into the house.                    (PV 122–27)

The passage is lyrical—simplicity itself, the work of a master,
the *ars celans artem* to which all art aspires. Mrs. Trilling,
contrasting the simplicity of Isherwood's style with that of
Steinbeck, Hersey, Katherine Anne Porter, reflects that "Mr.
Isherwood's style is a reflection neither of condescension nor of
assertion. It is the style of a free and generous creative intelligence, most happily balanced between self-tolerance and toler-
ance of others."[26] The writer for the *Times Literary Supplement*
observes that "In the final pages Mr. Isherwood reveals development. There the former detached analysis is replaced by an
understanding equally deep, and near to tenderness. This is a
rich, true quality which holds new promise. . . ."[27] Indeed, the
final pages carry the lyrical mysticism of a miniature *Bhagavad-
Gita,* the struggle for affirmation of Wordsworth's "Resolution
and Independence," even the transcendence of Tennyson's *In
Memoriam.*

At the spiritual center of *Prater Violet* is Bergmann, father to
Christopher or, in Vedantist terms, guru. Fictionally, Berg-
mann signifies the end of Isherwood's quest for a father figure.
It is important to note, however, that the novel's protagonist,
Christopher, is only beginning to recognize the full implica-
tions of Bergmann. As Isherwood points out, "because *Prater
Violet* was supposed to be a previous piece,"[28] the character
Christopher Isherwood could not hold beliefs in 1933 that he

did not have until 1940. Consequently, Christopher recognizes Bergmann only as father. Yet, because the search for a father and the search for a religion are inextricably bound in Isherwood's life, the novel cannot escape a luminous religious quality. Christopher may not know what he has stumbled upon, but Isherwood, after thirteen years of reflection, realizes the religious resonances of Bergmann's fatherhood.[29]

Perhaps because Isherwood's creative subconscious is responsible for the spiritual dimension in Bergmann, Bergmann is Isherwood's most successful portrait of a father-guru figure. Isherwood's deliberate attempt in "Paul," the fourth part of *Down There on a Visit,* is far less successful. Modeled on Huxley and Heard, the guru Augustus Parr is too self-consciously religious—he smacks of the confectionary "cosiness" critics find in Sarah and Gerda. Though Parr's appearance in "Paul" is brief, his function is as essential as Bergmann's in *Prater Violet.* Parr is Christopher's guru, someone whose presence and faith compel Christopher into belief. Nevertheless, in the book he comes off as little more than a cardboard saint.

The action of "Paul" occurs in Hollywood. There Christopher, involved in both Hollywood script-writing and Hindu spirituality, meets Paul, a dissolute male prostitute, a male version of Sally Bowles, but portrayed with far more complexity. When Christopher meets Paul, Paul's state is very similar to Christopher's in earlier phases of his life. Cynical and self-loathing, Paul is on the brink of suicide; in despair, he asks Christopher for assistance. With a convert's fervor, Christopher suggests that Paul should meet Parr. Reluctantly, Paul agrees.

In his first description of Parr, Isherwood seems to force Parr's spirituality: "Augustus reappeared in the doorway with the tea things, suddenly and silently, like an apparition" (V 228). With the same earnestness, he focuses on Parr's "supernaturally silent" (V 228) shoes; on Parr's "Christ-beard . . .

[which] . . . of course . . . he obviously trimmed . . . well, why shouldn't he for goodness sake!"; on Parr's "beautiful face," always pointing upward in "a heaven-seeking thrust" (V 228); and on his "pale, brilliant blue eyes which appear to lose focus and go blind—at least to the outer world" (V 229). Augustus is worldly enough to fuss over the tea things, yet spiritual enough to remind Christopher "of a radio operator with headphones over his ears, receiving a message which the people around him can't hear" (V 228). Like Sarah's prattle, Parr's is hackneyed and contrived:

> "What a curious thing it is, isn't it, when one says one is busy! So often it only means that one's afraid of having time taken away from one—like a dog growling over a bone it doesn't really want. One begins to growl before one even knows what the intentions of the person who is approaching are, save that he *is* approaching—getting within the zone of one's possessiveness."
>
> (V 223)

Isherwood's portrait of Parr has all the characteristics of high camp—a quality Isherwood finds lacking in the Quakers. High camp Isherwood defines as "a kind of extremely sophisticated humor about something in which you nevertheless firmly believe." Although humorous, "it must have an underlying seriousness. And it must imply an approval of its subject. In other words, it is not satire."[30] Even read as high camp, Parr's portrait is witless, occasionally even pretentious.

Only in *A Meeting by the River* does Isherwood create a convincing guru gifted with both the irresistible genius of Bergmann and the other-worldliness of Parr. The novel's action takes place in a Hindu monastery in India, which Isherwood visited with Swami Prabhavananda in Christmas of 1964. The novel is made up of the letters and diary entries of Oliver, about to take first vows, and his brother, Patrick, an enterprising *bon vivant,* visiting Oliver with the intention of knocking some secular sense into his brother's head. Oliver's guru, having died before the action of the novel occurs, is mentioned only briefly, but the pitch of his power rings in Oliver as well as Patrick who himself undergoes a reformation.

Oliver, the unpredictable son of a thoroughly middle-class English family, similar to the Lindsays, has left his home and a promising business career to engage in social work. While working in Munich for the International Red Cross, he accidentally meets a swami whose profound spirituality entrances him. Oliver's remarks parallel Christopher's first response to Bergmann:

> Something about him fascinated me, from the first moment; it was his very quiet unemphatic air of assurance. What I mean is, nearly all the other people who have ever struck me as having great assurance were also self-assertive and complacent, in fact downright stupid.                                    (R 16)

The guru is "a new sort of human being, almost" (R 16). He is not physically impressive, but "small and frail and skinny, with untidy grey hair cut rather short" (R 16); his robust inner being, however, flashes out: his eyes are "young, very clear and bright," possessed of an "extraordinarily calm assurance, without being in the least aggressive" (R 16). Isherwood's description of the swami's physical characteristics conveys far more successfully the inner strength of the man than the description of Parr's saintly idiosyncrasies.[31] Oliver describes his first talk with the swami as the most unsettling conversation of his life. But it is more than a mere conversation; it is a "confrontation with this individual who, just by being what he was, intrigued and mystified me and undermined my basic assumptions as no one else had ever done before" (R 17–18). Oliver begins to see that he is actually less unwilling than he realized

> to be receptive to this strange little man. Anyhow, as we went on talking, he somehow made me start questioning the very thing I

thought I was most certain about, my work and why it was
worthwhile. I began defending it even though he wasn't attack-
ing it, and whenever I found I couldn't make my defence hold
water I looked at him in dismay and he smiled!            (R 17)

Oliver encounters the swami—just as Isherwood met Swami
Prabhavananda—at that time in life when Oliver was most
open to a spiritual influence. Eventually, Oliver moves in with
the swami, the "usual title of a Hindu Monk who has taken the
final vows, just as you say Father to a Catholic priest" (R 18).
The swami is a father to Oliver—a relationship Oliver at first
finds awkward. He writes Patrick that he didn't know how to
conduct himself because "Father died when we were both so
young . . ." (R 20). The swami "took it all for granted, however.
And soon he began referring to me as his 'disciple'" (R 20).
Oliver's definition of discipleship recalls Isherwood's description in "What Vedanta Means to Me":

> To begin with, this [Oliver's discipleship] was more or less said
> as a joke, but then I realized that it was what he had been hoping
> for, ever since he had come to Europe from his monastery in
> India—a disciple in the literal Hindu monastic sense, a novice
> monk who serves his guru and is trained by him like a son, and
> who will become a swami himself in due course.            (R 20)

Oliver lives for eighteen months with the swami, receiving
instructions and rendering him service until the swami, frail
and unhealthy, dies peacefully in his sleep.

This time the Isherwood hero does not rebel against the
dead father, nor does he invent his own father; instead he
actually follows the plan this surrogate father had intended for
him: Oliver enters the monastery to become a monk. Though
dead, the swami is alive to Oliver, and because this presence is
real, Oliver survives his scruples and fears, secure in the
swami's rocklike assertion that he is with him. Near the novel's
conclusion, Oliver expresses his firm conviction that the swami

"is with me always, wherever I am" (R 173). Moreover, Oliver has a vision that "Patrick is in Swami's care and in Swami's presence—even though he himself may be utterly unaware of it now and for some time to come" (R 175). Looking into a mystery which surpasses human understanding, Oliver concludes that the power of the swami works in mysterious ways.

Unlike the heroic father of Philip or of Eric, and unlike Kathleen's version of Frank, Oliver's swami does not return to haunt, but to help and to heal. So does, as Isherwood calls him, the "real Frank." A visit to Ypres on November 11, 1935, confirms Isherwood once and for all in his belief that the real Frank was not enshrined in "the vulgar sarcophagus" (KF 505):

> Christopher decided that it was empty. No Hero-Ghost could ever come forth from it to delight them by disowning his unworthy son. The real Frank was beyond their reach. (KF 505)

The true Frank does not disown his son, but rather blesses him. Isherwood refers to a letter as proof of Frank's favor, interpreting it as Frank's last behest. Writing to Kathleen in 1915 about their son, Frank says:

> "I don't think it matters very much what Christopher learns as long as he remains himself and keeps his individuality and develops on his own lines . . ." (Christopher censored the rest of the sentence, about his laziness.) "The whole point of sending him to school was . . . to make him like other boys . . . I for one would much rather have him as he is." (KF 505)

Isherwood interprets this freely: "Don't follow in my footsteps! Be all the things I never was. Do all the things I never did and would have liked to do—including the things I was afraid of doing, if you can guess what they were!" (KF 505). It is Frank's mandate to Isherwood: "Be anything except the son The Others tell you you ought to be. I should be ashamed of that kind of son. I want an Anti-Son. I want him to horrify The

Others and disgrace my name in their eyes. I shall look on and applaud!" (KF 506).

In *Kathleen and Frank,* however, Isherwood, at peace with his version of Frank and with his lifelong rebellion, can honestly ask himself, what kind of father would Frank have made, had he not been killed? He wonders whether Frank would have been able to understand his homosexuality, his Freudianism, his Marxism, his pacifism. Of course he is only conjecturing, but he concludes that Frank probably would have forgotten he had ever wanted Christopher "to develop on his own lines" and quite possibly "would have ended by disowning this Anti-Son" (KF 505).

The truth, as Isherwood sees it, is that he did not need Frank as much as he needed Kathleen. "Speaking for himself, he could say that all he really required was his *idea* of a father— the Anti-Heroic Hero" (KF 505). Only then, with Frank as his ideal, or anti-ideal, could Isherwood retain his individuality, horrify the others, and escape from Kathleen—all the time with Frank's approval.

# CHAPTER

# 3

# ℘ The Idea of War ℘

Early in the summer of 1937, Messrs. Faber and Faber of London and Random House of New York commissioned Isherwood and Auden, flushed with their dramatic successes with Rupert Doone's Group Theatre, to write a travel book about the East, the choice of itinerary left to their discretion. With the outbreak of the Sino-Japanese War, they decided to go to China, leaving London in January 1938 and returning at the end of July.

*Journey to a War,* the result of their six-month collaboration, is a unique, highly original book, with an elaborate sonnet sequence by Auden on the evolution of the human race, and a brisk, impressionistic diary by Isherwood on their circuitous plodding toward the front line. The *Times* dutifully notes that "Mr. Auden and Mr. Isherwood, having made dramatic observations about more than one imaginary war, have now visited a real one together and have written a good book about it."[1] And Evelyn Waugh, although disparaging Auden's poetry in this book, lauds Isherwood's prose:

The style is austerely respectable; not only does he [Isherwood] never use a *cliché,* he never seems consciously to avoid one; a distinction due to a correct habit of thought. Anyone of decent education can revise his work finding alternatives for his *clichés;* a good writer is free from this drudgery; he thinks in other terms.[2]

Isherwood's diary is fragmented, deliberately unintegrated. On three occasions, however, Isherwood conspicuously reveals what is paramount in his mind, as he tries to define the nature of war.

Bound by river boat from Canton, Isherwood and Auden, in their sophomoric enthusiasm, scan the "river-banks eagerly, half expecting to see them bristle with enemy bayonets" (J 29). They pass a Japanese gunboat "murderously quiet":

> You could see the faces of her crew, as they moved about the deck, or polished the sights of a gun. Their utter isolation, on their deadly little steel island, was almost pathetic. Self-quarantined in hatred, like sufferers from a fatally infectious disease, they lay outcast and apart, disowned by the calm healthy river and the pure sanity of the sky. They were like something outside nature, perverse, a freak. Absorbed in their duties, they scarcely gave us a glance—and this seemed strangest, most unnatural of all.

Isherwood then concludes with his first definition of war: "This is what War is, I thought: two ships pass each other, and nobody waves his hand" (J 29).

Later, on their way to the front, Isherwood and Auden struggle to the top of a "shallow, stony pass," just outside of Lui Chuan. There they take a breather and look

> down on War as a bird might—seeing only a kind of sinister agriculture or anti-agriculture. Immediately below us peasants were digging in the fertile, productive plain. Further on there would be more peasants, in uniform, also digging—the unproductive, sterile trench.

"This," he conceives, "is how war must seem to the neutral, unjudging bird—merely the Bad Earth, the tiny, dead patch in the immense flowering field of luxuriant China" (J 107).

A few weeks later, Isherwood, for the third time and with parallel sentence patterns, tries to catch and fix a definition:

> War is bombing an already disused arsenal, missing it, and killing a few old women. War is lying in a stable with a gangrenous leg. War is drinking hot water in a barn and worrying about one's wife. War is a handful of lost and terrified men in the mountains, shooting at something moving in the undergrowth. War is waiting for days with nothing to do; shouting down a dead telephone; going without sleep, or sex, or a wash. War is untidy, inefficient, obscure, and largely a matter of chance. (J 202)

As Waugh writes, Isherwood's definitions are exquisitely hewn—but, more than ever, Isherwood is the outsider looking in, the *Berlin-Stories* narrator observing a holocaust in which he is not involved. Perhaps because he was unable to penetrate the enigma of the Orient, much less the enigma of man's violence to his fellows, his style is rhetorical, even rehearsed (Waugh's term was "respectable"). It is as if not only in dress but also in style, Isherwood is masquerading "as a war correspondent" (CK 301). In addition to lacking clichés, Isherwood's diary entries also lack the authenticity and anguish of his war novels. Perhaps his braced, deliberately wrought style derives from this fact—that to Isherwood, the *idea* of war is far more nightmarish than the actual *fact* of war.[3]

Although Isherwood was not a combatant in the Great War (perhaps it would be more accurate to say *because* he was not a combatant), he was a war casualty. As D. H. Lawrence writes in "Nightmare," the memorable chapter in *Kangaroo* in which he relives the horror of wartime England, it was at home that "the world was lost," at home that the proud human spirit collapsed and "sordid, rampant, raging meanness" triumphed. "The bite of a jackal is blood-poisoning and mortification," Lawrence rages, and at home stayed "all the jackals, middle-aged, male and female jackals. And they bit us all. And blood-poisoning . . . set in."[4] Blood-poisoned, subtly bullied by the war-mad, German-hating public whom Lawrence calls jackals, crippled by guilt at not having been old enough to fight, Isherwood cannot curb his own pathological war obsession from rearing its ugly head in his books. E. M. Forster's clear-eyed appraisal of English prose between the wars is pertinent here. Forster reads the books of that period as the "product of men who have war on their minds." Their works "need not be gloomy or hysterical—often they are gay and sane and brave—but if they have any sensitivity they must realize what a mess the world is in."[5]

War is the decisive, apocalyptic event, the ancestral curse inherited by Isherwood's generation, and like the past in Faulkner's novels it taints the atmosphere of a major portion of Isherwood's works. What Isherwood says about *The Memorial,* his first war novel, may also be said about *The Last of Mr. Norris, Goodbye to Berlin,* and Part III ("Waldemar") of *Down There on a Visit:* "It [*The Memorial*] was to be about war: not the War itself, but the effect of the idea of 'War' on my generation" (LS 296). George A. Panichas vividly spells out the effect of war on Isherwood's generation in his introduction to *Promise of Greatness,* a collection of retrospective essays about the Great War:

> After 1918 the values of a settled civilization were gone. The years of the war remained as the chief remembrance of things past, and the future was uncertain. The war had destroyed a sense of security and stability, and 1918 was to become a date signaling the crises of civilization that have marked the rest of the twentieth century. Those who lost their lives lost all their bitterness. But those who survived felt sorrow without end.[6]

The little lives of Isherwood's characters are rounded by nightmare: not yet recovered from the bitter sorrow of one war, they discover themselves madly careering toward another. There is nothing in Isherwood of the idea often found in Michael Roberts or Rupert Brooke or Rex Warner, that war would purge the country of pettiness and selfishness and eventually invigorate.[7] Rather, in Isherwood's world the idea of war conjures up a legion of Eumenides, or in Lawrence's terminology, a pack of jackals, hounding Isherwood's characters to the death. Richard Aldington expresses this sense of dread and disgust in *Death of a Hero,* a popular war book of the twenties:

> The death of a hero! What mockery! What bloody cant. What sickening putrid cant. George's death is a symbol to me of the whole sickening bloody waste of it, the damnable stupid waste and torture of it.[8]

One can still imaginatively experience the bewildering, even humiliating repercussions of the Great War on Isherwood and his generation by visiting Repton, Isherwood's public school. There, in the stark medieval courtyard, looms phantomlike the Repton War Memorial, one of the countless undistinguished obelisks and crosses erected in almost every English village, the product of what Robert Graves and Alan Hodge call "Memorial Craze."[9] In nearly every issue of *The Reptonian,*[10] the school newspaper, 1918–22, one finds references to the Memorial Cross:[11] its dimensions, building materials, site, the progress of its endowment. Gradually the Cross surrealistically assumes gigantic proportions symbolic of the cleavage between two generations, the way Isherwood was to use it ten years later in *The Memorial.* In fact, the entire ceremony of the Repton Memorial dedication, printed in *The Reptonian's* Special Number, December 1922, reads like a section from *The Memorial.* On the more distant side of the Repton Cross stand those whom Isherwood labels the Others with their "dishonest cant about loyalty, selfishness, patriotism, playing the game and dishonoring the dead" (LS 13). The Repton Headmaster proclaims the policy of the Others in a long oration, actually delivered the day following the Memorial dedication. The Headmaster commences by eulogizing the product of public school education, the public school man:

> The type . . . is easily recognizable; it is the man who plays for his side rather than for his own hand; the man who can take a beating without whining or argument, the man to whom defeat is but a challenge to fresh effort.

Such a man makes the ideal commander:

> With such men in the early days of the War our Army was officered, men who thought more of those under their command than of themselves, men who took more than their share of risk and hardship, that they might lead their fellows, men whose devotion called forth a ready response from those over whom they were set.

The Headmaster concludes his panegyric: "They were the typical production of our great Public Schools."[12] This spurs him to reminisce, to acclaim the "new impetus and new strength" the war has given the school. He boasts that of his five school friends who fought, three have been killed. He even quotes verse to immortalize them.

> The bravely dumb, who did their deed,
> And scorned to blot it with a name;
> Men of a plain, heroic, breed
> Who loved Heaven's silence more than fame.

The Headmaster then expatiates on the present, holding up "those who forgot themselves, and gave their lives for home and country," as examples whom "we remember . . . for their bravery, we thank for our deliverance, we . . . honor for their devotion and self-forgetfulness."[13]

The Headmaster virtually echoes the Bishop of Manchester's encomium the day of the Repton dedication. This address is more general and less "public schoolish": "Our brothers did in service of that cause all that could be done by the methods which they had to use." The Bishop avows that force has never succeeded; nonetheless, "The one cause for which they endured and suffered was the cause of God . . . we need the inspiration of our brothers, who have made their lives a sacrifice, and therein have found the secret of life." He finishes his tribute, "So we picture our brothers, who have found the secret of life in sacrifice, marching forward into the fuller life, and at their head Another, who also died in youth for the Kingdom that He served."[14]

On the other side of the Memorial, embittered, disillusioned, disinherited from that Kingdom the Bishop proclaims, stand Isherwood and his generation. A *Reptonian* editorial, printed two years before the Dedication, hints at the probable reception the younger generation would give to the Rupert-Brookean idealism of the Headmaster and the pietistic patriotism of the Bishop. The editorial, of which only a part is printed below, well could have served as a blurb for the Hogarth Press's first edition of *The Memorial*. Only sixteen months after the signing of the Armistice, the writer begins to see

> what is was unpatriotic to see during the War, that the world has not been made safe for democracy; we see, what it was impossible to see during the War, the full depth and agony of the suffering which tugs at the soul of the human race; we see— most terrible of all!—that the cause for which we fought, the ideals which justified five years' carnage on a scale unprecedented in history, have been ruthlessly discredited by the imposition of a Peace Treaty, the cynical character of which it is impossible to conceal. All this we see, with a gloom which it is hard to dissipate.

What does the youthful editorial writer foresee? Only hopelessness. His description of the predicament of postwar

England reads like psychological analyses of Eric Vernon and Edward Blake:

> We are, indeed, at the cross-ways: every way lies tragedy, every way sorrow; the world must choose between evil and lesser evil, but always evil. Politically we are wearied of brooding on a situation which deadens us with a sense of its own ghastliness; our mind tries to find matter outside, but cannot, and vacuously we fight a shadow of impending ruin, that looks terribly like our own.[15]

This boyhood nightmare, this understanding, even by public school boys that, as D. H. Lawrence writes, "We all lost the war,"[16] Isherwood freezes in the climax of *The Memorial,* the dedication of the Chapel Bridge War Memorial. This scene, so like the ceremony at Repton, brings to a pitch the horror and ironic loss of the postwar period. More than any other scene in the book it sums up "the atmosphere of pessimism" and of "impending ruin" pervading the novel. Again the Cross is a sign of separation. Obviously Lily and Major Charlesworth and old Mr. Vernon would sternly line up on the far side of the Cross with the Headmaster and the Bishop, while Mary and her children would presume to join the embittered young. Eric and Blake would be alone in the no man's land between both generations. With his main characters thus congregated around this death-dealing Cross, Isherwood laces his account of the Dedication proceedings with ironic references to the Cross of Christ.

Like the Bishop of Manchester, the Bishop in Isherwood's novel compares the Memorial Cross to the one true Cross:

> "O Lord our God, whose only beloved Son did suffer . . . the death upon the Cross, accept at our hands this symbol of His great Atonement, wherewith we commemorate the sacrifice which our brothers made. . . ."                (M 102)

From this Cross the lives of the main characters take definition. Lily typically fastens "the eye of her brain upon a needle-point of concentration. Richard, she thought, Richard" (M 102). To her the Cross symbolizes Richard, her life. She also seizes the moment to usher Mr. Vernon as chief mourner dramatically to the front of the Cross where he lays the first wreath of flowers. Mary sees the Cross as a hypocritical bore which must be shut out of her consciousness, lest she be haunted by the echoes of her goblin footfalls. Maurice is not even present. Eric, standing next to Anne, welters with guilt because he is not lucky enough to be one of the hallowed dead. Edward Blake vacantly loiters in the background, his mind hammered by the irrevocable loss:

> Richard is dead. And this is what remains, said Edward to himself, seeing the doll [Lily] in her black, the slobbering old man [Mr. Vernon], the gawky boy [Eric] getting into the carriage. This is what we've got left of Richard.        (M 141)

The Memorial Cross stands as a blasphemous antithesis to the Cross of Christ: its disciples are not filled with life, but sentenced to life-in-death. They are futile flesh-and-blood memorials to "that War [which] ought never to have happened" (M 294). Inheriting nothing but a "heap of broken images," they are debased figures crouched in the shadow of a sterile Cross.

Isherwood finished the first draft of *The Memorial* before departing for Berlin in 1929. Why did he go to Berlin? That question presupposes another: Why did Isherwood leave England? At the time, Isherwood, enrolled as a medical student at King's College, London, was absolutely miserable.[17] Medical School was "Cambridge again, but worse. Worse, because this time, I was honestly trying, seriously doing my best" (LS 288). He felt that his "Art was a flop, a declared failure in the open market. And I couldn't hide myself in Mortmere: Mortmere had failed us, dissolved into thin air" (LS 288). Thus he had reached the brutal conclusion that "I should never make a doctor. The whole thing had been a day-dream from the start. It was madness ever to have joined the medical school at all" (LS 288).

What, he agonized, was to become of him? "Was I to go back to tutoring until I got too old to impress the parents? Was I to try for another amateur-secretary job, and spend the rest of my life messing about on the outskirts of Bohemia? Was I, indeed, a total misfit, a hundred per cent. incompetent?" (LS 288).

Isherwood felt that he "hadn't advanced an inch, really, since those Cambridge days" (LS 304). He needed a change, a total break from England and the old life, the kind of severance Philip Lindsay and Eric Vernon unsuccessfully sought.

But why Berlin? In an article published in 1939 in *The New Republic*, "German Literature in English," Isherwood explains why Germany, and *a fortiori* Berlin, had such an irresistible power over his generation:[18]

> (1) After the War, the younger generation reacted against the blind chauvinism of the war years. Because the older generation claimed that the Germans were barbarians,[19] the younger inferred that they were the most civilized people in Europe.
>
> (2) Young people became pro-German because they sympathized with the unfair treatment of Germany after the War. "The New Germany was represented by a charming blond girl or boy who strode with open-necked shirt, harmlessly hiking through the Black Forest."
>
> (3) "Youth always demands its nightmares (perhaps in our case they were the horrible dreams of the war we had so narrowly avoided)": Germany supplied them. "Amateurs of the macabre, we reveled in the early Ufa films."
>
> (4) Youth delights in war novels, and Germany led the way for such fiction.
>
> (5) Youth's most admired writers were German: Hölderlin, Kafka, Rilke, and Mann.[20]

Most important, and a personal factor Isherwood would not have alluded to in his article in 1939, "Berlin meant Boys" (CK

2). As a homosexual, Isherwood could not "relax sexually with a member of his own class or nation. He needed a working-class foreigner" (CK 3). Introduced by Auden to Berlin's boy bars, the Cosy Corner in particular, and already "absolutely infatuated" from an earlier visit (CK 10) with a boy whom Isherwood calls "Bubbi" (Baby), Isherwood, on March 14, 1929, left London by the afternoon train for Berlin, there to join his own tribe. The trip profoundly altered the course of Isherwood's life: Berlin so stirred his creativity that, at least for his generation, Berlin would inevitably be his city, as Dublin is Joyce's and Paris Hemingway's. There Isherwood found himself both as a homosexual and as a writer: he enjoyed a prolonged affair with Heinz, the model for Otto Nowak and Waldemar, and there finished *The Memorial*, published it, and gathered material for *The Berlin Stories*.

Although Berlin was a break from medical school and furnished rich experiences for his best work, Berlin was not a break from the past. Indeed, Berlin was condemned by its past. The bitterness of defeat in a war which cost 1,773,000 lives in a losing cause; the Germans' bitterness in feeling that they had been betrayed into surrendering; the bitterness at the harsh terms of the Versailles Peace Treaty; spiralling inflation, social unrest, threats of revolution, the rise of the Nazis—all hurtled Germany into another world war. And Isherwood, a foreigner in a doomed capital, recorded what he saw: everywhere civilization crumbling, everywhere war more imminent.

Because Isherwood brilliantly recorded what he saw, *The Berlin Stories* is a valuable social document which provides an insight into Isherwood's handling of political themes.[21] It also gives us a purchase on Isherwood's use of fantasy, influenced by Mortmere and the German cinema, discussed in the next chapter.

Isherwood's stories achieve political significance not because of their ideological content, but because of their heightened sensitivity to the obscure dread, the vague, unnatural menace inherent in the last days of the Weimar Republic. Occasionally, Isherwood's narrator reports directly on the civil war in Berlin:

> Berlin was in a state of civil war. Hate exploded suddenly, without warning, out of nowhere; at street corners, in restaurants, cinemas, dance halls, swimming-baths; at midnight, after breakfast, in the middle of the afternoon. Knives were whipped out, blows were dealt with spiked rings, beer-mugs, chair-legs or leaded clubs; bullets slashed the advertisements on the poster-columns, rebounded from the iron roofs of latrines. In the middle of a crowded street a young man would be attacked, stripped, thrashed and left bleeding on the pavement; in fifteen seconds it was all over and the assailants had disappeared. Otto got a gash over the eye with a razor in a battle on a fair-ground near the Cöpernickerstrasse. The doctor put in three stitches and he was in hospital for a week. The newspapers were full of death-bed photographs of rival martyrs, Nazi, Reichsbanner and Communists. My pupils looked at them and shook their heads, apologizing to me for the state of Germany. "Dear, dear!" they said, "it's terrible. It can't go on."          (N 86)

Even in summations of this sort, as the extreme selectivity of detail suggests, Isherwood's method is to catch the unrest and shabby chaos of the larger life around him in the microcosm of the individual. Isherwood is not an archivist like Orwell, prying into totalitarian atrocities, but rather a seismographer capable of reading the subtlest tremors that ripple across his personal landscape. John Lehmann was the first to spot this capability.[22] Isherwood's comments on a short story, "My Enemy" by André Chamson, further reveal Isherwood's *ars politica*.[23] Chamson recounts the adventures of two French boys, avowed enemies, finding friendship by overcoming a common obstacle: they climb an arduous mountain and reach the top with new respect for each other. Once they descend, however, they resume their inveterate hatred, ashamed at being seen together. Isherwood writes to Lehmann that Chamson's story "makes one feel that a real artist can write about absolutely anything and still produce all the correct reflections about fascism, nationalism, etc. in the reader's mind, a trite observation but it always comes as a fresh surprise."[24] In this story the humanity of the two boys is stifled by the political atmosphere. No political speculations are necessary, for, in catching the truth about human nature, Chamson implies his political point. Hena Maes-Jelinek offers as an example of Isherwood's fictional treatment of politics his description of the people in front of the "Darmstädter und National" Bank on the day it is closed by the German Government:

> A little boy was playing with a hoop amongst the crowd. The hoop ran against a woman's legs. She flew out at him at once: "Du, sei bloss nicht so frech! Cheeky little brat! What do you want here!" Another woman joined in, attacking the scared boy: "Get out! You can't understand it, can you?" And another asked, in furious sarcasm: "Have you got your money in the bank too, perhaps?" The boy fled before their pent-up, exploding rage.                                                      (GB 57)

Maes-Jelinek's conclusion: "Isherwood does not discuss the consequences of the event but shows how it affects people."[25] Auden's poem "The Model" offers an insight into Isherwood's gift by summarizing a political method that fixes the eye of the reader on the "essential human element." In the poem Auden uses the analogy of a portrait painter and his female subject:

> So the painter may please himself; give her an English
>     park,
> Rice-fields in China, or a slum tenement;
>     Make the sky light or dark;
> Put green plush behind her or a red brick wall.
>     She will compose them all.
> Centering the eye on their essential human element.[26]

The "essential human element" in Isherwood's Berlin pieces composes all, gives the various genres a sustained, unified impact, and reveals the main lines of the epic he originally intended. As the political situation deteriorates, Isherwood's portraits darken. There is an increasing sense of suffocation, a sinking of human consciousness, as people discover themselves locked in hopeless situations, trapped by the approaching horror of Nazism. Indeed the subjects of Isherwood's portraits support Lehmann's assertions that anyone reading *Goodbye to Berlin* with *The Last of Mr. Norris* will catch "glimpses of the bigger work which never materialized,"[27] which Isherwood planned to name *The Lost,* or its German equivalent *Die Verlorenen.*

If we take *The Berlin Stories,* then, as the epic Isherwood intended, the first piece we encounter is a novel, *The Last of Mr. Norris,* narrated by Isherwood's namesake, William Bradshaw. Norris is an essentially comic character, a colorful *flaneur* delighting in mysteries, dabbling in communism and fascism, reveling in the decadence of wigs and scents and vintage wines.[28] Before the dressing mirror he displays all the vanity of Zuleika Dobson, tweezing his eyebrows, coloring his cheeks, and powdering his nose. His sexual tastes are comically perverse, his reading matter unashamedly pornographic, his manner clandestine and affected. Eventually, however, Norris' double-dealing and chicanery rebound, and he leaves Berlin, dogged by his servant, the Nazi-like Schmidt.

While Norris flits about with the epicene pomp of a *fin-de-siècle* aesthete, tragedy is all around him. For example, the Baron von Pregnitz (Norris and Bradshaw's communist friend) shoots himself in a railroad station lavatory. Meanwhile, as Isherwood had stated earlier, Berlin is in a state of civil war. But the reader's attention is focused on Arthur Norris' comic inferno and Bradshaw's amused toleration rather than on the tragedy. Even the ending is ironic, as Arthur, unable to elude the ubiquitous Schmidt, writes to Bradshaw, "*What* have I done to deserve this?" (N 191).

Perhaps the model for Norris, Gerald Hamilton, from whom Norris' absurd charm is derived, did not lend himself to tragedy. In *Christopher and His Kind,* Isherwood finds Hamilton "enchantingly 'period'" (CK 75). Auden, Spender, and others treat Hamilton "like an absurb but nostalgic artwork which has been rediscovered by a later generation" (CK 75), referring to him as "'a most incredible old crook'" (CK 75). As a "man of the world . . . Gerald had to hobnob with buyable chiefs of police, bloodthirsty bishops, stool pigeons, double agents, blackmailers, hatchet men, secretaries and mistresses of politicians, millionairesses even more ruthless than the husbands they had survived . . ." (CK 76). It is not surprising that Norris is comic.

The sequel to *The Last of Mr. Norris* is *Goodbye to Berlin,* which begins and ends with Isherwood's two Berlin diaries. Here the tonal change is immediately clear from the very first line, a sentence fragment: "From my window, the deep solemn massive street" (GB 1). The narrator Christopher Isherwood, unlike Bradshaw, senses the imminent menace of Nazism and himself feels its terror. To illustrate the gradual shift from edgy watchfulness to icy despair, Isherwood's four stories, or portraits, will be treated first; then the diaries will be discussed as focal points epitomizing the moods of the stories they frame. "Sally Bowles" follows "A Berlin Diary (Autumn 1930)." Sally, after Christopher himself, is the most memorable character in *The Berlin Stories.* Isherwood's Sally, however, has been so transformed by the art of other people—for example, Julie Harris in John van Druten's *I Am a Camera,* Jill Haworth in the stage musical *Cabaret,* and Liza Minnelli in the film version— that Isherwood, writing forty years after the publication of "Sally Bowles," cannot remember his first meeting with Jean

Ross, the real-life original of Sally, but only Sally the fictional character.

Like Arthur and like all Berliners, Sally is oblivious to the debacle around her. In Isherwood's story she is an English expatriate who lives for fast money and success as a cabaret entertainer. But like Arthur she is a poor actor, at once innocent and naughty, sophisticated and naive, gallant and frightened. In the end, she is duped by a sixteen-year-old con man who calls himself Paul Rakowski, a pretended European agent from Metro-Goldwyn-Mayer who promises her a leading role in a new movie. Like Arthur, she also manages to escape from Berlin.

But escape will soon be well-nigh impossible. "On Ruegen Island," which follows "Sally Bowles," is a pastoral interlude before the collapse in the final stories. This piece takes place away from Berlin: though fascism is present in a Nazi doctor, in flags on the beach, in a conversation at an ice cream shop, politics are not as obtrusive as they are in the earlier and later stories. Instead, the story centers on the conflict common to all relationships: love-hate. In this case, the lovers are homosexuals, Otto Nowak and Peter Wilkinson, observed by the uninvolved narrator, Christopher—in actual fact, however, Isherwood and Otto—Heinz in *Christopher and His Kind*—were lovers for many years. Peter is a warped, hypersensitive Englishman, about Christopher's age, unable to cope with the shallow, but violently sensuous Otto: they snap and claw at each other until Otto leaves. An apparently innocent game played on the beach compresses into a single episode the hostility of their relationship as well as the bullying tactics of the Nazis for those unable to meet their standards.

One afternoon a narrow-minded Berlin surgeon, who is vacationing on the island and whose Nazism has been a provocative nuisance throughout the story, literally coerces Peter,

Otto, and Christopher to join him in a game. The surgeon assumes control at once. Isherwood does not disclose the name of the game, but only the various reactions of the people involved:

> He [the surgeon] was very firm about this [the assigned places]—instantly ordering me back when I attempted to edge a little nearer, so as not to have such a long distance to throw. (GB 85)

Peter's play does not suit the doctor:

> Then it appeared that Peter was throwing in quite the wrong way: the little doctor stopped the game in order to demonstrate this.                                                        (GB 85)

Peter is amused at first, then annoyed; the thick-skinned doctor continues to bully Peter, correcting his stance, insisting that he relax, smugly catching his failures. As Peter continues to fail, the surgeon exults as if "this failure . . . were a special triumph for his own methods of teaching" (GB 85). Otto grins "understandingly," in collusion with the doctor. A simple, brief account, demanding only a few paragraphs, but, like the mountain-climbing in "My Enemy," like the closing of the "Darmstädter und National" Bank, this contest on a beach earlier cluttered with Nazi swastikas contains ominous rumblings and demonstrates Isherwood's assertion that a "real artist can write about anything and still produce all the correct reflections about fascism. . . ."

After "On Ruegen Island," the deluge: in "The Nowaks" and "The Landauers," the blood-dimmed tide is loosed upon Germany. Isherwood's characters are neither comic nor clowning, but pathetic, infected with the whimpering nihilism of T. S. Eliot's "The Hollow Men."

The Nowaks are a family living in the poorest section of Berlin, the Wassertorstrasse. From them Christopher, tempo-

rarily out of cash, rents a bed in an already crowded bedroom.
Now he is actually dwelling in "the immense, damp, dreary
town and the packing-case colonies of huts in the suburban
allotments" (N 87) described in *The Last of Mr. Norris.* The
description of the condemned apartment, with its tight quarters, its squalor and destitution, reveals more forcefully than
any sociological extrapolation of Isherwood's the inner poverty
of the Nowaks and of the majority of Berliners. Frau Nowak,
racked with tuberculosis, will soon be hospitalized. She and her
son Otto, whose cruelty had grieved Peter Wilkinson, squabble
throughout the story. Herr Nowak returns home drunk every
night, victimized by Berlin's inflation and social dissatisfaction.
Lothar, the older son, who has joined the Nazis, comes home
only to eat and sleep. Otto, when not spatting at home, pro-
cures his living in the streets. The lymphatic daughter, Grete,
vacantly lolls her days away. As the family deteriorates, Frau
Nowak's cough worsens. After she is sent to a sanatorium, the
family falls apart: Otto reverts permanently to the cabarets;
Lothar disappears; and Herr Nowak and Grete lapse into
more primitivistic existences.

Again, as in "On Ruegen Island," Isherwood captures the
plight of his characters with a single vivid emblematic scene.
Visiting the Nowaks a few days before Christmas, Christopher
stalks through the "long, damp street, patched here and there
with dirty snow" (GB 129), his path lighted by the "weak yellow
gleams" shining from cellar shops. He sees a knot of youths
"with raw, sullen faces" watching two boys fighting (GB 129).
At this point, Isherwood introduces a reflection which recurs
with increasing frequency as the stories draw to a close. Christopher wonders, "Did I really ever live here?" (GB 129). The
Nowaks' apartment is pitch dark because they have not paid
the light bill. Inside, Christopher finds Herr Nowak drunk and
Grete "shaking like a jelly, with tears of laughter pouring down

her cheeks" (GB 130). The house is miserably untidy. Isherwood's details are pertinent:

> Clothing of various kinds lay in a confused heap on one of the
> beds; on the other were scattered cups, saucers, shoes, knives
> and forks. On the sideboard was a frying-pan full of dried fat.
> The room was lighted by three candles stuck into empty beer-
> bottles.                                                (GB 130)

The Christmas tree is the smallest he has ever seen, so ema-
ciated that it holds only one candle and is decorated with a
single strand of tinsel. Attempting to light the candle, Herr
Nowak drops several lighted matches which Christopher fortunately stamps out. They croak "O Tannenbaum," and Isherwood gives his presents: cigars for Herr Nowak and chocolates
and a clockwork mouse for Grete. As he leaves, Christopher
hears them shrieking and roaring over the toy mouse: Herr
Nowak "and Grete were bending over it with the eagerness of
gamblers . . ." (GB 131).

The last story, "The Landauers," placed before the final
diary, with chilling horror brings the stories to the same conclusion as that of Joyce's *Dubliners*: paralysis. The Landauers
are a wealthy Jewish family, owners of a huge department
store. Christopher tutors their eighteen-year-old daughter,
Natalia, who introduces Christopher to her family—in particular, her cousin, Bernhard Landauer. Once Bernhard asks
Christopher to pay him a call, the focus of the story shifts to
Bernhard. Again, Isherwood's details become symbolic. On his
first visit, Christopher finds that Bernhard lives in consummate
solitude. His flat has four doors to insulate him from reality.
Bernhard is hermetically sealed from the world: inside, Christopher can hear nothing from without. Bernhard's Oriental
robes further stress his convoluted seclusion. Now Christopher
is at the very eye of the storm. Never does Bernhard speak
directly; instead he intimates through stories and oblique refer-

ences which shroud him in mystery. The causal connection
between character and environment is never more pro-
nounced than here. Bernhard's psychic make-up exhausts
even Christopher. Bernhard's is perhaps the most complete
statement of the theme of *The Lost*. He tells Christopher that

> "I am getting out of touch with existence. That is bad, of
> course. . . . One must preserve a sense or proportion. . . . Do you
> know, there are times when I sit here alone in the evenings,
> amongst these books and stone figures, and there comes to me
> such a strange sensation of unreality, as if this were my whole
> life? . . ."                                              (GB 180)

Bernhard's disjuncture and personal ambiguity are a dress
rehearsal of the coming debasement. The last time Christopher visits him, he hands Christopher a note:

> Bernhard Landauer, beware. We are going to settle the score
> with you and your uncle and all other filthy Jews. We give you
> twenty-four hours to leave Germany. If not, you are dead men.
>                                                           (GB 178)

But because Bernhard cannot act, he is already dead. He
enigmatically suggests that he and Christopher flee, now, at
once. Uncertain, Christopher demurs: "What about to-mor-
row?" (GB 181). Bernhard replies that tomorrow is too late.

It is. "Hitler came, and the Reichstag fire, and the mock
elections" (GB 182). Months later, Christopher overhears a
conversation in a Prague cellar restaurant: two Austrians are
boorishly arguing about the death by heart failure of Bernhard
Landauer and the sure collapse of Landauers' Department
Store. They are uncertain whether Bernhard is the son or the
nephew of old Landauer. They callously cap their story with a
joke about the "Jew and the Goy girl with the wooden leg . . ."
(GB 185). In death Bernhard is unknown, still lost.

The model for Bernhard was Wilfrid Israel, who did indeed
run the largest department store in Berlin. Unlike Bernhard,

however, Wilfrid heroically defied the Nazis, helped Jews to emigrate, and finally, in 1939, himself fled to England. In the novel he is a victim, not a hero, and his death, as Isherwood notes, "was merely a dramatic necessity. In a novel such as this one, which ends with the outbreak of political persecution, one death at least is a must" (CK 71). Though the timing of his death historically is wrong ("The Nazis would surely have waited long enough to prepare some false charges against him" [CK 72]), fictionally it is entirely right.

The opening and concluding Berlin diaries are like weather maps which record the increasing velocity of the approaching storm. Both diaries are well-planned inventions, intended to mesh with the tone and temper of the stories they intersperse—they are not on-the-spot, fragmented diaries like Isherwood's *Journey to a War* or like his "Waldemar" diary. They are personal notes from a Berlin underground with the chief character, the author, deliberately assuming the persona of the diary writer. In the early diary, as in *Mr. Norris* and "Sally," the narrator is abstracted, amused, fascinated by Berlin's demimonde, the excitement of crisis; in the latter diary, the tone shifts, again mirroring the change in the stories from comedy to pathos.

In "A Berlin Diary (Autumn 1930)," inserted between *Mr. Norris* and "Sally," Christopher parries a student's question about his reasons for remaining in Berlin by answering that he thinks Berlin politics very interesting (GB 15). In "A Berlin Diary (Winter 1932–3)," Christopher's cool curiosity has changed to horrified incredulity: "The sun shines, and Hitler is master of this city . . . and dozens of my friends . . . are in prison, possibly dead" (GB 207).

At the beginning, Christopher observes the glee of Frl. Schroeder, his landlady, and Frl. Mayr, a tenant, eavesdropping on Frl. Glanterneck, a Galician Jewess, who is being whipped by a butcher in the flat below. By the winter of 1932–33, this petty intramural spat has swelled into Nazi murders of Jews, a Jewish boycott—everywhere arrests of Jews.

In the autumn of 1930, Christopher finds the Troika club garish and grand, laughs at the glitter of Berlin on the make. In the last diary, because the Nazis are shutting down all night clubs, he pays them a farewell visit. Otto Friedrich fittingly comments in his portrait of Berlin in the twenties, *Before the Deluge*, "This [1933] was to be the last year of the Weimar Republic, the last year of Berlin's freedom."[29]

Even Isherwood's imagery darkens. In the opening diary, the objects of Frl. Schroeder's living room augur the ferocity of Nazi Germany: the hatstand is made of three halberds "heavy and sharp enough to kill" (GB 2); the candlesticks are "shaped like entwined serpents" (GB 2); from an ashtray emerges the "head of a crocodile" (GB 2); a paper knife is copied from a Florentine dagger. Isherwood then speculates on the objects:

> What becomes of such things? How could they ever be destroyed? They will probably remain intact for thousands of years: people will treasure them in museums.                   (GB 2)

Or, he suggests, "perhaps they will be melted down for munitions in a war." Their menacing solidity is like "an uncompromising statement of her [Frl. Schroeder's] views on Capital and Society, Religion and Sex" (GB 2). In the final diary, Isherwood turns inward, from the various items of Frl. Schroeder's ménage to the texture of his soul. Now the serpents, the dagger, the halberds no longer menace but strip and flay both Isherwood and Berlin, as Isherwood identifies himself with the great unreal city:

> Berlin is a skeleton which aches in the cold: it is my own skeleton aching. I feel in my bones the sharp ache of the frost in the girders of the overhead railway, in the ironwork of balconies, in

bridges, in tramlines, lamp-standards, latrines. The iron throbs
and shrinks, the stone and the bricks ache dully, the plaster is
numb.                                                    (GB 186)

Berlin is lost—as Alfred Kazin writes in his review of *Goodbye to
Berlin,* "More than Rome, Berlin has become the very emblem
of lost cities. . . ."[30] As in Bradshaw's prophetic nightmare in
*The Last of Mr. Norris,* the world has suddenly filled with
swastikas and become unmistakably brown (N 181). Initial
premonitions materialize into Nazi monstrosities. Auden's lines
from "Lullaby" sound the funeral knell for Berlin:

> Certainty, fidelity
> On the stroke of midnight pass
> Like vibrations of a bell,
> And fashionable madmen raise
> Their pedantic boring cry:
> Every farthing of the cost,
> All the dreaded cards foretell,
> Shall be paid. . . .[31]

Isherwood leaves Berlin in its nightmarish horror. War,
which had slain his father and had crippled Isherwood from
childhood, continues to harrow him with torment. John Lehmann, Isherwood's intimate friend and colleague, particularly
during the thirties when Isherwood was coeditor of *New Writing,* reports on Isherwood's condition:

Christopher, exiled from the Germany he had made his home,
suffered acutely from now on from traumatic anxiety about the
explosive state of Europe. He pitched his tent in various European cities—Lisbon, Copenhagen, Brussels, Amsterdam—
never staying very long, listening to the darkest prognostica-
tions of the refugee friends from Berlin who nosed him out,
prostrated every seven days by the grisly international low-down
that Claude Cockburn [*sic*] served up in his skillful little news-
letter *The Week.*[32]

The burden of Isherwood's letters, Lehmann discloses, was always the same: "What do you think of Europe? . . . I am utterly unable to judge, having lapsed even deeper into a state of utter inert horror. I read all the newspapers and listen in to the wireless in all languages, even those I don't understand; hoping somehow I shall get a clue from the peculiar intonation with which the Lettish announcer pronounces the word Alexander. . . ."[33] In another letter, Isherwood asks, "Is there going to be a war? This question may well be answered before you read it. Anyhow I can't judge anything from the scrappy paragraphs at the back of the Athens *Messenger*. . . ."[34]

Isherwood's habit of reading that "grisly international lowdown," *The Week*, edited by Claud Cockburn, certainly would not have ameliorated his mental health, for *The Week* specialized in ferreting out clandestine intelligence about every event or scandal. During the Munich Crisis, *The Week* carried this copy:

> People in London who talk about next spring now rate as practically fanatical optimists—in private of course: for in public it is still the Fleet Street fashion to claim that nothing of this kind will happen and we shall all live happily ever after, or anyway till 1940.[35]

Though impaired by his war complex, Isherwood was not numbed into the passivity of Bernhard Landauer. He could at least plunge into his work. *The Last of Mr. Norris* was published in 1935; "Sally Bowles" in 1937; "The Nowaks" and "The Landauers" and "Berlin Diary (Autumn 1930)" were published in separate issues of *New Writing;* the complete *Goodbye to Berlin* was issued in 1939. During this time, Isherwood also collaborated with W. H. Auden on three plays, all of which won, if not acclaim, at least generous recognition for their Brechtian experimentalism and political radicalism. In addition, the trip to China gave him another chance to slake his morbid war curiosity.

When he returned to England to finish *Journey to a War,* Isherwood found England crouched in fear, darkened by "The sudden shadow of a giant's enormous calf."[36] Indicative of the times was T. S. Eliot's resignation from the editorship of *The Criterion.* In "Last Words," Eliot prefaces his statement of resignation with the following:

> In the present state of public affairs—which has induced in myself a depression of spirits so different from any other experience of fifty years as to be a new emotion—I no longer feel the enthusiasm necessary to make a literary review what it should be.[37]

A few months later, after the war had begun to rage, Cyril Connolly was to describe the "present state of public affairs" as follows:

> The moment we live in is archaistic, conservative and irresponsible. . . . At the moment civilization is on the operating table and we sit in the waiting room.[38]

The Sudetenland crisis, in August and September 1938, inflames Isherwood's old sickness unto death. Time does not soothe but, rather, exacerbates his wounds. Nor is it the crisis only which plunges Isherwood into despair. Ever since his lover Heinz had been refused admission into England on January 5, 1934, Isherwood had been desperately trying through Gerald Hamilton, a host of lawyers, and various desperate schemes, to obtain a permit allowing Heinz into England. But his efforts were frustrated at every turn: "Everything seemed to be slipping away down into a bottomless black drain" (CK 245).

Isherwood records these months of fear and loss in "Waldemar," the third section of *Down There on a Visit.* Isherwood's neurotic fright of war, his anger and guilt at having lost Heinz, give "Waldemar" an anguish and passionate despair that recall Quentin Compson's breakdown in William Faulkner's *The Sound and the Fury.* "Waldemar" is one prolonged, desperate scream from beginning to end. Edward Munch's expressionistic lithograph "The Cry" pictorially approximates the tormented style of this psychological no man's land.

Isherwood is so engrossed with himself that he does not see his despair macroscopically reflected in Europe's; instead, he sees England's and Europe's problems mirrored in his own manic behavior. Isherwood writes in *Christopher and His Kind* that "these entries are actually more often about Christopher than about the political situation. His diary-keeping was a discipline designed to shame himself out of giving way to panic-depression, sloth, overdrinking, oversmoking, masturbation, and nervous pottering around" (CK 320).[39]

But "panic-depression"—because Heinz is lost, war is imminent—is rampant throughout the diary. A telling contrast may be pointed out by juxtaposing extracts from Isherwood's diary, which forms a great part of "Waldemar," with extracts from another journal, *Journal Under the Terror, 1938,* kept that same year by an older writer, a novelist, a classicist, and a combatant in the First World War—F. L. Lucas. Lucas' diary is calm, studied, almost Arnoldian in its attempt to view events clearly and wholly; Isherwood's is incoherent, self-conscious, at odds with itself.

Lucas' motive in keeping a diary is historical and altruistic:

> It is an attempt to give one answer, however fragmentary, to the question that will surely be asked one day by the unborn with the bewilderment, one hopes, of a happier age: "What can it have felt like to live in that strange, tormented and demented world?"[40]

Isherwood's purpose is a therapeutic cry for help: "If the ship really is sinking, one ought to be sending out wireless signals. But to whom? . . . bulletins, addressed to no one in particular, sent without any hope of help, for the sake of one's own sanity" (V 159).

Lucas can dispassionately analyze the present: "Today the world feels nearer the breaking point than ever before in the nineteen years since the Great War."[41] Isherwood can only picture himself and the world as insane: " . . . we are all mad here—the crisis is our madness . . ." (V 177).

Finally, Lucas can calmly scrutinize the future, "Who knows if the world will last three years?"[42] The thought of the future hurtles Isherwood into despair:

> The future . . . *un jour sans lendemain,* a day without a morrow.
> This time we are living through now, this doom-heavy summer,
> is *un jour sans lendemain,* or my fear whispers that it may be; and
> everything one does seems to have a tomorrowless quality about
> it. . . .                                                    (V 142–43)

"Waldemar" records Isherwood's descent into a personal inferno: the escapes and attitudinizings, obsessions and superstitions he excoriates in *The Memorial* are desperately embraced as alternatives to his weary gloom. But sex is "cold and tragic and desperate" (V 176); Marxism disgusts him (V 182); religion nauseates him ("when I hear the word God I want to vomit" [V 142]); the cinema fails to blunt his time-and-place sense (V 171); laughter is "crisis-laughter" (V 170). The past is even more stultifying: visiting his ancestral home he exclaims, "Oh the squalor of the terrible diseased old house" (V 174).

War incites Isherwood, toxic with the crisis, to take a hard look at himself. He finds that he possesses the subtlety of Talleyrand (V 140) and the arrogance of Lawrence of Arabia: he is ruthless and completely cynical, charming and well-mannered. His work is not vulgarly famous, but chic (V 140). Yet he chafes, pricks himself: "Why do I do it? Why do I take all the trouble?" He cannot answer these questions, but can only vacillate, can only dilate his problem into a cosmic *memento mori.*

The political crisis stokes Isherwood's personal crisis. Though studded with citations from newspaper pundits, his diary is really another mirror in which Isherwood can glare at his sweating self. Stylistically, the selections shudder with self-interrogations, curses, and ranting *non sequiturs*. Occasionally the diary blares with yellow-journalism insistence: "September 26. The Czechs have refused Hitler's terms. Roosevelt has cabled Berlin urging moderation; but will Hitler take any notice?" (V 177). It is as if Isherwood's war phobia produces a disjunctive, telegraphic manner of writing, a crisis style or anti-style. Sentences are frequently retarded by interruptions: "And I keep remembering that phrase—It's from Balzac—*un jour sans lendemain . . .*" (V 142). This same edginess is achieved by throwing the objective complement forward before the sentence kernel: "Those crow's feet at the corners of my eyes I got them from constant, anxious squinting ahead, like a sea captain in a fog" (V 140). Observe the following contrapuntal thought pattern. Isherwood declares a thesis: "All I tell you is, I'm spinning." He denies it: "That sounds like the statement of a madman, or at least of someone in the depths of despair. Not a bit of it!" He then suddenly affirms the thesis just denied: "Take a good look at me standing there. Do I seem defeated, downcast, dismal? Anxious—yes." He then confirms his claustrophobic mirror-madness by eyeing the crow's feet in his cheeks, concluding with a contradictory thesis: "But my eyes are bright, my face is still youthfully lean, and a stranger would be surprised to hear I shall be thirty-four at the end of the month" (V 140).

When his paragraphs strain toward completion, the conclusions are feckless and subversive:

Am reading Clausewitz on war, because Dr. Fisch told me to and because it is so horribly seasonable. After a couple of dozen pages he brings the reader, with relentless logic, to the point

where he is forced to accept Clausewitz's thesis: that the purpose
of war is to defeat the enemy.                          (V 162)

Or: "Fisch said on the telephone: 'War is inevitable. London
will be bombed within two or three days.' I went to bed and
took a sleeping tablet" (V 175).

Perhaps too cleanly dovetailed with his crisis pangs is the
story of Dorothy and Waldemar. When not writing about his
personal torment, Isherwood tells the story of these two would-
be lovers—himself and Heinz in disguise. Dorothy is an
English girl whom Christopher met in Berlin. She brings Waldemar, a ne'er-do-well opportunist, whom Christopher also
knew in Berlin, home to her stiffly middle-class family and
announces their engagement. Dorothy has no idea that Waldemar is a scoundrel. Her family responds as any middle-class
family would. Waldemar is a *persona non grata* to them, hardly
better than a servant. After futile attempts by Dorothy to
salvage their engagement, Waldemar sizes up his situation,
finds it not at all profitable, and abandons her. To Christopher,
Dorothy's family represents all he detests in England—Kathleen's England which has "rejected Heinz" (CK 160); and
Waldemar's predicament mirrors Christopher's plight, for
Christopher too is an undesirable alien, bereft of home, country, and creed.

The Dorothy-Waldemar relationship is principally a way for
Isherwood to write about Heinz. After Waldemar abandons
Dorothy, he visits Christopher at home, asks him to take him to
America. Isherwood's love for Heinz, his frustration, his guilt,
are all thinly veiled in this farewell scene. Heinz startles Christopher violently one morning by appearing in the bathroom
doorway while Christopher is bathing. Drunk, he asks Christopher to take him to America:

"Will you take me with you, Christopher?"
I smiled weakly, pretending I thought he wasn't serious.
"Christoph—do you remember those old days? Perhaps you've

forgotten, but *I* haven't. I remember everything. We were just boys then. We were so happy, weren't we? ... Who wants to have women along? They're no fun. ... Those were the best times, weren't they, with just the two of us?"    (V 186–87)

But, as Isherwood knows, the relationship is finished. He gives this realization to Heinz-Waldemar, however, who says:

"We shan't meet again. Ever."
"What nonsense!"
"It's no good. I just know it, that's all. Good-by. Enjoy yourself in Amerika."    (V 188)

Heinz-Waldemar departs. "I got a sudden, violent feeling that it was my duty to stop him. ... But if I ran downstairs and shouted after him, naked except for a small bath towel, what would the taxi driver think? To hell with the taxi driver. ..." But Isherwood guiltily reflects: "My hesitation had been only momentary, but it had been sufficient. For now I heard the taxi driving away" (V 188).

If Isherwood's guilty, paranoid lines do nudge toward a conclusion, it is to undertake still another journey, this time to America. Placed before the final section, "Paul," which deals in part with Isherwood's Vedanta experience in California, "Waldemar" serves both as Isherwood's most personal statement of his spiritual desolation and as an explanation for his trip to America—a delayed answer to his critics. As we have seen in the last chapter, Isherwood and Auden's crossing of corrosive seas did ease their hearts' disease,[43] but stung their contemporaries into vindictive retaliation. *Reynolds* sneered at Huxley, Heard, and now Isherwood, "who have gone to California to contemplate their navels."[44] Stephen Spender, one of Isherwood's dearest friends, reviewing Gerald Heard's *Pain, Sex and Time*, indicts Huxley, Heard, and by implication, Isherwood:

One cannot read their books without asking is it right that they should be living in Hollywood and wondering whether one couldn't oneself submit to yogi exercises in such a pleasant climate.[45]

Cyril Connolly morosely writes that the "departure of Auden and Isherwood to America . . . is the most important literary event since the outbreak of the Spanish War." He continues,

> It is extremely unfortunate that they began to settle in their new surroundings and sent word home, just as we went to war with Germany, for it puts . . . Isherwood's profession of faith in Yogi into a weapon that reactionary papers such as *Action* have used against him.

Later, Connolly even brands them as opportunistic:

> Auden is our best poet, Isherwood our most promising novelist. . . . They are far-sighted and ambitious young men with a strong instinct of self-preservation, and an eye on the main chance, who have abandoned . . . European democracy, and by implication the aesthetic doctrine of social realism that has been prevailing there. Are they right? It would certainly seem so. Whatever happens in the war, America will be the gainer . . . England will be poverty-stricken, even in victory.[46]

In literary terms, Connolly views their migration as a reaction against social realism, as necessary and salutary as the reaction from the Ivory Tower writers of the earlier generation.

With more breadth, Lehmann states that actually Isherwood had left England much earlier, in 1929, after he had settled in Berlin. He even senses that Isherwood had "left Europe in spirit long before, rejecting at last the categories of its conflicts and dimly discerning that California might reveal itself as the home he had looked for in vain since the break-up of his Berlin life and German circle of friends."[47] Lehmann records a letter he received from Isherwood in May 1941:

> I myself am in the most Goddamawful mess. I have discovered, what I didn't realize before, or what I wasn't till now, that I am a

pacifist. That is one reason why I am going out to Hollywood, to talk to Gerald Heard and Huxley. Maybe I'll flatly disagree with them, but I have to hear their case, stated as expertly as possible.[48]

That startling confession, Lehmann declares,

quite clearly and sadly, wrote the epitaph to our friendship as we had known it, and as I had imagined it continuing into the future, a friendship that had been the pivot of my life as a writer and editor-publisher for nearly seven years.[49]

With even more poignancy and sense of loss, Lehmann regrets that the Mortmere novels and a trilogy of novels, sequels to *The Lost,* all which Isherwood had so vividly "talked aloud," would never be written. Again Auden's lines approximate Isherwood's state of soul:

> Coming out of me living is always thinking
> Thinking changing and changing living.[50]

Lehmann, looking back after sixteen years on Isherwood's departure, can only concur with Auden's sentiments: "Christopher was changing too fast; and so was the world."[51]

# CHAPTER

# 4

# ～Mortmere～

In spite of dire warnings Isherwood received not to visit Berlin, "shabby, violent and morally corrupt Berlin" was strangely enough the most suitable place for a writer of Isherwood's temperament.[1] Berlin answered not only his quest for intellectual and sexual freedom, his desire to shock the Others, but also, and more important, his need for the bizarre and the grotesque—nurtured, oddly enough, at Repton and Cambridge, of all places.

At Repton, Isherwood met Edward Upward and immediately fell under the spell of this young anarchist. Both boys joined in rebelling against the narrow elitist values of public school life by escaping into their own world of make-believe, a world of macabre fantasy alternately called the Other Town, the Rat's Hostel, and finally, at Cambridge, Mortmere.

Because his mother, invoking his dead father, wanted him to attend and because an award given by the Others enabled him to attend with the highest scholarship of his year, Isherwood had no choice but to detest Cambridge. In *Lions and Shadows,* he calls it a "city of perpetual darkness . . . the country of the dead" (LS 23). He vigorously rejected Cambridge and in its place substituted, with Upward, his own imaginary country of the dead, located somewhere near the Atlantic and peopled with a menagerie of ghouls. This macabre fantasy of Mortmere schooled Isherwood for the real nightmare he was to encounter in pre-Hitler Berlin.

Mortmere became the mad nursery in which Isherwood and Upward grew up as writers. The extent of Isherwood's involvement in Mortmere can be seen from the following statement in *Lions and Shadows:* "My official education was, it is true, at a standstill: but Chalmers [Upward] was educating me all the time" (LS 73). What Isherwood writes in his foreword to Upward's "The Railway Accident," the only Mortmere story to be published, applies to himself as well: "no further evaluation of his [Upward's] work will be able to ignore it [Mortmere]."[2]

With its aberrant characters, pornography, and gothic plots, Mortmere is as flamboyantly bizarre as a Dali painting, its stories clever pastiches of Sir Thomas Browne, the Brothers Grimm, Edgar Allan Poe, Lewis Carroll, Conan Doyle, Beatrix Potter, Anatole France, and many others.

In *Lions and Shadows,* Isherwood pens quick portraits of this gallery of monsters. Mortmere's Rector, the Reverend Welken, resembles a diseased goat who, in punishment for moral offenses committed as an altar boy, is visited by his dead wife in the form of a succubus. His intimate friend, Ronald Gunball, is "a frank unashamed vulgarian, a keen fisherman, a drunkard and a grotesque liar" (LS 102). Gunball's world is "the world of delirium tremens" (LS 102): he sees horrors all about him, lives placidly amidst two-headed monsters, "downpours of human blood and eclipses of the sun" (LS 102–3). Dr. Mears, the Mortmere physician, is at work on a novel classification of the human race into "Dragoons" and "Dorys" (LS 111). Sergeant

Claptree keeps the Skull and Trumpet Inn; Mr. Wherry is the architect whose railway tunnel under the downs collapses just as the first Mortmere express puffs through; Henry Belmare is a Mortmere landowner; Miss Belmare, his crabbed sister, wears "starched blouses and a small steel padlock inside her stiff collar" (LS 112). Is it any wonder that this fictional world became more vivid for Isherwood and Upward than the real world? G. H. Bantock, deploring the surrealist element in the Mortmere fantasies, notes that "the surrealist movement itself was not only symptomatic of a state of disintegration but sprang in many cases from a subconscious desire to avoid the responsibility of making coherent sense of the external world."[3]

Isherwood and Upward eventually repudiated Mortmere precisely because they were unable to connect its lunacy with the prose of everyday life. They gave it up, however, reluctantly, and only after repeatedly trying to impose sense on its essential nonsense. In *Lions and Shadows,* Isherwood tells of their abortive attempts to prune Mortmere of its excesses. At one point, hoping to forge a link to reality, they experimented with a narrator called Hearn, a composite of two earlier grotesques, Hynd and Starn, protagonists of such Mortmere tales as *The Javanese Sapphires* and *The Garage in Drover's Hollow* (LS 106). Hearn, at the beginning of this comparatively tame version, is merely an inventive young man moving into a quiet village to recuperate from a nervous breakdown. Walking to a tea party, Hearn composes a preposterous letter to a friend in which he ascribes "imaginary characteristics, freak vices and miraculous attributes upon his mildly eccentric but really quite normal village neighbours" (LS 164). But because Hearn seemed flat and commonplace, Isherwood and Upward couldn't resist turning Hearn into a monster, and thus dashing their original plan of rationalizing madness: " . . . suppose [Hearn is] . . . a dangerous madman? Suppose, at the end of the book, he has a violent attack, burns down the church, blows up the parish hall and kills everybody in the village?" (LS 165). Like all Mortmere tales, this one is also perversely exciting, but its outcome is still no more than mere Arabian-Nights escapism. Mortmere remains only an autistic feast of surrealist violence.

At Cambridge, Isherwood and Upward were incapable of toning down Mortmere's sensationalism. But more than twelve years later in *Lions and Shadows*, Isherwood, still worrying at an alternative, conjectures that "a modified, less extraordinary version of the story could certainly have been written; if only we had seen that the vital clue to the action was contained in Hearn's relations with the village characters *as ordinary people*" (LS 165). Isherwood then details his tea-table nightmare: a young writer, neither mad nor ill, settles in a village of normal people. Naturally observant of the villagers, the writer constructs "a novel, in which his neighbours are distorted into the characters of an extravagant and lurid fable, and their mild impulses, lukewarm emotions and timid half-intentions are developed into fantastically violent acts" (LS 166). For a while, the world of art—the writer's novel—coexists with the real world—the life of the village. But when the writer reads parts of his work to the villagers, disaster strikes. The people, horrified, scandalized, indignant, but profoundly, guiltily excited, suddenly turn into the depraved anomalies of Mortmere. Life imitates art. The writer, bewildered, flees from the village he has unwittingly destroyed as all the sophomoric depravity of the original Mortmere erupts. At the end, only the writer remains "from first to last, a quiet undistinguished ordinary young man" (LS 167).

As university students, however, Isherwood and Upward did not consider this solution—if this solution was indeed viable. Hence Isherwood's final verdict on Mortmere: "Mortmere . . . brought us to a dead end" (LS 273).

Upward, however, according to Isherwood, needed Mortmere "at all costs. I did not. That, as writers, was the essential difference between us" (LS 273–74). Because Upward had created Mortmere out of "his own flesh and blood," he could never abandon it altogether; "if he did so, he was lost" (LS 274).

Upward struggled to reconcile Mortmere with Marx—but unsuccessfully. He produced two Marxist fantasies, "The Colleagues" and "Journey to the Border," but soon faced another dead end and lapsed into a nineteen-year silence. While Upward fled, even hid from the looking-glass world of fantasy, retreating into the flat land of communism, Isherwood serendipitously stumbled toward the very Mortmere he thought he had closed the book on. When he boarded a train whose final stop was Berlin's Zoo Station, he found the vital connection between reality and fantasy, fact and fiction. Rather than to an impasse, fantasy led Isherwood to a Germanic—but, in the end, to an intensely personal—Mortmere. The prophecy of Mr. Lancaster, Christopher's distant relative in *Down There on a Visit,* is more than fulfilled:

> "Christopher—in the whole of *The Thousand and One Nights,* in the most shameless rituals of the Tantras, in the carvings on the Black Pagoda, in the Japanese brothel pictures, in the vilest perversions of the Oriental mind, you couldn't find anything more nauseating than what goes on there, quite openly every day. That city is doomed, more surely than Sodom ever was."
>
> (V 35).

Mr. Lancaster is not the only witness to the Hieronymus Bosch nightmare of Berlin. D. H. Lawrence, passing through Germany on his way to France, felt his flesh creep. In a remarkable letter of 1924, Lawrence vividly sketches the horror of Germany's atavistic darkness.

> Immediately you are over the Rhine the spirit of the place has changed. There is no more attempt at the bluff of geniality. The marshy places are frozen. The fields are vacant. There seems nobody in the world. . . .

The moment you are in Germany, you know. It feels empty
and, somehow, menacing. So must the Roman soldiers have
watched those black, massive round hills: with a certain fear and
with the knowledge that they were at their own limit. A fear of
the invisible natives. A fear of the invisible life lurking among
the woods. A fear of their own opposite.[4]

Lawrence is aghast at the change that has come over Germany
in only two years, the time of his last visit, when Germany was
open to the West. Now Germany leans toward the destructive
East that produced Attila. Soon a Germanic night will shroud
all of Europe:

> But at night you feel strange things stirring in the darkness,
> strange feelings stirring out of this still-unconquered Black
> Forest. . . . There is a sense of a danger. . . . Out of the very air
> comes a sense of danger, a queer, *bristling* feeling of uncanny
> danger.
> Something has happened. Something has happened which
> has not yet eventuated. The old spell of the old world has
> broken, and the old, bristling, savage spirit has set it.
> . . . But something has happened to the human soul, beyond
> all help. The human soul recoiling now from unison and mak-
> ing itself strong elsewhere. The ancient spirit of prehistory
> Germany coming back, at the end of history.
> It is a fate; nobody can alter it. It is a fate.

Lawrence concludes his doom-heavy letter with this final
judgment: *"Quos vult perdere Deus, demantat prius."*[5]

Two of Isherwood's closest friends confirm Lawrence's perceptions. Spender, sitting in a Berlin café with his brother
Michael, records the following observation:

> "There isn't a girl sitting in this place who hasn't got scars on her
> wrist where she has cut her veins in an attempt to commit
> suicide."[6]

Lehmann, in 1932, walking the streets with Isherwood, is speechless when he sees what might be considered the abomination of abominations: huge pictures of Hitler arranged in windows, illuminated by devout candles, like altars dedicated to some primitive demon-cult.[7]

No wonder then that Berlin with its Mortmere monstrosities uncannily pandered to Isherwood's predilection for the grotesque. In *Christopher and His Kind*, Isherwood describes the sexual perversions he found at the Hirschfeld Institute, a museum and laboratory, where Isherwood first lodged, dedicated to the study of homosexuality. Again the details seem lifted straight from an early Mortmere story:

> Here were whips and chains and torture instruments designed for the practitioners of pleasure-pain; high-heeled, intricately decorated boots for the fetishists; lacy female undies which had been worn by ferociously masculine Prussian officers beneath their uniforms. Here were the lower halves of trouser legs with elastic bands to hold them in position between knee and ankle. In these and nothing else but an overcoat and a pair of shoes, you could walk the streets and seem fully clothed, giving a camera-quick exposure whenever a suitable viewer appeared.
>
> (CK 16)

John Whitehead wisely connects Mortmere with *The Berlin Stories* when he writes, "It is only a step from the Rev. Welken and Gunball to Baron von Pregnitz and Mr. Norris himself."[8] In fact, Isherwood's "modified, less extravagant" attempt to salvage Mortmere, which would feature a young writer whose psychotic musings transform a village into an asylum, sounds very much like Isherwood's rationale in *The Berlin Stories*—with two exceptions. Fantasy does not alter reality; rather, reality in Berlin assumes the Caligari-like perspective of dream and surpasses even fantasy's tendency toward extremism: life heightens art. And life drastically alters the writer. The callous observer of *The Berlin Stories,* whom Isherwood repudiates in the late fifties and sixties, not only describes the Mortmere monstrosities about him, but, by the time of *Down There on a Visit,* actually becomes a monster. In "Ambrose," part II of *Down There on a Visit,* the narrator, essentially the same observer, flees to a Greek island where Berlin finally catches up with him. As with Germany and all of the West, "something has happened" to his soul, beyond all help. He is utterly lost.

Isherwood's technique, as he himself expounds it, is that of a camera; however, too many readers stress the objectivity of the camera, forgetting that the Isherwood camera is subjective, highly expressive, and, in fact, Germanic. The influence of German film on Isherwood's writings is no surprise—Isherwood cites German film as captivating his generation. Indeed, before the Nazis ruined German film by using it for propaganda, the German pictures led the way in Europe, producing more features in 1927 (241) than any other European country.[9] Thrillers such as Fritz Lang's *Doctor Mabuse, the Gambler* (1922) and G. W. Pabst's *Pandora's Box* (1929), surrealist films such as F. W. Murnau's *Nosferatu* (1922), based on *Dracula* and called "the most intense concentration of horror of which the screen is capable,"[10] fairy-tale films such as Henrik Galeen's *The Student of Prague* (1926), and of course Robert Wiene's daring and expressionistic *The Cabinet of Dr. Caligari* (1920)— these and more were acclaimed successes. The peculiar German contribution to film was the creative use of the camera— what the gestures of the actors could not communicate was to be conveyed by the symbolic language of the moving camera which "had the power of giving meaning even to lifeless things."[11]

In the following passage I have combined various statements of Paul Rotha on the German film before its Nazification, and, in the place of film-makers and their films, I have freely substituted Isherwood's name and the titles of his Berlin works.

By taking such liberties with Rotha's text, I hope to show that the camera of German film-makers is also Isherwood's camera:

> The easily recognizable characteristic . . . of [Isherwood's stories] . . . is the freedom of the camera as an instrument of expression, assuming the status of an observer and not of a spectator. . . . [Christopher Isherwood's *Mr. Norris*] was again a simplification of detail, a centralization of incident into small units of space and time, decorated by a fantastic touch. [*Goodbye to Berlin*] was yet another example. Nearly all the stories contain the fantastic element. They were seldom wholly tragic or wholly comic: they were often melodramatic, as in the case of [*Mr. Norris*]. . . . [These stories] . . . in using the expressionistic technique exploited the age-old German love for fantasy and the macabre which a hundred years before had surged through Romantic literature.[12]

This does not pretend that the camera as a metaphor for Isherwood's technique is identical with the actual camera of film-making. The two art forms are vitally different and, of course, Isherwood achieves certain effects which can be produced only by the choice and arrangement of individual words. As G. S. Fraser notes, Isherwood has style.[13] However, the characteristically visual properties of this style are achieved by Isherwood's placing his so-called camera in the proper position at the proper time. Lehmann supports this assertion by seeing *The Berlin Stories* as "outstanding" examples of novels which have been influenced by the "tempo, cutting, and visual primacy of the cinema."[14]

The very simplicity of *The Berlin Stories*—in plot, lack of clutter, and use of cogent incident only—may well be a result of Isherwood's schooling in the German cinema. On its simplest level, *The Last of Mr. Norris* is a serial biography of Arthur Norris who, surrounded by lesser characters, commands the reader's eye. In the first eight chapters, William Bradshaw is utterly fascinated, charmed, and scandalized by Norris. This first section of the novel ends when Norris leaves Berlin. The second part (chapter 9) begins, appropriately, only with Norris' returning to Berlin, entangling Bradshaw in an espionage jaunt to Switzerland, and becoming so embroiled in Berlin politics himself that he must flee. Thus, from beginning to end, resourceful, shiftless, impossible Arthur Norris, in or out of action, is the unmistakable center of attention.

The novel's action is episodic, bracketed into single chapters or a series of chapters, like sharp cuts in a film, often with little connection to preceding incident. For example, chapter three opens with: "A few days after Christmas I rang up Arthur (we called each other by our Christian names now) and suggested that we should spend *Silversterabend* together" (N 21). The chapter concludes when the party ends. Chapter four, beginning "Frl. Schroeder, my landlady, was very fond of Arthur" (N 32), has no link to the earlier chapter. The progression of the book resembles a film serial in which each installment presents, almost independently, another phase in the life of its picaresque hero.

In *Goodbye to Berlin,* Isherwood abandons the novel form to compose what he feels he can write best, a sequence even simpler and more compact—individual portraits. Against the bleak but garish background of a falling city, Sally Bowles, Peter and Otto, the Nowaks, the Landauers, and other Berlin denizens shuffle through their shabby cabaret choreography. Even more compressed than *The Last of Mr. Norris,* these portraits are succinct and direct. It is as if Isherwood, rather than making a full-length feature as he did in *Norris,* contents himself with shooting vivid, loosely joined shorts, startling in their severity and power.

Rotha also writes that the German camera is not an objective spectator, but almost a sentient observer. Enough has been said about the remove provided by the camera technique. Here it is important to note that the camera technique itself embodies the theme of *The Berlin Stories,* for, as Hitler's grasp on the city tightens, the narrator becomes more remote. In the beginning of *The Last of Mr. Norris,* Bradshaw feels excluded from a communist meeting, standing "outside it. One day, perhaps, I should be with it, but never of it" (N 48–49). By the time of "Sally Bowles," however, the narrator is isolated from the mass of men:

> In a few days, I thought, we shall have forfeited all kinship with ninety-nine per cent. of the population of the world, with the men and women who earn their living, who insure their lives, who are anxious about the future of their children. Perhaps in the Middle Ages people felt like this, when they believed themselves to have sold their souls to the Devil. It was a curious, exhilarating, not unpleasant sensation: but, at the same time, I felt slightly scared. Yes, I said to myself, I've done it, now. I am lost.                                                                    (GB 49)

In "Ambrose," this personal detachment dilates to cosmic proportions.

But what separates Isherwood's camera from the documentary camera which churned out reel after reel of undistinguished footage is the way Isherwood's camera is highly sensitive to nuance, capable, because of its selectivity, its angles, its juxtaposition of light and dark, of catching what Stephen Spender calls "the terrifying mystery of cities."[15]

Isherwood's camera captures the terror of Berlin very early in *The Last of Mr. Norris.* Bradshaw's walk to a New Year's party in chapter three is actually an archetypal journey to the land of the dead. So closely allied is Isherwood's technique with that of the early German film-makers that, merely by the insertion of camera directions and a slight rearrangement of the text, Isherwood's account of a New Year's festivity could have been excerpted from an early fantasy feature similar to *Dr. Caligari.*

In this expressionistic scenario, the camera first picks up William Bradshaw in the cloak room of the Troika club where, looking into the mirror, he is shocked to discover that he has been wearing a false nose—his mask for entry into the underworld.[16] He then finds himself in what is clearly the region of the dead. The camera follows Bradshaw's gaze through a room so crammed and smoke-filled that "it was difficult to say who was dancing and who was merely standing up" (N 22). Dancers "locked frigidly together, swayed in partial-paralytic rhythms under a huge sunshade suspended from the ceiling . . ." (N 23). Cut to Arthur's table where Bradshaw meets his guide to the underworld, the Baron von Pregnitz, "fishy and suave" (N 22). The Baron leans his head toward Bradshaw, "like a cod swimming up through water" (N 22). As the Baron gets progressively intoxicated, his face seems "slowly to disintegrate. A rigid area of paralysis formed round the monocle" (N 24). Here Isherwood's camera focuses on details that unsettle the viewer: the shiny black oil-cloth curtains in the alcoves are oddly cold to Bradshaw's touch; the table lamps are Alpine cow-bells; a fluffy white monkey perches above the bar. The whole smoke-filled inferno is irradiated by the light cast from "bottles filled with coloured liquids brilliantly illuminated from beneath, magenta, emerald, vermilion" (N 23). Drunk and wearing a false nose, Bradshaw has become one of the dead. He has a blasphemous vision of what life really is: "It had something, I remember, to do with the revolving sunshade. Yes, I murmured to myself, let them dance. They are dancing. I am glad" (N 23). As the music surges and dies, the conversation, like everything else, collapses into absurdity. The Baron asks Bradshaw:

"Excuse me, please. May I ask you something?"
"By all means."
"Have you read *Winnie the Pooh,* by A. A. Milne?"        (N 24)

The camera reels, shows Bradshaw standing: "What had happened? It was midnight. Our glasses touched" (N 24). He is startled by "a tremendous crash. . . . Like a car which has slowly, laboriously reached the summit of the mountain railway, we plunged headlong downwards into the New Year" (N 24).

After midnight, a montage of chaotic scenes follows. Bradshaw draws the scenario: "The events of the next two hours were somewhat confused. We were in a small bar, where I remember only the ruffled plumes of a paper streamer, crimson, very beautiful, stirring like seaweed in the draught from an electric fan. We wandered through streets crowded with girls who popped teasers in our faces. We ate ham and eggs in the first-class restaurant of the Friedrichstrasse Station. Arthur had disappeared" (N 25). The film then cuts to a taxi crossing several bridges and passing a gas works, driving "along a street bounded by a high dark wall" (N 25). Close-up in the taxi on Bradshaw and the Baron. The Baron squeezes Bradshaw's hand; with his other hand, Bradshaw fishes in his pocket and puts on his false nose. Spotting a cross over the top of a high wall, Bradshaw exclaims: "Good God, are you taking me to the cemetery?" (N 25). The Baron smiles, and Bradshaw has to "stop the taxi under a lamp-post in order to be sick" (N 25).

Finally the taxi screeches to a stop, "having arrived, it seemed, at the blackest corner of the night" (N 25). Bradshaw and the Baron stumble into a courtyard where a house is scarcely visible, except for a few windows from which "snatches of gramophone music and laughter" emanate (N 26). The atmosphere seems even more sinister, as Bradshaw and the Baron have moved from the sleazy-colored dance floor to utter darkness: "A silhouetted head and shoulders leant out of one of the windows, shouted: *'Prosit Neujahr!'* and spat vigorously. The spittle landed with a soft splash on the paving stone just beside my foot" (N 26). Another splash, this time from an emptied beer-mug.

Cut to a crammed room with "people dancing, shouting, singing, drinking, shaking our hands and thumping us on the back" (N 26). Now the tempo of the film quickens, the noise increases, the camera movements become more jerky. Once again as Bradshaw's gaze circles the room the camera picks up significant details—"a bowl of claret-cup in which floated an empty match-box, a broken bead from a necklace, a bust of Bismarck on the top of a Gothic dresser—holding them for an instant, then losing them again in general coloured chaos . . ." (N 26). In the midst of this turmoil, in a big armchair, "with a thin . . . sulky-looking girl on his lap," is Norris, without his wig, almost "perfectly bald" (N 26). Bradshaw is in this nightmare, but not of it—the next day he calmly steps over the drunken bodies strewn about the room, walks home, and sleeps it off. But soon he too will have no exit. *Goodbye to Berlin* and particularly *Down There on a Visit* show that the Isherwood narrator will not always walk away from Mortmere. Ultimately he carries it within him wherever he goes.

The potential of Isherwood's Germanic camera as an instrument of expression is almost unlimited. In this description of the Wassertorstrasse, the poor section in which the Nowaks live, Isherwood first focuses on the "big stone archway, a bit of old Berlin, daubed with hammers and sickles and Nazi crosses and plastered with tattered bills which advertised auctions or crimes . . . a deep shabby cobbled street, littered with sprawling children in tears" (GB 100). He calmly picks up woolen-sweatered youths whooping at girls passing with milk-jugs. The acute camera angle of the final sentence, however, is stunning: "At the end of it [the street], like a tall, dangerously sharp, red instrument, stood a church" (GB 101).

As the examples demonstrate, Isherwood's camera fulfills Joseph Conrad's injunction that prose should make the reader, above all, see,[17] by directing the eye to the telling symptom, the give-away gesture, the revealing detail. In this shot of Bernhard Landauer's flat, Isherwood's camera stamps inanimate objects with psychological import. After Christopher rings the bell to Bernhard's flat, a "gnome-like caretaker" stares at Christopher "through a tiny basement window ... with profound mistrust" (GB 154). Suspiciously, the caretaker presses a button that mysteriously releases the lock of an outer door. The stark, faithful recording of details renders them symbolic:

> This door was so heavy that I had to push it open with both hands; it closed behind me with a hollow boom, like the firing of a canon. Then came a pair of doors opening into the courtyard, then the door of the Gartenhaus, then five flights of stairs, then the door of the flat. Four doors to protect Bernhard from the outer world.                                      (GB 154)

The camera's use of light and dark lends a hallucinatory quality to Christopher's visit to a tuberculosis sanitorium. Fittingly, his visit occurs near the end of "The Nowaks," after the family has disintegrated, now that Frau Nowak is hospitalized. When Christopher and Otto, Frau Nowak's son, arrive, they are blinded by the brilliant sun:

> The bus stopped. Otto and I were the last passengers to get out. We stood stretching ourselves and blinking at the bright snow: out here in the country everything was dazzling white. (GB 132)

The patients hobble out to greet the bus, "awkward padded figures muffled in shawls and blankets, stumbling and slithering on the trampled ice of the path" (GB 132). They appear dazzling and happy, but something is obviously wrong, for light and laughter only cloak their distress. Inside, the sanitorium is faintly nauseating, "like soiled linen locked in a cupboard without air" (GB 135), and the women are playful and shrill like overgrown schoolgirls. Christopher and Otto spend what appears to be a normal day with Frau Nowak and her friends: they dance, take tea with them, visit an animal cemetery, have a snowball fight. But something is amiss. To convey this scene's mounting catastrophe, the camera is gauzed, even silent, as it slowly swivels about the room:

> Everything which happened to me to-day was curiously without impact: my senses were muffled, insulated, functioning as if in a vivid dream. In this calm, white room, with its great windows looking out over the silent pine-woods ... these four women lived and moved. (GB 134–35)

As the ward darkens, the truth assails the dazed Christopher. Erna, a lonely inmate, Christopher's companion for the day, tries to make love to him: "her big dark eyes fastened on to mine like hooks; I could imagine I felt them pulling me down" (GB 136). She puts Christopher's arm around her waist, whispers his name and kisses him (GB 137). But Christopher has no sensation of contact: "All this was part of the long, rather sinister symbolic dream I seemed to have been dreaming throughout the day" (GB 137). Five minutes later, visiting hours end. Now the camera, in a flash, exposes the truth. Frau Nowak weeps, begs them to return. "And suddenly she started coughing—her body seemed to break in half like a hinged doll" (GB 138). The nightmare climaxes as the bus leaves: the patients, huddled around the bus, resemble the insane hooded subjects of Goya's black paintings; their faces, lit from the headlights of the bus, are "ghastly like ghosts" against the black trunks of the pines:

> This was the climax of my dream: the instant of nightmare in which it would end. I had an absurd pang of fear that they were going to attack us—a gang of terrifyingly soft muffled shapes— clawing us from our seats, dragging us hungrily down, in dead silence. But the moment passed. They drew back—harmless, after all, as mere ghosts—into the darkness, while our bus, with a great churning of its wheels, lurched forward towards the city, through the deep unseen snow. (GB 139)

This same masterful juxtaposition of light and dark concludes *The Berlin Stories,* though here the dark is not physical, but psychological. Again, light is opaque and hides Berlin's darkness:

> The sun shines, and Hitler is master of this city. The sun shines, and dozens of my friends . . . are in prison, possibly dead. . . .
>
> No. Even now I can't altogether believe that any of this has really happened. . . .                                    (GB 207)

Nonetheless, even after Berlin's nightmare, Isherwood's narrator is still as uninvolved as he had been after the New Year's party in *Norris*. When he catches his reflection in a store front, he is quite shocked to see himself smiling. In *Down There on a Visit,* however, the same narrator is not so detached. Then looking into the mirror, he is startled by his terrible transformation. Although Isherwood's narrator flees Berlin's Mortmere atrocities, he cannot escape them—for the truth, as Isherwood discovers, is that Mortmere is not a place, but a state of soul, more pernicious than his wildest imaginings at Cambridge.

But this evocation of a Mortmeresque nightmare Isherwood reinterprets, as he has reinterpreted every other aspect of his life and art. In his introduction to *Mr. Norris and I,* written by Gerald Hamilton, the model for Arthur Norris, Isherwood views himself with unexpected acerbity. He says that having heard of Berlin from Mr. Lancaster, he began dreaming of it "as unrealistically as a child dreams of the jungle; he hopes to meet tigers and pythons there, but doesn't expect them to hurt him" (E 86). As a touchstone for his experiences, he chooses a line from *Othello:* "There's many a beast then, in a populous city,/ And many a civil monster."

> I arrived in Berlin on the lookout for civil monsters. And, since my imagination had very little contact with reality, I soon persuaded myself that I had found several.

Now, looking back, he is repelled by *Mr. Norris,* that "heartless fairy-story about a real city in which human beings were suffering. . . . The only genuine monster was the young foreigner who passed gaily through these scenes of desolation, misinterpreting them to suit his childish fantasy" (E 86–87). In "Mr. Lancaster" and "Ambrose," parts II and III of *Down There on a Visit,* written more than thirty years after Isherwood's Berlin experience and which could well be entitled *Berlin Revisited,* Isherwood reassesses the world of the lost and sees his young, heartless narrator in a harsh light.

A review in *The New Yorker* caricatures Mr. Lancaster as a "protean bore—an argumentative bore, a mystifying bore, a patronizing bore, a querulous bore, a pompous, didactic, poetic, philosophical, and Philistine bore."[18] Christopher, young and mischievous, would have relished painting him in Fauvist colors as a civil monster; but instead, in "Mr. Lancaster," the older Isherwood, with cool clarity, concentrates on the cruelty of the young writer who tolerated Mr. Lancaster only for the sake of his fictional possibilities. This second look centers not on the Mortmere distortions of Mr. Lancaster, but on those of the young writer who evades the truth about both himself and Mr. Lancaster. Christopher is incapable of entering into Mr. Lancaster's lonely world—to the detriment of both men. As one reviewer writes, "He has turned the camera on himself . . . and the image is frightening";[19] what he sees is not a young man, but a "genuine monster."

Approximately a year before his trip to Berlin, Isherwood is taunted by Mr. Lancaster, a distant relative, to visit him in a northern German city (probably Hamburg): "I'm willing to wager, most excellent Christophilos, that you've never seen the inside of a tramp steamer" (V 12). Let go of your mother's apron strings, he teases. "Show us you can rough it. Let's see you eat bacon fat in the middle of a nor'easter. . . . It might just possibly make a man of you" (V 12). Because he loathes Mr. Lancaster, Christopher cannot refuse this challenge. It is a Test, he concludes, and speedily concocts an epic drama, "adapted freely from Conrad, Kipling, and Browning's 'What's become of Waring?'" in which Christopher plays the lead (V 13).

Before embarking on his epic journey, Isherwood trains his camera on the young Christopher. The world is before him. He has just published his first novel, *All the Conspirators*. But he is alone and forever play-acting, "isolated by his self-mistrust, anxiety and dread of the future" (V 14), inflating his life into epic proportions. Genuinely a rebel, he knows that only by rebellion will he ever learn and grow, and ultimately, more than thirty years later, be able to judge himself dispassionately. In many ways, the young Christopher is a stranger to the writer now evoking his presence; he is even, practically speaking, dead. Isherwood promises not to apologize for his callowness or superficiality, for "after all, I owe him some respect. In a sense he is my father, and in another sense my son" (V 14).

Arriving in Mr. Lancaster's city after an uneventful trip converted into a fantastic voyage by imagination and sea-sick pills, Isherwood loathes Mr. Lancaster even more: "No—I could find no beauty in him . . . I reminded myself with approval of one of . . . Hugh Weston's dicta: 'All ugly people are wicked'" (V 21). Mr. Lancaster quickly establishes himself as one of the Enemy: he bores Christopher, detests modern literature, exacts a promise from Christopher that he will never "commit" a novel, and takes cold showers. Beside himself, Christopher decides to "make the best of Mr. Lancaster" (V 36). After all, Christopher reasons, he is a novelist, and hadn't he and Chalmers in school been fond of exchanging the watch-word "All pains!" by which they used to remind each other that, "to a writer, everything is potential material and that he has no business quarreling with his bread and butter" (V 37).

While Mr. Lancaster is at work, Christopher, alone in Mr. Lancaster's flat for the first time, stealthily searches for "clues," but finds few: a British army captain's uniform and a "locked writing desk which might possibly contain secrets."

One afternoon, however, Christopher's Sherlock Holmes activities finally yield results: an army service revolver and a "thick notebook with a shiny cover" (V 42) which, it is not surprising, echoes the shiny black decor of the *Norris* New Year's party. Thrilled because the notebook contains several poems written by Mr. Lancaster, Christopher scribbles down a long Wordsworthian piece which he plans to ridicule later with Chalmers.

Then, two days before he returns to England, Christopher has his final clash with Mr. Lancaster on a fishing expedition. Provoked by Mr. Lancaster's playing the role of a British Admiral and expert fisherman, Christopher malevolently wrecks the boat and Mr. Lancaster's naval persona. The incident begins when, heading toward land and carrying on in the best tradition of windy old salts, Mr. Lancaster complacently remarks on his own foresight in calculating a timetable that set them flowing with the tide both ways.

> Suddenly he screamed: "SAND! SAND AHEAD! PUT HER ABOUT! HARD! HARD OVER!"
> What happened next was quite unplanned. At least, I had no conscious knowledge of what I was going to do. Nevertheless, I did it. I had the feel of the tiller by this time; I could sense pretty well how much it would stand. All I did was to obey Mr. Lancaster's order just the merest shade too energetically. I swung the tiller hard over—very hard. And with the most

exquisitely satisfactory, rending crack, the crosspiece to which
the outboard engine was clamped broke off, and the engine fell
into the water.                                                    (V 51)

They had to sail the rest of the way; and this time, Mr.
Lancaster, glum, did the steering. Christopher however was
ecstatic:

> . . . at the very instant when that engine had splashed into the
> water—I had had a visitation. A voice had said: "The two
> women—the ghosts of the living and the ghosts of the dead—
> the Memorial." And, in a flash, I had seen it all—the pieces had
> moved into place—the composition was instantaneously *there*.
> Dimly, but with intense excitement, I recognized the outline of a
> new novel.                                                      (V 52)

As the young Christopher had intuited, it is only by rebellion
that he will learn and grow. In this instance, his defiance of Mr.
Lancaster goes a long way toward furthering his development
as an artist.

Later, in London, Christopher tries to caricature Mr. Lancaster, but finds that he just "did not have the key to him . . ."
(V 55). Even his poetry "wasn't bad enough in the right way" (V
55). In his own heartlessness, he would have forgotten Mr.
Lancaster, had Mr. Lancaster toward the end of that same year
not shot himself. (Thus was the gun a telling "plant" when
found in the drawer with the notebook.) The following year in
Berlin, Waldemar, who had worked for Mr. Lancaster, informs
Christopher that Mr. Lancaster had often spoken of him, had
praised his book, had denounced its hostile critics, and had
even claimed Christopher as his nephew. "I believe he was
really fond of you. . . . Who knows, Christoph, if you'd been
there to look after him, he might have been alive today!" (V
57). Twenty-five years later, Isherwood knows that life is more
complicated than Waldemar's optimism allows. He realizes
now that Mr. Lancaster's scornful invitation was "his attempt to

re-establish relations with the outside world" (V 57). But ensconced in his own sounding box, singing his epic song of himself, Mr. Lancaster "didn't need me. He didn't need any kind of human being; only an imaginary nephew-disciple to play a supporting part in his epic" (V 57). However, Isherwood concludes, Mr. Lancaster ceased to believe in his epic. "Despair is something horribly simple . . . in his case, I hope and believe, it was short-lived. Few of us can bear much pain of this kind and remain conscious" (V 57).

In "Ambrose," whose action occurs five years after that of "Mr. Lancaster," Isherwood anatomizes his own horribly simple despair. The many-stranded, saturnalian plot seems lifted from the pages of Mortmere, as Isherwood recalls his personal nightmare through narrative and through frequent excerpts from his diary.

Fleeing from the Nazis in 1933, Christopher accompanies Waldemar to a Greek island where Waldemar is to work for an eccentric young Englishman, Ambrose. For Christopher, Ambrose is more than just another acquaintance: he is a mirror in which Christopher sees the monster he is becoming. Although Ambrose is about Christopher's age, his face is "shockingly lined as though life had mauled him with its claw" (V 71). The story grows more Mortmeresque by the page. Ambrose is bargaining to purchase the entire island of St. Gregory. Unfortunately the island is owned by 311 cantankerous Greek villagers who cannot agree on settlement terms. Nevertheless, Ambrose, combining, as one critic says, "the characteristics of Prospero, Dorian Gray, and Holden Caulfield,"[20] begins building a perverse monastic commune on the island. With him are Geoffrey, a wooden, truculent young Englishman, who advises Christopher that if he is not hiding from the police to leave at once; Hans, who, like Waldemar, is a bisexual opportunist; and a crew of assorted fiends, led by

Theo and Petro. The crew is "swinishly dirty, inhumanly destructive and altogether on the side of the forces of disorder" (V 106). Their antics are inane and satanic. They pull the feathers off a live owl, suffocate a rabbit in a box without holes, dynamite fish in the ocean, and festoon surrounding bushes with toilet paper. Over the improbable island and its hellish crew, like an exiled mythological king (V 103), Ambrose sets himself up as the Lord of Misrule, the center which paradoxically holds together the widening gyre of passionate confusion. But Ambrose is already dead, he repeatedly informs Christopher, and his "charming Devil's Island" (V 81) is surrounded by death.

Christopher should know, for he has seen nothing but death, even before his arrival. Vultures are everywhere, and Christopher and crew are ferried across the waters by a Charon-like old man. They are not met by Ambrose's boys because, as Geoffrey rants, "the little Sodomites . . . were screwing somebody or something . . ." (V 90). Starting up a hill, the crew carries a tent "like an enormous dead body" (V 88); its lanterns lend the procession "an air of nocturnal melodrama . . . like a painting of the descent from the cross—except that we were going uphill . . ." (V 88)—an indication of the religious perversion to come. Even the animals on the island suggest death: there is a goat "like a lean, black, shaggy-legged devil with goblin teeth and slanting Levantine eyes" (V 91), and there are rats swarming "all over the inhabited part of the island. . . . They are as bold as dogs, and nothing is safe from them" (V 107). The island escape sought by Philip Lindsay in Isherwood's first novel is finally revealed for what it is: a world of Kafkaesque fantasy, sequestered from humanity.

As the story progresses, Christopher falls under the spell of this island of death. His sense of time and place blurs; even his sense of self, his individuality, fades and begins to merge with that of Ambrose. Like Bernhard Landauer, Christopher

begins to lose even the realization that he is lost. Ambrose, as
the center of corruption, represents the temptation to ultimate
despair. This final temptation, after the horror of Berlin, and
anticipating what C. Day Lewis in his autobiography calls the
coming "delirium of nations,"[21] momentarily paralyzes Christopher. Later, during the Sudeten crisis, Christopher suffers.
But then, his very anguish and indecision, recorded in the
"Waldemar" diary, are a sign of hope, because the writer still
cares about the future. Marooned on Ambrose's island, however, he is anesthetized to despair. His sea-change does not
save but damns him.

After a meal of roasted chicken, one of Ambrose's crew hints
that, before killing the chicken, he had raped it. Recording this
in his diary, Christopher is startled to find himself grinning. At
the end of *The Berlin Stories,* Isherwood's narrator shrugs off
his grin: "You can't help smiling, in such beautiful weather"
(GB 207). Now, the older writer allows his narrator no such
excuse, as Christopher asks: "What is this island doing to me?"
(V 109). Daily, Christopher answers this question as he finds
himself more and more like Ambrose: he even discovers that
he had known Ambrose at Cambridge and that they were
fellow-recalcitrants. Ambrose had hated Cambridge, the poshocracy, the world of academia, England—in fact, all of Christopher's Enemies.

This island life, ultimately a projection of Ambrose's ada-
mantine will (Christopher calls Ambrose a steel-winged butter-
fly [V 95]), is disrupted by the arrival of a prostitute, Maria
Constantinescu, whose power and promiscuity usurp
Ambrose's misrule. She also brings Christopher to a moment
of truth. One morning, she asks Christopher whether he hates
her:

> "Of course I don't! I'm rather fascinated by you. You're a
> kind of monster I've never met before."

"Oh, wonderful! Then we can be like brother and sister. Because, my dear, you too are a monster, I find! Do not pretend! Admit now!"

"All right," I said. "I'm a monster." I felt rather flattered.

"Yes!" Now I see it more plain than ever! *Tu es vraiment gentil, mon petit.* You look so young. You have such nice clear eyes. But you are an old, old monster, like me. . . ." (V 124)

With startling insight, she unmasks Christopher's motivation, the motivation which prompted him to settle in Berlin and now prompts him to remain with Ambrose: " . . . monsters are heartless, *mon vieux!* You know this—do not be so hypocrite! You cannot hold a monster by his emotion, only by puzzling him. As long as the monster is puzzled, he is yours" (V 125).

Having plundered the stronghold of Ambrose's homosexual kingdom, Maria kidnaps Geoffrey and runs off. Christopher even catches her in the act, but can only watch. The demon of the place possesses him; he has forfeited any sense of consequence. His final diary entries, unlike his rantings during the Sudeten crisis, are sparse and passionless. Like the aphasic half lines in Eliot's "The Hollow Men," they remain unfinished because Christopher is incapable of finishing them.

Sun. Island. Gramophone. Sea. World without adjectives. Except—hot, hot, hot.

. . .

Saw today what this island is. Words no good.

. . .

If one could only—
What *am* I doing here?

. . .

Oh, Jesus, my head.

. . .

Last night, perfect calm. Sitting on benzine can in moonlight, watching sea. Ambrose understands. (V 129)

With these whimpers, the diary ends, and the older Isherwood
again turns his camera on himself: What does the nightmare
mean? Life on the island, he sees, was unreal; he had ceased to
be himself or anyone else. Why did he remain, aping
Ambrose's absurd mummery? Here Isherwood plunges
deeper into himself than Maria Constantinescu had. He
remained to assure himself that he wasn't alone. Ironically,
Ambrose contributes to his salvation. He insists that they are
worlds apart: "One's always alone, ducky. Surely you know
that" (V 134). Christopher leaves because fortunately Ambrose
does not ask him to stay. Ambrose can no longer make a
positive gesture. Looking back on the island, as he did on
Berlin, Christopher cannot believe that it had all happened:
"Imagine—someone actually lives there—alone, in the midst
of the wilderness" (V 135). In a hotel on the mainland, Christopher looks in the mirror and for the third time answers his
question, "What is this island doing to me?"

> My hair was long and matted, my beard had started to grow, I
> was sunburned nearly black, my face was puffy with drinking
> and my eyes were red. All that, of course, could soon be tidied
> up. But there was also a look in my eyes which hadn't been there
> before. (V 135)

Like Welken and Gunball of the Cambridge fantasies, like Mr.
Lancaster and Ambrose, Christopher too is lost, has become a
character out of Mortmere. And after more than thirty years,
Isherwood does not permit his narrator to apologize or grinningly to bow out of reprisal. Rather, his narrator looks in the
mirror and, like George in *A Single Man*, sees not a face but a
predicament. With Christopher's realization and acceptance,
Isherwood, at long last, and only after having immersed himself in the destructive element, repudiates Mortmere, not
because of its fantasy but because of its reality.

# CHAPTER

# 5

# The Hero

Throughout his career, Isherwood has constantly been reassessing and reinterpreting his life and work. For a writer who sought escape from the past, this continual remembrance of things past is, as we have seen, an unexpected irony. The rebellion against Kathleen and Frank, the camera technique of *The Berlin Stories*, which won him instant acclaim, the bizarre Mortmere fantasy of those stories, the concealment of his homosexuality—of these Isherwood, as an older man, takes a second, very different view. With his conversion to Vedanta he even revises his conceptions of character and conflict, conceptions basic to the work of any novelist.

Very early in his career, as he relates in *Lions and Shadows*, Isherwood formed four concepts which fired his creative imagination and which were to figure in his major fiction: the Enemy, the Test, the Truly Weak Man, and the Truly Strong Man. These concepts are also the props upon which Auden, from his close association with Isherwood, and the so-called "Auden group" (composed of Louis MacNeice, Stephen Spender, C. Day Lewis, and Rex Warner) constructed an elaborate cloak-and-dagger mythology of spies and frontiers. For Isherwood, as we have seen, the first Enemy was his mother, and later, all those busybodies—headmasters, schoolmasters, Cambridge dons, and preachers—who minimized the present by drumming into the young Christopher his obligations to Frank the hero-father, thus aggravating the guilt and shame Christopher felt at not having fought in the Great War. Gradually Isherwood stretched this term, the Enemy, to cover the Cambridge poshocracy (the social and academic elite), the bourgeois, those who frowned on Freudianism, Marxism, Socialism, homosexuality, modern literature—as C. Day Lewis bluntly writes, anyone who was so tone deaf that he could not hear the entrance of a new theme into the world.[1]

The enthusiastic rebels of the postwar generation viewed life, as Auden writes in his birthday poem to Isherwood, as an extraordinary game of spies played with the ingenuity of precocious Sixth Formers.[2] But their iconoclastic bravura and impatient anticipation of the brave new world left many young rebels disaffected and spiritually destitute.

As an adolescent and young adult, Isherwood suffered keenly from his renunciation of tradition. Because he required a principle against which he could measure himself, he devised his own criterion which he called "the Test" and which was war in a "purely neurotic sense" (LS 76):

> The test of your courage, of your maturity, of your sexual prowess: "Are you really a Man?" Subconsciously, I believe, I longed to be subjected to this test; but I also dreaded failure. I dreaded failure so much—indeed, I was so certain that I *should* fail—that, consciously, I denied my longing to be tested, altogether. I denied my all-consuming morbid interest in the idea

of "war." I pretended indifference. The War, I said, was
obscene, not even thrilling, a nuisance, a bore.          (LS 76)

In spite of his attempt to debunk war, Isherwood continually
imposed giddy, daredevil trials on himself. At Cambridge, the
Test first "transposed itself into a visible metal contraption of
wheels, valves, cogs, chains and tubes, smartly painted black": a
1924 A.J.S. motor-bicycle. Motorcycle rides down narrow,
crowded Cambridge lanes were pure terror: "How I loathed
and enjoyed those rides . . . no sooner had I released the grips
of the clutch than I seemed to shoot forward like a bullet . . ."
(LS 84). After three or four masochistic escapades, Isherwood
basely walked his bike out of the city. "I thus began to fail the
Test almost before it had begun" (LS 84). But once on the open
road, he would accelerate to speeds of fifty-five. "I clung on,
horribly scared, with the wind screaming in my ears: I wasn't
allowed to reduce speed until I had counted up to a hundred,
at least" (LS 84).

His most humiliating mishap occurred when, with a girl
riding pillion, he crashed and she, not he, was injured. "Everyone was very nice about the accident, but I noticed, or imagined, contemptuously pitying glances; and, two days later,
received, at my own request, an urgent telegram from London,
recalling me home" (LS 96). Isherwood had again failed the
Test and was, for the time, "comfortably and ignobly resigned"
(LS 96).[3]

He replaced the motorbike with a journal, modelled upon
Barbellion's *Diary of a Disappointed Man.* Isherwood's unsur-
mountable difficulty was that, unlike Barbellion, he was not
dying of some obscure paralysis—"though, in reading some of
my more desperate entries, you would hardly suspect it . . ."
(LS 97). Failing another Test, he then posed as an aesthete,
Isherwood the Artist, affecting to be above the Test, which was
"something for the common herd" (LS 97). In reality, he had

only exchanged the old Test for a new one which he botched whenever he made an addition to the journal: "the self-imposed Test of his integrity as a writer" (LS 97).

As discussed in the previous chapter, Isherwood's most sustained and sophisticated escape from responsibility and respectability and from his own puerile principles was Mortmere, the surrealist world he and Edward Upward created. But, like all his escapes, that too was short term.

Though Isherwood tried to gloss over his failure of the Test, the Test, like Welken's wife, clung like a succubus to Isherwood's subconscious. His first attempt at a novel, an unpublished *Lions and Shadows*, "dreadfully long, longer than anything I've ever written before or since,"[4] was a fiasco because his subconscious had rigorously censored him from spilling out his dread of war and the Test. Impossible to pass, the Test doomed Isherwood to continual aberrations in behavior. To get sent down from Cambridge, he deliberately failed his Tripos by composing puns and limericks; out of school, he pursued a career in Bohemia as a kind of secretary-factotum for the Mangeot family's musical group; he flatly flunked medical school; and by the time of the General Strike, he was psychologically paralyzed. To his jaundiced eyes, the strike was a "dress rehearsal of 'The Test': and it found me utterly unprepared. I wanted to lock myself away in a corner and pretend that nothing was happening" (LS 179). Until Isherwood's departure for Germany, his career, as Hena Maes-Jelinek summarizes it, is a "record of failure . . . revealing his instability and illustrating the conflicting tendencies of his temperament."[5] Even the flight to Berlin is a search for the ultimate experience, the absolute Test, as the squeamish public school boy willfully samples the perversion of a foreign capital.

In Isherwood's early fiction, the Test exists only for the Truly Weak Man, Isherwood's version of the modern neurotic hero, feckless and impetuous, plunging where angels fear to tread. Yet, "no matter whether he passes it [the Test] or whether he fails, he cannot alter his essential nature" (LS 207), for he is damned by his ponderous sense of failure and inadequacy. His antithesis, the Truly Strong Man, is

> calm, balanced, aware of his strength, sits drinking quietly in the bar; it is not necessary for him to try and prove to himself that he is not afraid, by joining the Foreign Legion, seeking out the most dangerous wild animals in the remotest tropical jungles, leaving his comfortable home in a snowstorm to climb the impossible glacier ... [he] travels straight across the broad America of normal life, taking always the direct, reasonable route.                                    (LS 207–8)

But "the broad America of normal life" is precisely what the Truly Weak Man dreads:

> And so, with immense daring, with an infinitely greater expenditure of nervous energy, money, time, physical and mental resources, he prefers to attempt the huge northern circuit, the laborious, terrible north-west passage, avoiding life; and his end, if he does not turn back, is to be lost forever in the blizzard and the ice.                                    (LS 208)

That these concerns were with Isherwood from his very beginning as a writer can be seen in a short story entitled "The Hero," published in *Oxford Outlook*, June 1925.[6] The story, set at Rugonstead, Isherwood's fictional Repton, is an ironic tale about adolescent hero-worship. This pedestrian subject gains force from Isherwood's four key concepts. Isherwood contrasts Gerald Wayne, uncertain and unheroic, the Truly Weak Man, with Wayne's best friend, Thompson, a recognized athlete, the Truly Strong Man. Smarting because of Thompson's *éclat* and his own inferiority, Wayne yearns to prove his pluck in one smashing stroke. His chance comes one rainy day when Thompson, conveniently unable to swim, falls into the river.

Wayne dives into the water but, once in the flood-swollen river, panics and tries to save himself only. Thus he fails the Test. After both boys are rescued, however, everyone lionizes Wayne, and the Headmaster publicly dubs him a hero. Wayne, who knows the truth, accepts his undeserved status, but loses Thompson as a friend. As in the beginning, Wayne is alone and miserable.

All of Isherwood's early characters—those conceived during his English period, before he left for America in 1939—easily slip into the categories of the Truly Weak Man and the Truly Strong. Philip Lindsay, Eric Vernon, William Bradshaw, Christopher Isherwood, to name the protagonists, are all Truly Weak Men. Their prototype is Edward Blake of *The Memorial.* Significantly an airman and, like Auden's Airman, irrevocably wounded, Blake is an apathetic wastelander: ragged at school, unsure of his manhood, confused and unpopular, periodically living with his wife, Margaret, more often with homosexual pick-ups, he wanders the demimonde. Eliot's line sums up his fitful existence: "I read, much of the night, and go south in the winter."[7] In *The Memorial,* Blake even "mucks" his attempt at suicide. The events before and after his pathetic failure are recounted in a severe, asyndetic style, which emphasizes Blake's desolation:

> He closed his eyes. Immediately the blood-beats in his head quickened to a smooth, rushing, roaring sound. Louder and louder. He had the feeling that he was losing consciousness. Dug the muzzle hard against his palate. Further back. No, it didn't matter. A tremendous roar. Like falling. The first time you jump with a parachute. Yes. Quick. Now. Raising himself upon one elbow, he fired.                                    (M 58)

Sometime later he regains consciousness:

> A bright surface. Pattern of cubes. The bright edge intersected the dark. A solid oblong shape bulging toward the top.

The wardrobe seen from the floor.
. . . O Christ, thought Edward, I've mucked it.     (M 58–59)

In the early books, the few Truly Strong Men such as Allen Chalmers and Richard Vernon do not receive the attention given to the neurotic heroes; if anything, Chalmers and Vernon are foil characters whose sanguine self-assurance highlights the others' Sisyphian struggles for self-fulfillment.

Isherwood's characters and conflicts are no more than the desperate attempts of a Truly Young Man straining to exorcise his demons, for the fictional possibilities of this early scheme lead nowhere. The Truly Weak Man is on an endless journey without a destination. He can retreat to the snug womb of home and mother, as does Philip Lindsay, or stumble into religion, as does Eric Vernon, or abortively attempt suicide, as does Edward Blake, or hide behind the austere objectivity of the camera, as does the Bradshaw-Isherwood narrator. In all cases, the options, in terms of the novel, are cramped, even solipsistic.

The options of the Truly Strong Man seem equally feeble for a novelist. In Isherwood's early career this figure suffers from such superficiality that he is a mere heroic cutout: Allen Chalmers is a cynic with a peripheral role in *All the Conspirators,* and Richard Vernon is an unapproachable Olympian in *The Memorial.* In spite of the stunted promise, however, these concepts of character and conflict do not harden into sterile categories, as one might predict; but they mellow and deepen as Isherwood himself develops. Because Isherwood is an autobiographical writer, his continuing search for fulfillment can spell only larger dimensions for his characters. In fiction as in life, Isherwood's quest for meaning is rewarding because, in Audenesque terms, he is willing to experiment, to venture down blind alleys, to pursue false clues. In one of Auden's quest poems, "Atlantis," only because the pilgrim in the poem persists does he discover his goal, Atlantis. Auden sums up the pilgrim's experience, as well as Isherwood's, as follows:

> ... unless
> you become acquainted now
> with each refuge that tries to
> counterfeit Atlantis, how
> will you recognize the true?[8]

Isherwood, as we have seen, recognizes the true Atlantis in Vedanta. Thus, in the books of his American period, or more properly his Vedanta period, beginning with the publication of *Prater Violet,* his characters become markedly more interior as Isherwood discovers more potential in them. Bergmann in *Prater Violet* is the first indication of Isherwood's deeper understanding of the Truly Strong Man. Alternatively, Stephen Monk in *The World in the Evening* is as spoiled as Philip Lindsay *(All the Conspirators),* as lost as Eric Vernon *(The Memorial),* and as miserable as Edward Blake *(The Memorial).* But Stephen does learn the futility of imposing harebrained tests on himself, because the Test for the deeper Isherwood hero is inward and the Enemy is his own deficiency, not his mother or his father or his two wives. In *Down There on a Visit,* Paul, reputed to be the most expensive male prostitute in the world, embraces Vedanta and undergoes a short-lived reformation. Even though he later recedes into opium and lassitude, nonetheless, like Bergmann and Monk, Paul enjoys a greater extension of character. Near the end of the novel, Isherwood hints that perhaps Paul is true to himself in exploring personal depths which would dizzy other men—he certainly understands the Isherwood narrator. Paul accuses him of his greatest sin: that of being an observer. When Paul offers Chris a pipe of opium, Chris accepts, but he insists on one pipe only. At this, Paul censures Christopher for his tentativeness:

> "You're exactly like a tourist who thinks he can take in the whole
> of Rome in one day. You know, you really *are* a tourist, to your
> bones. I bet you're always sending post cards with 'Down here
> on a visit' on them. That's the story of your life. . . ." (V 315–16)

At best, Paul's pronouncement is a half-truth, for even the
Bradshaw-Isherwood narrator matures from a cameralike
robot into a fuller, more human person. This growth illumines
and reaffirms the contrast between the early and the later
Isherwood conceptions of the novel.

Isherwood first used his namesake as a narrator because he
felt that only in this way could he be true to his experiences.
Apprehensive of employing his own name, he used William,
his middle name, and Bradshaw, a family name which, until he
chose to discard it, was joined by a hyphen to his present
surname. But Isherwood deems this first attempt at relating
personal experiences through his namesake a failure. In a
lecture delivered in 1963, he claims that William Bradshaw was
a fundamental mistake from the very beginning, because by
identifying himself with Bradshaw he was not telling the truth
but instead was

> lying about the nature of my experiences . . . a thing I have
> never done since then; I mean I was making myself participate
> in a kind of way I didn't in order to assist at certain criminal
> procedures which were going on . . . I was made a great deal
> dumber than I ever had been because I would have seen right
> through these people and had nothing to do with them and so
> William Bradshaw turned out to be unsatisfactory as a vehicle
> for my perceptions.[9]

That William Bradshaw turned out to be unsatisfactory as a
vehicle for Isherwood's perceptions may be true for the writer
personally. As a method for recording impressions of the
people and events around him, however, Bradshaw and the
Herr Issyvoo of *Goodbye to Berlin* are, as the reviewer for the

*Times Literary Supplement* notes, highly successful lenses "through which to focus a real or imaginary world," an expert use of the first person narrator, bettering the achievements of rival practitioners in this mode like Maugham.[10]

In *Goodbye to Berlin,* Isherwood employs his own name and elucidates his role as narrator at the beginning with certainly the most quoted passage in all of Isherwood's books:

> I am a camera with its shutter open, quite passive, recording, not thinking. Recording the man shaving at the window opposite and the woman in the kimono washing her hair. Some day, all this will have to be developed, carefully printed, fixed. (GB 1)

Although the narrator Christopher Isherwood is more involved than Bradshaw in the lives of Berliners, the difference is marginal. Isherwood in the sixties also belittles the narrative method of *Goodbye to Berlin,* for there his namesake either apologizes for his glaring indifference or overlooks it.[11] In a recent interview Isherwood acknowledges that Cyril Connolly's astute observation that he has a terrible inclination to apologize to the reader turns out to be "one of the most perceptive things anybody has said about my writing, in a negative way."[12] Thus Isherwood judges the narrative apparatus of *The Berlin Stories* as posing insoluble problems:

> of course you can't go right through a book being a camera and people started getting involved with the camera, talking to it, getting mad at it, even sometimes making passes at it, and the question was, How does the camera respond?[13]

Or, in more philosophical terms, the question is, Who is Christopher Isherwood? The camera is turning into a human being and, by the time of *Prater Violet,* the novel in which Isherwood thinks the camera method works best, there is no suppressing Christopher's inner life, magnificently revealed in the book's penultimate scene.

The third, "and, as I at present believe, the last time" Isherwood focuses through Christopher is in *Down There on a Visit*. But now the task has become almost intractable: the camera confines the narrator to recording life from a safe distance, but Isherwood's Vedantism urges him toward interpretation of, and involvement with, his young narrator and the people he meets. Hence to be true to his youth and to his identity at the time of writing, Isherwood cannot present himself merely as an inert onlooker. The events of the book, which span the years 1928–52, have been developed, carefully printed, fixed. Maintaining his allegiance to technique and to religion, he avails himself of a "bi-focal vision in . . . [which] . . . I try to show myself now writing about the situation and also at the same time, the I, other than myself, who was involved at that time with these characters, and so I attempt a kind of autobiography in depth."[14] In the following paragraph, Isherwood establishes this double view:

> And now before I slip back into the convention of calling this young man "I," let me consider him as a separate being, a stranger almost, setting out on this adventure in a taxi to the docks. For, of course, he *is* almost a stranger to me. I have revised his opinions, changed his accent and his mannerisms, unlearned or exaggerated his prejudices and his habits. We still share the same skeleton, but its outer covering has altered so much that I doubt if he would recognize me on the street. We have in common the label of our name, and a continuity of consciousness; there has been no break in the sequence of daily statements that I am I. But *what* I am has refashioned itself throughout the days and years, until now almost all that remains constant is the mere awareness of being conscious.     (V 13–14)

In spite of the revamped technique, Isherwood told Leon Surmelian he was still dissatisfied by the experiment:

> The truth is that Christopher cannot by his very nature be a character like the other characters in a novel. He is merely a

kind of scanning device which is being operated at long-distance by the author. So I am forced to conclude that the whole I-Christopher experiment is a failure, in the last analysis.[15]

Isherwood is a harsh critic of his work, but not necessarily an accurate one, particularly in the sixties when his disavowal of William Bradshaw and Herr Issyvoo stems from moral, not aesthetic concerns. Contrary to Isherwood's disclaimers, the I-Christopher experiment was innovative and effective—as long as the writer remained content to focus on the outer world and work within the stringent limits of the technique. Once he turned its truth-showing eye on himself, then he was compelled to abandon or modify his camera. Rather than a failure, the experiment, seen from current perspective, is untenable, since Isherwood's narrator has outgrown the camera, becoming "more human, more agonizingly involved with his characters, existing on their level 'down there!'"[16] Thus, a dozen years after *Goodbye to Berlin,* the writer for the *Times Literary Supplement* composes a joyful epitaph for the occasion of *Down There on a Visit:* "In short, Herr Issyvoo is dead: long live Christopher Isherwood."[17]

It is clear, then, from the maturing view taken of the narrator and from the depths of the author's later characters that, at least from the time of *Prater Violet,* Isherwood is writing from an altered perception of what a novel should be. The convictions formulated in *Lions and Shadows,* the matrix for his early fiction, he reassesses and recasts in an article published in 1946, "The Problem of the Religious Novel."[18] At the same time that his terminology undergoes change, the basic ideas of the Enemy, the Test, the Truly Weak and Truly Strong Men, though still with him, become modified. Now Isherwood's Truly Strong Man is a saint, the most interesting subject to write about because a saint responds to life more creatively than anyone else.

Because the saint is not a recognizable social type, the author must use "utmost persuasiveness, deftness, and cunning"[19] to refute preconceived notions of him as a stodgy, hair-shirted eccentric. Thus, Isherwood says the writer must establish that his saint-to-be is really like Jones or Smith or Brown. (Isherwood lauds Somerset Maugham for portraying Larry, the young man who adopts Vedanta in *The Razor's Edge,* as a quite ordinary person.)

The crux, in Isherwood's late view, however, would be to show dramatically that "decisive moment at which my hero becomes aware of his vocation and decides to do something about it"[20]—or, in terms of *Lions and Shadows,* when the hero becomes aware of the Test. But the Test is no longer the somber spectacle of insurmountable odds, the Truly Weak Man's inevitable failure. By now Isherwood has grown to view the Test as the risk-taking inherent in maturing into one's better self. The northwest passage is within; the Test is more akin to a conversion than to an ordeal. The conversion of Father Zossima in Dostoevsky's *The Brothers Karamazov* is, Isherwood thinks, a perfectly executed scene, rendered "without the least sentimentality, in terms almost of farce, yet with such warmth, insight, and naturalness!"[21] This is the kind of realistic scene Isherwood hopes to bring to a novel. Visions he rules out, at least in the beginning, as contrived and dishonest; except for historical fiction like *The Song of Bernadette,* visions and visitations are undesirable "because they excuse the author from explaining what is happening in his hero's mind."[22]

Once the hero is converted, Isherwood sees the writer's task as demonstrating that the saint is not insane when he turns his back on "the whole scheme of pleasures, rewards, and satisfactions . . . accepted by the Joneses, the Smiths, and the Browns, and goes in search of superconscious, extraphenomenal experience."[23] If the hero impresses the reader as being merely muddleheaded, then the world is fragmented into two camps, that of the Enemy and that of the saint, and Isherwood's original purpose is wrecked. Instead, Isherwood writes, he must show that the average person is always searching "however unconsciously, for the same fundamental reality of which X has already had a glimpse"—searching in the wrong places and with random methods.[24] Nevertheless this groping, this gnawing doubt about their lives, Isherwood explains, may one day "be their salvation. It is the measure of their kinship with X. For the evolving saint does not differ from his fellow humans in kind, but only in degree. That is why X can only be understood, artistically, when his story is related to that of the Joneses, the Smiths, and the Browns."[25] The greater part of this novel, Isherwood says, would concern itself with X's struggles towards sainthood. Although the path of the aspirant saint is formidable, Isherwood sees no reason "to sentimentalize his hero's sufferings, or to allow him to indulge in self-pity."[26] Sportswriters find no pathos in the training rigors of a boxer. Certainly, then, a saint's self-imposed sufferings should not be enfeebled by sentimentality or bathos. Instead, his trials of purification should be made plausible by humor: "Surely the mishaps and setbacks which beset the path of spiritual progress can be recounted with some of the humor which invests one's failure in cookery or falls in learning to ski?"[27]

What about the portrait of the perfected saint? Here Isherwood despairs, for nothing short of genius can succeed in such a task:

> For the mystical experience itself can never be described. It can only be written around, hinted at, dimly reflected in word and deed. So far, the novelists have given us nothing but brilliant glimpses—the incident of the Bishop's candlesticks in *Les Misérables,* the few interviews with Father Zossima, Huxley's sketch of Bruno Rontini.[28]

Isherwood concludes: "Perhaps the truly comprehensive religious novel could only be written by a saint—and saints, unfortunately, are not in the habit of writing novels."[29]

This new depth and awareness of saintly possibilities are

salient characteristics in Isherwood's last two novels, *A Single Man* and *A Meeting by the River*. Although *The World in the Evening* was influenced by his reflections on the religious novel, its protagonist, Stephen Monk, is so entangled in his own egotism and so preoccupied with outgrowing his adolescent dependence on mother figures that I have preferred to treat that novel in my chapter called "Mothers and Sons," and to read it not from a specifically religious viewpoint, but from the humanistic angle provided by Edwin Muir's excellent article.

Though radically different in technique, *A Single Man* and *A Meeting by the River* both point to an extra dimension, a "super-conscious, extraphenomenal" aspect in reality. In *A Single Man*, Isherwood presents a day in the life of a Truly Lonely Man, George, a middle-aged homosexual and professor of English literature. George is very much like Jones or Smith or Brown, for his life is not particularly rich or luminous: if he is different, it is only in degree. His homosexuality, his education, his pathetic mourning for Jim, his dead lover, actually intensify George's very human condition of loneliness. The spiritual, even mystical aspects of George's life are suggested by Isherwood who, throughout the novel, sustains a delicate dialogue with the reader. Isherwood's description of George's late-night encounter with Kenny, one of his students, as a symbolic Platonic dialogue, defines the book's narrative method: a symbolic dialogue between the author as a kind of guru and the reader as a disciple meditating on the ephemera of George's day.[30]

George has no idea that his confusion and monotony contain mystical ramifications; he is the early Isherwood hero as he might have been without Isherwood's conversion. The dialogue remains between author and auditor only—George is unaware of his dimensions. In *A Meeting by the River*, two brothers hold another "dialogue" which is vividly reported through the book's epistolary format. The sparks struck by the clashing diary entries of Oliver, preparing to take vows in a Hindu monastery, and the letters of Patrick, his entrepreneur brother, kindle the reader's awareness of the suprasensible. Here both brothers seek religious experience, Oliver deliberately and Patrick unwittingly.

*A Single Man* begins with George's awakening: fitfully, almost resentfully, George emerges from the pacific oblivion of sleep:

> Waking up begins with saying *am* and *now*. That which has awoken then lies for a while staring up at the ceiling and down into itself until it has recognized *I,* and therefore deduced *I am, I am now. Here* comes next, and is at least negatively reassuring; because *here,* this morning, is where it has expected to find itself: what's called *at home.*                    (SM 9)

"It" rises, empties its bladder, weighs itself, gazes into the mirror:

> What it sees there isn't so much a face as the expression of a predicament. Here's what it has done to itself, here's the mess it has somehow managed to get itself into during its fifty-eight years; expressed in terms of a dull, harassed stare, a coarsened nose, a mouth dragged down by the corners into a grimace. . . .
>                                                             (SM 10)

Isherwood's use of the first person plural pronoun formally begins the dialogue with the reader: "The creature we are watching will struggle on and on until it drops. Not because it is heroic. It can imagine no alternative" (SM 10). The "creature" obediently washes, shaves, brushes its hair, because it accepts its responsibility to the Others, and "it is even glad it has its place among them. . . ." It even knows its name: "It is called George" (SM 11). Isherwood's opening sentences, which at first lack a personal subject, mirror the circular journey of George's day: from unconsciousness, to self-awareness, back to the lack of personhood, the Vedantist ideal.

As George prepares for his day, Isherwood's use of the second person pronoun involves the reader in George's musings:

> He crosses the front room, which he calls his study, and comes down the staircase. The stairs turn a corner; they are narrow and steep. You can touch both handrails with your elbows, and you have to bend your head, even if, like George, you are only five eight. This is a tightly planned little house. . . . there is hardly room enough to feel lonely.
>
> Nevertheless . . .                                          (SM 12)

Addressing the reader, Isherwood recreates George's hidden life with Jim:

> Think of two people, living together day after day, year after year, in this small space, standing elbow to elbow cooking at the same small stove, squeezing past each other on the narrow stairs, shaving in front of the same small bathroom mirror, constantly jogging, jostling, bumping against each other's bodies by mistake or on purpose, sensually, aggressively, awkwardly, impatiently, in rage or in love—think what deep though invisible tracks they must leave, everywhere, behind them. . . . here, nearly every morning . . . George, having reached the bottom of the stairs, has this sensation of suddenly finding himself on an abrupt, brutally broken off, jagged edge—as though the track had disappeared down a landslide. It is here that he stops short and knows, with a sick newness, almost as though it were for the first time: Jim is dead. Is dead.                     (SM 12–13)

Throughout George's day, Isherwood continues the dialogue with the reader, sometimes by direct questions: "He has gone deep down in himself. What is he up to?" (SM 36); "But does George really hate all these people?" (SM 40). Sometimes Isherwood uses the second person pronoun: "No sooner have you turned off the freeway onto San Tomas Avenue than you are back into the tacky sleepy slowpoke Los Angeles of the thirties" (SM 41). Sometimes he employs an informal manner to maintain the dialogue; after the class's discussion of Huxley's novel, Isherwood introduces their comments in the following informal manner: "Here are some of its [the class's] findings . . ." (SM 68).

George lives apart from others, his distorted life a Giacometti study in personal distance, the void in which men suffer remote from their fellows. A paragraph from *The Reptonian*, March 1922, outlines George's predicament. Isherwood probably read the article and perhaps even subconsciously culled his title from it:

> The individual man cares much more for the things that touch his individuality than for those that touch his manhood . . . there is many a prig and many a fool who possesses so large a love of mankind that he has not a grain of his tender emotion to spare for a single man. And Humanity and the single man are divided by the largest gulf; the single man is the smallest integral division of humanity. . . . [31]

In the first half of the novel, George is certainly the "smallest integral division of humanity." Toward the end of the novel, however, the single man advances toward a letting go of consciousness and of self and toward a merging with Being Itself.

As day declines, the pace of the novel slackens. Changes of scene occur less frequently, less suddenly. The high point of George's waking day is the symbolic dialogue with Kenny. This leads to their sacramental swim in the sea, symbolic of death and prologue to George's actual death.

In a beach bar, the Starboard Side Inn where he first met Jim, George runs into Kenny Potter. Kenny, who has been dumped by his girl friend, had been particularly kind to George earlier in the day: he had sought out his companionship after class and, in a boyish gesture, had bought George a yellow pencil sharpener. In the bar, George buys Kenny a drink; as they drink and talk, their conversation approaches the symbolic Platonic dialogue:

> . . . not a Platonic dialogue in the hair-splitting, word-twisting, one-up-to-me sense; not a mock-humble bitching match; not a debate on some dreary set theme. You can talk about anything and change the subject as often as you like. In fact, what really matters is not what you talk about, but the being together in this particular relationship.                          (SM 154)

George cannot imagine such a relationship with a woman "because women can only talk in terms of the personal" (SM 154). Nor with a man of his own age, unless there were "some sort of polarity; for instance, if he was a Negro" (SM 154). The dialogue partners must be opposites, for by its nature the dialogue is impersonal, symbolic, an encounter in which "you can say absolutely anything. Even the closest confidence, the deadliest secret, comes out objectively as a mere metaphor or illustration which could never be used against you" (SM 155). In the case of George and Kenny, the polarity is age and youth.

The two achieve the phatic communication attained by Christopher and Bergmann, though here it is not a father-son relationship but, as Isherwood notes, an age-youth symbolic relationship. "George can almost feel the electric field of the dialogue surrounding and irradiating them. . . . As for Kenny, he looks quite beautiful. *Radiant with rapport . . .*" (SM 155). George even passes the Test Kenny proposes:

> "Let's go swimming," says Kenny abruptly, as if bored by the whole conversation.
> "All right."
> Kenny throws his head right back and laughs wildly. "Oh— that's terrific."
> "What's terrific?"
> "It was a test. I thought you were bluffing, about being silly.

So I said to myself, I'll suggest doing something wild, and if he
objects—if he even hesitates—then I'll know it was all a bluff."

(SM 160–61)

Unlike Christopher in *Down There on a Visit* whose response to
the proffered opium was a qualified "one pipe," George
responds wholeheartedly. Thus George and Kenny, age and
youth, bolt for the ocean, stripping as they go, and pitch
themselves into the surf. The moment is jubilant and unconscious, a madcap midnight escapade which Isherwood turns
into a religious experience, symbolic of George's and Kenny's
mergings with the Greater Consciousness, for which both
yearn. Isherwood's syntax—the long, right-branching second
sentence—and the diction—"blackness," "mysteriously," awfully"—communicate the mystical quality of the experience:

> As for George, these waves are much too big for him. They
> seem truly tremendous, towering up, blackness unrolling itself
> out of blackness, mysteriously and awfully sparkling, then curl-
> ing over in a thundering slap of foam which is sparked with
> phosphorus.                                   (SM 162)

Immersed in phosphorus, George laughs at the sparks all over
his body, which seems "bejeweled. . . . Laughing, gasping,
choking, he is too drunk to be afraid . . ." (SM 162). George,
"intent upon his own rites of purification . . . wide-open-
armed" receives "the stunning baptism of the surf. Giving
himself to it utterly, he washes away thought, speech, mood,
desire, whole selves, entire lifetimes . . ." (SM 162–63). And
then, foreshadowing the book's conclusion, a prodigious wave
roars forward, as climactic as death, as great as Being Itself,
and swallows the single man into its mysterious utter vastness:

> And now, suddenly, here is a great, an apocalyptically great
> wave, and George is way out, almost out of his depth, standing
> naked and tiny before its presence, under the lip of its roaring

upheaval and the towering menace of its fall. He tries to dive
through it—even now he feels no real fear—but instead he is
caught and picked up, turned over and over and over, flapping
and kicking toward a surface which may be either up or down or
sideways, he no longer knows. (SM 163)

By his imagery Isherwood shows that George is completely
given over to Being Itself—George now possesses what he
sought for in Jim, what he seeks for in Kenny, who he hopes
will be another Jim—but he is singularly unaware of this. As
one critic writes, "It is fitting that we never know his [George's]
final name. Neither does he."[32] Nonetheless George's search
for something better gives him kinship with Isherwood's saint.

Kenny finally drags George out of the ocean, and both
stumble toward George's house. In drunken clarity, George
divines why Kenny was in the Starboard Side Inn—he wanted
to talk to him:

> "The point is, you came to ask me about something that really
> *is* important . . . You want me to tell you *what I know*. . . . Oh
> Kenneth, Kenneth, believe me—there's nothing I'd rather do!
> But I can't. I quite literally can't. Because, don't you see, *what I
> know is what I am?*" (SM 176)

And what he is, George insists, Kenny must find out for
himself, for George is like a book that must be read in order to
discover its contents: "A book can't read itself to you. It doesn't
even know what it's about. I don't know what I'm about" (SM
176). Kenny, George vatically rages on, is the single boy he has
met on campus who could know what George is about. Could
Kenny be another Jim? Unfortunately no, for Kenny cannot be
bothered to read George and will commit the inexcusable
triviality of calling him a dirty old man, thus diverting this
potentially precious night into a flirtation:

> "You don't like that word, do you? But it's the word. It's the
> enormous tragedy of everything nowadays: flirtation. Flirtation

instead of fucking, if you'll pardon my coarseness. All any of
you ever do is flirt. . . . And miss the one thing that might
really—and, Kenneth, I do not say this casually—*tranform your
entire life*—" (SM 176–77)

George then passes out, his state of unconsciousness rendered
in imagery which echoes Blake's suicide attempt and harkens
back to the midnight swim:

> For a moment, Kenny's face is quite distinct. It grins, daz-
> zlingly. Then his grin breaks up, is refracted, or whatever you
> call it, into rainbows of light. The rainbows blaze. George is
> blinded by them. He shuts his eyes. And now the buzzing in his
> ears is the roar of Niagara. (SM 177)

Later, George awakens to find a coy note from Kenny; then,
before falling asleep, he enjoys an intense sexual climax by
masturbating. He begins by conjuring Kenny and his girlfriend,
then Kenny and a tennis player he had watched earlier that
day; they flirt, grapple, flirt. Because Kenny does not take
himself seriously, George substitutes the other tennis player,
and, finally, comically, himself: "He is either. He is both at
once. Ah—it is so good! Ah—ah . . . !" (SM 180). Then, slowly,
George submerges into the ocean of unconsciousness from
which he originally surfaced. George sinks deeper; only "Partial surfacing. . . . Partial emergings, just barely breaking the
sheeted calm of the water. Most of George remaining sub-
merged in sleep" (SM 181). George's brain, barely awash,
cognizes darkly, not in its daytime manner, for now, incapable
of decision, it can become aware of certain decisions not yet
formulated: "Decisions that are like codicils which have been
secretly signed and witnessed and put away in a most private
place to wait the hour of their execution" (SM 181). In a
catechetical question-answer format similar to Bloom and Stephen's post-brothel dialogue in *Ulysses* (though Isherwood's
diction is infinitely simpler), George reviews his day, his life.

Unlike Kenny, George resolves that he will not flirt with life, that he will find another Jim, that he will not truckle to old age:

> *Why does George believe he will find him* [Jim]?"
> He only knows that he must find him. He believes he will because he must.
> *But George is getting old. Won't it very soon be too late?*
> Never use those words to George. He won't listen. He daren't listen. Damn the future. Let Kenny and the kids have it. Let Charley keep the past. George clings only to Now. It is Now that he must find another Jim. Now that he must love. Now that he must live. . . .                    (SM 182)

Isherwood begins to close the circle toward which the story line has been curving since its beginning. As in *Prater Violet,* the book concludes with a Vedantist epiphany, particularly trenchant here because both the ocean imagery and the dialogue technique are resumed. With "this body known as George's" (SM 183) asleep, Isherwood asks, "But *is* all of George altogether present here?" (SM 183). He answers his question with an extended analogy which summarizes George's entire day:

> Up the coast a few miles north, in a lava reef under the cliffs, there are a lot of rock pools. You can visit them when the tide is out. Each pool is separate and different, and you can, if you are fanciful, give them names. . . . Just as George and the others are thought of, for convenience, as individual entities, so you may think of a rock pool as an entity; though, of course, it is not. The waters of its consciousness—so to speak—are swarming with hunted anxieties, grim-jawed greeds, dartingly vivid intuitions, old crusty-shelled rock-gripping obstinacies, deep-down sparkling undiscovered secrets, ominous protean organisms motioning mysteriously, perhaps warningly, toward the surface light. . . .                    (SM 183–84)

For the rock-pool image, Isherwood is clearly indebted to Cyril Connolly's 1936 novel *The Rock Pool.* There Connolly

uses the rock pool as a metaphor for his protagonist's impersonal observation of a colony of decadent artists. Searching for
a viewpoint, Connolly's narrator settles on " . . . *The Rock
Pool*—a microcosm cut off from the ocean . . . aquarium similes
were the rage now. . . ."[33] Isherwood, however, converts the
image into a rich religious parable. Just as the ocean floods the
rock pools at the end of the day, so over George and the others
in sleep comes "that other ocean—that consciousness which is
no one in particular but which contains everyone and everything, past, present and future, and extends unbroken beyond
the uttermost stars" (SM 184). Extending his analogy, Isherwood prepares for George's death by describing the mysterious
dying of the rock-pool creatures. In the dark of the full flood,
surely some of the creatures are "lifted from their pools to drift
far out over the deep waters" (SM 184), never to return again.
What can they tell us about their nocturnal journey? "Is there,
indeed, anything for them to tell—except that the waters of the
ocean are not really other than the waters of the pool?" (SM
184). Centering the reader's attention back on George's body,
Isherwood uses the imagery of a ship and its crew which easily
doubles as medical terminology:

> Within this body on the bed, the great pump works on and
> on, needing no rest. All over this quietly pulsating vehicle the
> skeleton crew make their tiny adjustments. As for what goes on
> topside, they know nothing of this but danger signals, false
> alarms mostly: red lights flashed from the panicky brain stem,
> curtly contradicted by green all clears from the level-headed
> cortex. But now the controls are on automatic. The cortex is
> drowsing. . . .                                           (SM 184–85)

Isherwood then invites the reader to fantasize George's death
("Just let us suppose, however . . ." [SM 185]). Isherwood
ironically traces its beginning to the moment in which George
felt most alive: his first glorious meeting with Jim in the Starboard Side Inn.

> Let us then suppose that, at that same instant, deep down in one of the major branches of George's coronary artery, an unimaginably gradual process began. Somehow—no doctor can tell us exactly why—the inner lining begins to become roughened. . . . Thus, slowly, invisibly, with the utmost discretion and without the slightest hint to those old fussers in the brain, an almost indecently melodramatic situation is contrived: the formation of the atheromatous plaque.    (SM 185)

Again Isherwood invites the reader to imagine George's death: "Let us suppose this, merely. . . . This thing is wildly improbable. You could bet thousands of dollars against its happening, tonight or any night. And yet it *could*, quite possibly, be about to happen—within the next five minutes" (SM 185–86). Together both writer and reader put George to death: "Very well—let us suppose that this is the night, and the hour, and the appointed minute" (SM 186). Isherwood traces the gradual necrosis of George's body by beginning with his favorite word, the word on which he based his life:

> *Now—*
> The body on the bed stirs slightly, perhaps; but it does not cry out, does not wake.    (SM 186)

Cortex and brain stem are murdered in the blackout . . . throttled out of their oxygen . . . the lungs go dead, their power line cut. The great ship of George's body founders, sinks, as "one by one, the lights go out and there is total blackness" (SM 186).

What about George the single man? His body "is now cousin to the garbage in the container on the back porch. Both will have to be carted away and disposed of, before too long" (SM 186), for George's spirit can no longer associate with what lies on the bed. It must, at long last, follow the current of George's life and merge with the Greater Consciousness—what, as Isherwood has shown throughout the novel, George has yearned and searched for in the wrong places and by the wrong methods. In death, George is no longer the single man.

Who is George? Isherwood's Everyman: for in his humanity and desire for wholeness, George is no different from anyone else. Thus Isherwood's dialogue, which George thinks must be conducted by opposites, is resolved into a unity. The protagonist and the reader, as well as the novelist, do not "differ in kind, but only in degree."

In *A Meeting by the River,* however, Isherwood abandons any stylistic individuality in favor of an epistolary novel—it's as if in his last novel he is trying to bring the book as near as possible to the experiences of the Joneses, the Smiths, the Browns, by casting the book in the form of letters and diary jottings. The style here is simple, energetic, but in comparison with the subtle, delicate prose of *The Memorial, The Berlin Stories, Prater Violet, A Single Man,* it is deliberately undistinguished.

In contrast to the circular structure of *A Single Man, A Meeting by the River* is composed of two lines which merge, intersect, snarl, and finally separate and shoot off in parallel paths. One line traces the adventures of Patrick, an ambassador of pragmatism who stops off at Oliver's monastery en route to Singapore to tour shooting locations for a film. Patrick is determined to shock Oliver back to his senses, which means a return to England, mother, and a posh position in a bank. However, like Lambert Strether in Henry James's *The Ambassadors,* Patrick himself is quickened to a change of viewpoint. The other line of the novel maps Oliver's course. Oliver is scandalized by his unmortified ego and by Patrick's florid insincerity; nonetheless, he emerges from the clash determined to follow his vocation.

The separate lines of their lives quickly entangle when Oliver writes Patrick requesting him to inform their mother that he is in a monastery, is healthy, and will soon take first vows. Shocked, Patrick informs Oliver that luckily he will find it convenient to pay him a visit. Once Patrick arrives, the plot becomes unthinkably knotted.

The epistolary format in which the novel is written complicates the entanglement, for the diary entries and letters highlight the contradictory sides of both brothers. Within the one line are many potential lines. Oliver unrealistically labors to eradicate his old, worldly, brother-of-Patrick self, in love with Penelope, Patrick's wife, and distrustful of Patrick. Patrick, the *poseur non pareil,* masters innumerable disguises: he indites letters to his mother in the tone of a British imperialist touring a former colony; he splatters his letters to Penelope, wise like Elizabeth Rydal in matters of the spirit, with superficial cocktail allusions to Hinduism and Meister Eckhart; to Tommy, a homosexual infatuation in Los Angeles, he scalds his letters with middle-aged lust. The results are charged, as Isherwood notes,[34] with all the turmoil of a lawsuit—a lawsuit further complicated by the absence of a narrator to salvage the truth, by the confusion of the characters, and by the essentially internal nature of their struggle.

What begins as a dispute ends in a fraternal dialogue as Isherwood deftly manipulates the double viewpoints to fulfill his chief requirements for a religious novel. He makes his saints-to-be very much like Messrs. Jones, Smith, and Brown. More important, Isherwood surpasses his own expectations, for the novel's thrust is that both Oliver and Patrick are incipient saints, brothers in the deeper sense that both are seeking sanctity. It is not the richly evocative language of *A Single Man,* but Isherwood's placing of the letters and feuilletons of the brothers which contrasts their individual strivings and thus makes two points intrinsic to Isherwood's conception of the religious novel: that Oliver's behavior is not at all insane but, in essence, is similar to that of Patrick; that Patrick's flamboyance is not merely mindless bustle but actually an expression of his longing for the same realities Oliver seeks. Their two paths, therefore, represent complementary roads to holiness, the religious and the worldly.

The spiritual kinship of the brothers—who prefer to think that they are incompatible—is striking. Frightened by his similarity to Patrick, Oliver would like to snip any ties to him: "Heredity has made us part of a single circuit, our wires are all connected . . . I get afraid that I'll start behaving like him and lose my identity altogether" (R 115). Both brothers love Penelope, and both have like spiritual experiences. For example, after reading a pornographic book from Tommy, Patrick writes his lover:

> What I want to tell you tonight is this—as far as I'm concerned, our relationship seems to keep on growing stronger and deeper, although we're apart. I mean this literally! It's very strange, something I have never experienced before with anyone. (R 130)

Patrick's description sounds like Oliver's account of his experience of his dead swami. In the passage below, Oliver describes his state as he sits in the swami's favorite outdoor niche:

> And then, very soon, the seat began to draw me to it. I began going at night or in the early morning to sit there with my beads. A few times I've felt Swami with me there, so strongly that I've shed tears of relief. . . . (R 80)

From his intense experience of Tommy's presence, Patrick, uncertain what to call it, glimpses his goal:

> I've had plenty of sexual dreams, of course, but never anything like this one. This was much more than a dream, it was so intense it was a sort of vision . . . it's all so hard to describe. . . . I *can* tell you one thing—this life I got a glimpse of was of such a closeness as I'd never even imagined could exist between two human beings, because it was a life *entirely without fear*. (R 130–31)

Thus Patrick devises all sorts of schemes to keep Tommy near. He even considers leaving Penelope.

Oliver also wants fulfillment. Muddled by scruples and self-doubt, he, like Patrick, cannot puzzle out a coherent scheme to follow. Like Patrick, pushed to extremes, Oliver ponders renouncing the monastic life. Slapstick confusion reigns; both men have stumbled into each other's trap.

Such misapprehension brings the brothers to a turning point. A drunken phone call from the lovesick Tommy leads to a frank, unsettling dialogue between Oliver and Patrick. Tommy's phone call is mistakenly taken by Oliver who, surmising Tommy's relationship with Patrick, conveys the call to Patrick. Afterwards, Patrick, guilty and embarrassed, makes a last crafty effort to change Oliver's mind about monastic life. Under the guise of confessing everything, he sketches his relations with Tommy in such pornographic detail that Oliver, suspicious and bewildered, is physically and mentally disturbed. In good faith, Oliver then advises Patrick to leave Penelope, who represents only duty, and live with Tommy. Confronted with that reality, Patrick is thunderstruck: *"Leave Penelope! You simply can't mean that!"* (R 149). But this brotherly strife is not yet over. Patrick again turns the tables on Oliver by drawing a psychological portrait of him as a tyrant, a Machiavellian despot—the side of his character Oliver is trying to escape by burying himself in the monastery. The result of this conversation is utter bafflement. No one has advanced; both are depleted, still groping—or so it seems.

But from such garbled ideas comes sure direction. Just as Patrick has a dream-vision which clarifies his needs, so Oliver experiences a visitation from the swami, more tranquil than Patrick's but similar nonetheless. Isherwood continues to stress the spiritual kinship of both brothers. Oliver construes his vision in terms of a dream, whereas Patrick has read his dream in terms of a vision.

... Presumably it was a few moments before waking that I saw
Swami.

Yes, I can say I did literally see him, although this wasn't a
vision in the waking state. But seeing him was only a part of the
experience of his presence, which was intensely vivid, far more
so than an ordinary dream. Also, unlike a dream, it didn't
altogether end when I woke up. It is losing strength now, but it's
still going on inside me at this moment.                (R 172)

The vision bolsters the sagging morale of Oliver and assures
him that all is well with Patrick. Although Patrick is in trouble
"so serious as to be almost ridiculous . . . *he would be all right*" (R
175). As for himself, Oliver intuits that he will never be alone,
that he can pursue his life entirely without fear: swami *"is with
me always, wherever I am* (R 173).

Disturbed by the confrontation with Oliver in the garden,
perhaps even mystically aided by Oliver's swami, Patrick at
long last realizes that his dream-vision can be attained only with
Penelope. He gives up Tommy, not Penelope. He writes an
honest letter to Penelope, hinting at his homosexual shenani-
gans, cautioning her not to be upset by a long-distance call
from Los Angeles. In short, Patrick begs Penelope to accept
him for what he is: a well-intentioned scoundrel.

At the center of both dream-visions is another person, either
dead or still living, who provides a link to the world of spirit.
For Patrick, the bridge is Tommy, or even Penelope; for
Oliver, his dead swami. Indeed it seems essential to Isherwood's conception of the saint that he be joined to the world of
spirit through another person who, like Mrs. Wilcox in *Howards End* and Mrs. Moore in *A Passage to India,* reconciles the
spiritual with the physical realm. For Christopher in *Prater
Violet,* Bergmann arises as the spiritual middle person; for
Stephen Monk in *The World in the Evening,* Elizabeth Rydal, his
dead wife; for Christopher in *Down There on a Visit,* Augustus
Parr; for George in *A Single Man,* his dead lover, Jim. In

Isherwood's own life, this Fosterian connection is Swami Prabhavananda, whose faith in God makes it impossible, he claims,
for him to disbelieve. In this light, then, Lily in *The Memorial*
and Ambrose in *Down There on a Visit* are anti-saints: their ties
to the spiritual confer only death.

Nor are the visions and dreams Patrick and Oliver experience a form of *deus ex machina* or of literary cheating, for they
confirm and clarify the intimations both had previously sensed
in themselves; moreover, the visions are presented not as
extraordinarily rare occurrences, but experiences quite properly common to the average person—illuminations with which
sensitive men are rewarded during moments of heightened
awareness.

This spiritual awakening of two brothers is not recounted
without what Isherwood considers a *sine qua non* of the religious novel, humor: Patrick is a lovable rascal, an Arthur-
Norris rogue. Oliver's reactions to Patrick are equally humorous and touching. For example, visiting Patrick after his
arrival, Oliver is mortified by the lavish spectacle of Patrick's
nude exercising. He is particularly shocked by Patrick's deliberate grin and his "rather big penis slapping against his bare
thigh as he jumped" (R 70–71). Because Patrick is naive and
out of place at the monastery, his good-willed attempts to adapt
are farcical. He unwittingly spoils Oliver's anonymity by con-
tracting a magazine to run a picture story on Oliver, the
"English Monk." His observations of monastic life are offbeat
and comic. Oliver's robe is "crumpled shoddy cotton sheeting
. . . it makes him seem rather pathetic, like a hospital patient in
a nightgown, deprived of his trousers" (R 61). Patrick finds the
superior's underwear disconcerting: "Is it that all monks are
still to us what Victorian ladies used to be—are their undergar-
ments 'unmentionables' which mustn't even be thought about?"
(R 95). He explains Oliver's asceticism as follows: "We must
remember that converts are always apt to be more royalist than
the King!" (R 99).

The book's humor typifies India's religion. As E. M. Forster
wisely observes in *A Passage to India,* Indian worship is always a
gallimaufry of human emotions and aspirations:

> There is fun in heaven. God can play practical jokes on Himself,
> draw chairs away from beneath His own posteriors, set His own
> turbans on fire, and steal His own petticoats when He bathes. By
> sacrificing good taste, this worship achieved what Christianity
> has shirked: the inclusion of merriment. All spirit as well as all
> matter must participate in salvation, and if practical jokes are
> banned, the circle is incomplete.[35]

Understood in this sense, the book is a serious practical joke
played by Isherwood on himself. It is Isherwood's way of
drawing the chair from under his own *bêtes noires,* for the book
reinterprets Isherwood's four key concepts, not with the guilt
and rancor of his youth but with the sobriety of his maturity.
Abetted by Oliver's prayers and questions, Patrick ultimately
views the Test as an entirely personal proposition: it does not
entail flagrantly living with Tommy and challenging the
Enemy, but calmly sifting his desires and needs and acting in
accordance with them. Likewise, Oliver perceives that his Test
is similar to his brother's: Patrick's clumsy intrusion forces him
to question and eventually to reaffirm his decision to become a
monk. The Enemy is no longer the majority, those who resent
Patrick's bisexuality, but those unable to fathom the depth and
complexity of his relationship with the all-forgiving Penelope.
For Oliver, the Enemy is not, as one might expect, the outside
world: withdrawal from the world, Oliver realizes, actually
binds him to the world's people by his love of them. Hence, the
Enemy, or the Others, no longer implies spite, but a neutral
recognition of difference. This difference, in the last analysis,
is one of degree, not of kind.

A similar positive displacement affects the Truly Strong and
the Truly Weak Men. Isherwood no longer simplifies these
ideas into mutually exclusive black-and-white categories.

Instead, he discerns them as capacities residing simultaneously within a person. Throughout *A Meeting by the River,* Patrick and Oliver do not act as if they were tailored to fit a narrow notion: their inconsistency borders on the farcical. According to Isherwood's review of Edward Upward's *In the Thirties,* their behavior is heroic, similar to that of Upward's protagonist, Alan Sebrill:

> Alan is, first and last, an individual. Although he keeps accusing himself of weakness, he is in fact heroic and strong. He fights like a hero to master his predicament and to find meaning in life for himself and others: and he will shrink from no measure, however drastic, if it will help him to achieve this end. That his heroism is utterly unconscious and partly comic only makes it seem nobler.[36]

Both Patrick and Oliver are trying to master their predicaments by mastering the warring selves within. In religious terms, they are casting off the old man to put on the new.

Does Isherwood give us the portrait of the perfected saint? No. But he does present the Isherwood hero as no longer lost, but as having found himself; if he is still an outsider, he is so not because of neurotic hostility but because of spiritual growth. And, at the end of the novel, though not the complete saint, Oliver is "taller than usual . . . wonderfully handsome and every inch a holy man, with the long flame-coloured robe falling to his feet" (R 187). In a letter to his mother, Patrick writes: "You would have been proud of him I know, and happy to see how well he seems suited to his new role in life. I was so proud to walk beside him and know that everybody knew he was my brother" (R 187). After the vow ceremony, Patrick, with his instinct for melodrama, drops to his knees and bows to Oliver. But Isherwood gives Oliver the last word. Touched by Patrick's humility, Oliver relates that, suddenly lifted outside of himself, he sees Patrick, the swami, the onlookers, himself "all involved in this tremendous joke. . . . And everybody was smiling and murmuring, as much as to say how charming it was of Patrick to play this scene according to our local Hindu rules, and how very right and proper it was that we two brothers should love each other" (R 190–91).

# The Homosexual ⁓ as Hero ⁓

That Isherwood should in the seventies attempt a frank and factual revelation about his life is not at all surprising. *Christopher and His Kind* conforms easily to the pattern Isherwood has traced since his conversion to Vedanta: beginning with *The World in the Evening* and continuing through *Down There on a Visit, A Single Man,* and *A Meeting by the River,* Isherwood has systematically re-examined and revised his past. Always his bent has been toward fidelity to the complexity of experience and, in the later works, toward an investigation of his place as a homosexual in an intolerant society.

In both style and substance, Isherwood, in his latest works, leans toward a frank divesting of disguise. The mannered Isherwood of the thirties and forties would never have put such words as these into the mouth of a character: " . . . the enormous tragedy of everything nowadays: flirtation. Flirtation instead of fucking . . . " (SM 176). The upshot of this new candor is the epistolary novel, *A Meeting by the River*, and the autobiographies, *Kathleen and Frank* and *Christopher and His Kind*, the armatures of which are Isherwood's prolix journals.

What *is* surprising is the belatedness of Isherwood's homosexual revelation. A first avowal in print appeared only in 1971 in *Kathleen and Frank*: "Heterosexuality wouldn't have suited him [Christopher]; it would have fatally cramped his style" (KF 380) Late though his confession may have been, confession was never, he quickly underscores, either vexing or guilt-ridden:

> . . . for me it was really No Sweat, you know. I lived in a writer's world where everybody knew I was gay. I lived with—I always shrink from the word lover, because it sounds as if they loved *you*, but you didn't love them—but anyway, a lover, and everyone knew it.
>
> I told my mother quite early on. It might have been more difficult with my father, but he died in World War I.[1]

Nor is Isherwood's frankness a commercial ploy to exploit contemporary license in sexual matters or to ride on the crest of the gay liberation movement. Simply put, before *Kathleen and Frank*, Isherwood possessed no compelling reason to lay bare his homosexuality. But in *Kathleen and Frank*, Isherwood feels obliged

> . . . to be absolutely open . . . because this is really the first time that I have written a genuinely autobiographical story. . . . I was compelled to say everything about myself, and it would have been impossible to speak about my relationship with my mother without explaining that I was homosexual.[2]

Writer-critic Dennis Altman, himself a homosexual, concurs with Isherwood's rationale, finding it fitting

> . . . that in writing about his parents Isherwood makes an open affirmation of his homosexuality, for it is in relation to one's family that the peculiar nature of our stigma cuts most deeply.

> Unlike those stigmatized by colour or caste our homosexuality is
> not shared by our family: unlike physical defects, there remains
> always the suspicion that we could rid ourselves of it if we
> wanted to enough.[3]

Even if we lay Isherwood's personal life aside, we must see
that heterosexuality would have fatally cramped the anti-myth.
Had Isherwood's alienated heroes not been homosexuals, they
could not have been completely different from, and absolutely
"other" than, the Enemy, or the Others. They would not have
been irreparably damned. But because anti-sex and anti-sex-
uality were before the sixties subterranean and unacceptable,
Isherwood's heroes are beyond redemption: never between the
homosexual and the Others could there have been reconcilia-
tion. Thus, like many of Byron's cursed brooders, the homosexual hero is doomed for eternity to be an outsider, if not by
choice, then by his very nature. In the early novels, Isherwood's treatment of the homosexual is, at best, conventional;
only later, as Isherwood's own vision deepens, does he alter his
vision of the homosexual's place in the world.

Not surprising, Isherwood's first references to homosexuality in *All the Conspirators* are, like other aspects of the novel,
strained and self-conscious. In homosexual imagery that is coy
and sophomoric, Isherwood describes Colonel Page taking
holiday photographs. There seems to be no good reason for
such a clutter of suggestive imagery. As a jab meant to punc-
ture the Kiplingesque masculinity of the Colonel, the passage is
blunted by its lack of restraint and taste:

> On one of these rocks knelt Colonel Page, cramped in his
> cache of stones, peering forward through a chink, breathing
> heavily and gripping the pipe between his teeth in his excite-
> ment, as his heavy fingers toyed with the rubber bulb of the
> camera shutter. Peninnis stands amidst its own enormous
> ruins. . . .                                        (AC 19)

This type of preposterous description yields to clumsy *double entendre* in Philip's stream-of-consciousness remembrance of an experience in the school lavatory:

> May I ask how much longer you Juniors propose to hang round the lavatories? Out before I count two. We're coming, sir. Sorry sir. Oh, *sir.* All clattered away.                    (AC 34)

Philip is likewise repulsed by women, but, as with so many motifs in this book, Isherwood does not pursue this theme:

> The typists began to appear in their summer dresses, wearing bangles on their bare arms with a handkerchief stuffed inside. This trick of carrying the handkerchief offended Philip. . . . He disliked the aroma of the girls' increased sexual vitality, their whispered holiday schemes, giggled anecdotes and the snapshots which they passed around for their friends' inspection.
> (AC 124)

In later novels, Isherwood picks up the notion of women as the homosexual's enemy, but not here. Uncertain of himself and his writing, Isherwood has not yet fixed upon the artistic possibilities inherent in the theme of homosexuality.

By the time of *The Memorial* and *The Berlin Stories,* however, homosexuality has become a staple of the anti-myth, a characteristic of both the Truly Weak Man and of the Lost, who are alike shunned by society. Edward Blake in *The Memorial* is severed from society by the nightmare of the Great War and by his sexual preferences. Blake's homosexuality, though, is a perversion characteristic of his peculiar malaise. Blake's wife, Margaret, who feigns sympathy to dominate him, even suggests potential lovers. On one occasion, Blake barks that he doesn't need her to "pimp" for him. The Truly Weak Man, Blake is in awe of the suave impeccability of his hero, Richard Vernon, and is probably secretly in love with him. Vernon is, in many ways, a young Colonel Page—smug and gruffly masculine. As expected, woman is again the Enemy: Richard is so dominated by his wife, Lily, that he declines to help his sister, Mary, who is eloping. Blake is crushed, disillusioned by what he interprets as his paragon's surrender to the destructive Lily.

Though repressed, Eric Vernon's homosexuality is a symptom of his psychological disorder. Riven by both love for and hate of his mother, he promises as a child never to marry but to remain always with Lily. As an adult, he cannot commit himself to anyone or anything, nor can he endure his mother's smothering presence. Having lost a father in the war, Eric is in love with Blake, a surrogate father; under the guise of concern for his cousin Maurice, he demands that Blake end his affair with Maurice, stammering, " . . . you're old enough to be his father" (M 224).

Later he recognizes that he is consumed by jealousy. Blake complies with Eric's request, however, and though Eric and Blake do not yield to their mutual attraction, their truncated relationship satisfies a need in both: Blake assumes for Eric the role of Richard Vernon, Eric's father; and Eric, in turn, becomes Blake's son and idealized lover, a substitute also for Richard Vernon. In this novel Isherwood introduces two threads which he later explores: the wife as confidante to her husband's sexual indiscretions, and the homosexual's despondency because of his lover's failure to meet his expectations.

In *The Berlin Stories,* homosexuality takes on a new dimension and becomes a resonant metaphor for Berlin's Mortmeresque depravity. Isherwood's portrait of the Baron Kuno von Pregnitz, for example, like all the Mortmere parodies, is a caricature of perversion: loathed by Bradshaw, the Baron is drawn as a sinister storybook monster. His advances to Bradshaw are always made to appear farcical. In this scene, Norris has coyly departed to enable the Baron to seduce Bradshaw. Bradshaw, sensing the Baron's intention when his foot is pressed under the table, politely demurs:

"You know," I said. . . . "I really ought to be getting home. . . ."

"Oh, surely not."

"I think so," I said firmly, smiling and moving my foot away. He was squeezing a corn.

"You see, I should like so very much to show you my new flat. . . ."

"I should love to see it; some other time."

He smiled faintly.

"Then may I, perhaps, give you a lift home?"

"Thank you very much."                          (N 108)

The Baron's advances on the way to Bradshaw's flat are ingratiating and trivial. In his car, the Baron grabs Bradshaw's hand. His manner is ridiculously urbane; and, as the hand-squeezes increase in frequency and pressure, the scene approaches slapstick:

"You're still angry with me," he murmured reproachfully.

"Why should I be?"

"Oh yes, excuse me, you are."

"Really, I'm not."

Kuno gave my hand a limp squeeze.

"May I ask you something?"

"Ask away."

"You see, I don't wish to be personal. Do you believe in Platonic friendship?"

"I expect so," I said guardedly.

The answer seemed to satisfy him. His tone became more confidential: "You're sure you won't come up and see my flat? Not for five minutes?"

"Not to-night."

"Quite sure?" He squeezed.

"Quite, quite sure."

"Some other evening?" Another squeeze.

I laughed: "I think I should see it better in the daytime, shouldn't I?"                          (N 108–9)

The Baron's fantasy of a deserted island where he leads a Robinson-Crusoe existence attended by several Fridays, his villa estate where he is catered to by muscular athletes, his authorship of numerous homoerotic novels in which he is the dashingly handsome hero—all contribute to Isherwood's caricature of the Baron. Like many other characters in the novel, the Baron is only another freak in an exhibition of freaks—the types of portraits Isherwood later regretted because of their patent insensitivity.

Throughout *Goodbye to Berlin* homosexuality's latent force affects all of the narrator's relationships. It is always an unspoken barrier between Christopher and Sally. In this scene in which Sally visits Christopher, Isherwood shamelessly toys with the scene's erotic possibilities—but only toys. When Christopher compliments Fr. Schroeder on her elaborate preparations for Sally's visit, she teases, "Oh, yes, Herr Issyvoo. You can depend on me! I know what pleases a young lady!" (GB 32). Sally flits in with a "page-boy cap stuck over one ear" (GB 32) and issues an open invitation: "Do you mind if I lie down on your sofa, darling?" Christopher replies in his noncommittal manner, "No, of course not." Comfortably and enticingly settled, Sally bursts: "I'm most terribly tired. I didn't sleep a wink last night. I've got a marvellous new lover." Throughout her risqué outpouring, Christopher is only pouring tea, and responds indifferently that her affairs are no business of his (GB 32–33). Exasperated, Sally exclaims, "Oh, for God's sake . . . don't start being English!" Christopher scolds, "Well, then, if you want to know, it rather bores me" (GB 33), and the scene eventually dissolves into laughter. Later Sally asks Christopher whether he is in love with her:

> "Then do you like me, Christopher darling?"
> "Yes, of course I like you, Sally. What did you think?"
> "But you're not in love with me, are you?"
> "No, I'm not in love with you."

"I'm awfully glad, I've wanted you to like me ever since we first met. But I'm glad you're not in love with me, because, somehow, I couldn't possibly be in love with you—so, if you had been, everything would have been spoilt."

"Well then, that's very lucky, isn't it?"                    (GB 34)

The knotty issue of homosexuality is briskly evaded. Commenting on this scene in *Christopher and His Kind,* Isherwood is still elusive:

The "somehow or other" may be taken to suggest that Sally knows instinctively that Christopher is homosexual—or it may not. As for Christopher, he once says vaguely that he has wasted a lot of time "hunting for sex," but he doesn't say which kind.

(CK 62)

Unlike the film and stage versions of the story, Isherwood's version at least does not misrepresent the relationship by making them lovers. Isherwood flirts both with turning them into lovers and with betraying Christopher's homosexuality, but finally eschews both options.

In "On Ruegen Island" homosexuality is a cruel lever between Otto and Peter. Again the narrator is an isolated observer. In reality, however, Otto was a lover of Isherwood's, and Isherwood, in the following description, barely conceals his admiration of Otto:

Otto has a face like a very ripe peach. His hair is fair and thick, growing low on his forehead. He has small sparkling eyes, full of naughtiness, and a wide, disarming grin, which is much too innocent to be true. When he grins, two large dimples appear in his peach-bloom cheeks . . . Otto moves fluidly, effortlessly; his gestures have the savage, unconscious grace of a cruel, elegant animal . . . Otto is outrageously conceited . . . Otto certainly has a superb pair of shoulders and chest for a boy of his age—but his body is nevertheless somehow slightly ridiculous. The beautiful ripe lines of the torso taper away too suddenly to his rather absurd little buttocks and spindly, immature legs. And these struggles with the chest-expander are daily making him more and more top-heavy.    (GB 78–79)

Again Isherwood blurs a possible clue to his own homosexuality or that of his narrator by the arch reference to Otto's "slightly ridiculous" body. In *Christopher and His Kind* Isherwood discusses this guarded description, which he wrote almost forty years earlier:

> The fictitious Isherwood takes the attitude of an amused, slightly contemptuous onlooker. He nearly gives himself away when he speaks of "the beautiful ripe lines of the torso." So, lest the reader should suspect him of finding Otto physically attractive, he adds that Otto's legs are "spindly." Otto's original in life had an entirely adequate, sturdy pair of legs, even if they weren't quite as handsome as the upper half of his body. (CK 42)

The final pages of "A Berlin Diary (Winter 1932–3)" epitomize Isherwood's early handling of the homosexual motif. A party of drunk Americans ask Fritz and Chris in one of Berlin's dives,

> "Say . . . what's on here?"
> "Men dressed as women," Fritz grinned.
> The little American simply couldn't believe it. "Men dressed as *women*? As *women* hey? Do you mean they're *queer*?"
> "Eventually we're all queer," drawled Fritz solemnly, in lugubrious tones. The young man looked us over slowly. . . .
> "You *queer*, too, hey?" demanded the little American, turning suddenly on me."
> "Yes," I said, "very queer indeed."    (GB 192–93)

As an early critic perceptively notes, this theme of "queerness" runs through *The Berlin Stories* "like an accompaniment . . . not merely the advertised, painted boys of the notorious brothels, but the more poisonous homosexuality that is comradeship

and masculinity gone awry."[4] Isherwood's recent reflections on
Berlin confirm the notion that his use of homosexuality as a
symbol of depravity is only a literary technique and not a
realistic representation. Isherwood recalls that Berlin's atmosphere was, surprisingly, not at all sinister. Indeed, it was
"incredibly down to earth, unkinky, undecadent, and natural."
On one bourgeois level, the bars were terribly stuffy:

> everybody was sitting up at their tables and there was an orches-
> tra and you went up to one of these cute boys you fancied,
> bowed to him, bowed to his friend, and said, "May I?" It was
> more like the middle of the nineteenth century.[5]

Even in *Prater Violet,* when, near the end of the book,
Christopher's inner life is revealed, Isherwood resorts to a
nineteenth-century evasion by representing the narrator's lovers not by names, but by letters of the alphabet.

Thus the sexuality of Isherwood's withdrawn narrator—
precisely because of Isherwood's conspiratorial reticence—is
questionably heterosexual. On reflection now, it seems preposterous that Bradshaw-Isherwood could stagger through Berlin's bacchanalia; hobnob with homosexuals, heterosexuals,
and pansexuals; fend off countless propositions from both
men and women; and still retain his neuter innocence. Isherwood's artistic reason for turning Bradshaw-Isherwood into
what many consider a chaste prig are well-intentioned and
understandable. To have made the narrator heterosexual
would have been to capitulate to the heterosexual dictatorship
and to distort his own experience; to have made him homosexual would have been to affront his readers and to detract from
the story.

> Therefore, the Narrator could have no explicit sex experi-
> ences in the story. ("This sexless nitwit," one reviewer was to call
> him.) The unlucky creature is, indeed, no more than a demi-
> character. It is as if Christopher has told him: "Don't call any

unnecessary attention to yourself; don't get more involved with
anybody than you absolutely have to."            (CK 186)

But this state of abnormal celibacy would soon become intolerable for the writer. As the narrator began to develop into a
human being in the later novels, and as Isherwood's own
understanding of how he might use homosexuality as a theme
in his novels matured, the fictional treatment of the narrator
drastically altered. Rather than a Mortmere curiosity, the narrator becomes a human being. As Dennis Altman comments,
Isherwood as an older man "is less afraid to reveal both lust
and pain."[6]

In *The World in the Evening,* for the first time, Isherwood
begins to probe the perilous dilemma of the homosexual in an
intolerant society. He gamely attempts to draw Bob Wood, Dr.
Charles Kennedy, and Michael Drummond as complex human
beings who are also homosexuals. Their loneliness and aliena-
tion are unmerited: they suffer because they are different. But
like almost every other character in the book, they are cardboard figures, another series of exhibitions. Nonetheless, Isherwood's failure here shows an advance in his handling of
homosexuality: he has indeed tried to imbue them with flesh-
and-blood characteristics. They are not, at least, observed by a
cold, distant narrator, nor are they monsters of a perverse
fantasy. Like Stephen Monk, they too must learn to be alone,
that love is not dependency. Whether they learn these lessons
or not, Isherwood doesn't reveal. They are, however, Truly
Weak Men with the possibility of changing. Seeking salvation
in a malevolent society, they have not abandoned hope. No
such options existed for the early woebegone Edward Blakes
and Eric Vernons.

Bob Wood, the lover of Dr. Charles Kennedy, is Isherwood's
angry militant. His rantings, however, only torture and frus-
trate him. Guilty and schizophrenic, he regards himself as a

professional criminal. Monk's first impression of Wood calls attention to his unremitting isolation:

> What struck me chiefly about him, always, was his quality of loneliness; and this was even more apparent when he and Charles came to visit me together. When, for example, Bob was fixing our cocktails, his slim figure with its big shoulders bending over the bottles would look strangely weary and solitary, and he seemed suddenly miles away from either of us. He was like a prospector preparing a meal in the midst of the wilderness. (WE 115)

Raised as a Quaker, Bob resents the sect's wholesomeness and disregard for his plight. Moreover, with World War II imminent, Wood is tormented by his questionable draft status: should he declare himself a homosexual, a conscientious objector, or should he enlist? By novel's end he joins the Navy, declining noncombatant status because "if they declared war on the queers—I'd fight" (WE 281) and because he wants to prove that queers are fit "for their beautiful pure Army and Navy" (WE 281). How he arrives at this decision and how this resolves his conflicts Isherwood does not explore. Stephen's reflection that the style of Quaker camp would be the only possible solution to Bob's problems is painfully inadequate.

Isherwood also exposes, then overlooks, the conflicts of Dr. Charles Kennedy. In love with Wood, Kennedy informs Stephen that were Bob to join the Navy "he wouldn't know what he'd do" (WE 112). Bob joins the Navy; yet, at a dinner party before Bob's departure, Kennedy appears serene and victorious. Like Mrs. Lindsay, however, he has no reason to beam. How did he acquire this fortitude? Isherwood chooses not to tell, and the reader remains perplexed.

Michael Drummond may well be the most complex character in the novel—his predicament demands not a few fleeting pages but probably an entire novel to dramatize fully. An ex-

public school boy, a solitary Byronic adventurer, he is portrayed as an earnest young man, capable of commitment—
unlike Stephen. He falls in love with Stephen, lures him into
bed, and even confronts Elizabeth with their affair, demanding
that Stephen run away with him. But Elizabeth with preterna-
tural coolness understands Stephen well enough to realize that
he will not walk out on her. "The reasons why Stephen
wouldn't leave me for you—or anybody else—certainly aren't
ones that I can be proud of. They're actually quite humiliating—or would be, if I hadn't lived with them for so long . . ."
(WE 208).

Nonetheless, in spite of Drummond's complexity, the question arises: Why has Isherwood entangled Stephen in a homosexual affair? Certainly the reader needs no more proof of
Stephen's dependence on Elizabeth, his inability to commit
himself—all this is already evident. The question becomes
more pressing when one considers Isherwood's squeamish
handling of homosexuality. The treatment of the bed scenes is
almost coy. On the first occasion in which Stephen and Michael
approach intimacy, Isherwood, as he has so frequently done in
the past, resorts to laughter as an evasion: the bed collapses,
bells ring out:

> But this was too much for the crazy old bedstead. It back legs
> collapsed. In fact, the whole back part of the bed fell right off
> and hit the floor. And, exactly at that moment, deadening what
> would otherwise have been a crash sufficient to rouse the whole
> household, there was a tremendous clash of bells from the
> church tower.                                          (WE 190)

Michael finally bribes Stephen into bed. Clinging spread-
eagle to a precipice, while he and Stephen are on a climbing
expedition, Michael extorts a promise. Stephen pleads,

> "Oh, for God's sake, come down!"
> "What'll you give me if I do?"

"What do you want?" I asked, humoring him as if he were a
madman.

"Will you give me anything I want?"

"Anything I can—within reason."

"Do you swear that?"

"All right. If you'll come down at once."

"You've promised, remember!" Michael was gleeful with
triumph.                                    (WE 192–93)

Their first night of love-making, however, means little to Stephen—at this point in the novel he is still too self-centered to
care about anyone but himself:

> In the darkness I remembered the adolescent, half-angry
> pleasure of wrestling with boys at school. And then, later, there
> was a going even further back, into the nursery sleep of child-
> hood with its teddy bear, or of puppies or kittens in a basket,
> wanting only the warmness of anybody.          (WE 194)

Disillusioned, like Blake, by his lover's inability to live up to his
expectations, Michael joins the International Brigade. When
he and Stephen meet years later, Michael has matured into a
confident, sensitive adult; Stephen has remained the perennial
adolescent.

Ambrose in *Down There on a Visit* and George in *A Single Man*
are portraits of the homosexual at the end of his tether. Thus
far, Isherwood has tarried on the periphery of the homosexual's plight; now he is dead center. For Ambrose and George,
an island fantasy similar to the Baron von Pregnitz's is a
nightmarish reality: Ambrose actually tries to organize an
island kingdom which will be completely detached from the
world, a perverse monastery. A young man without hope, he is
one of the lost, a castaway from Isherwood's Berlin. In
George's case, the Baron's island is a state of mind. He too is
lost and isolated, but his salvation consists in his yearning to
find fulfillment. Unlike the homosexual lovers in E. M. Fors-

ter's *Maurice,* George finds his happy ending not in life but in
death. His character is shaped in the healing light of Vedanta.

 Hapless Ambrose can find no place in society. Even more
than Blake, Wood, or the other homosexual characters, he is
always in transit. At Cambridge, his room frequently ran-
sacked, he was constantly plagued and tormented:

> It made me realize that I didn't understand Cambridge or
> England at all. I might as well have been living among a lot of
> Eskimos. We just didn't make sense together. (V 112)

But Cambridge is only England in microcosm: "England's
impossible. . . . I'm never going back there. Never. Whatever
happens" (V 111). Thus Ambrose is always on the move. He
finds no home, no country, yet abhors moving: "It's *never*
because I want to! I even feel depressed when I have to leave a
hotel room, or a cabin on a boat. But they won't *let* one stay—
*anywhere*—" (V 110). "They" of course are the "completely
hateful" Enemy who want everybody "to conform to their
beastly narrow little ways of looking at things." If one is different, "one's treated as something unspeakable. And then there's
nothing for it but to leave at once—" (V 110). Without family
or friends, Ambrose determines to build his asylum according
to his own specifications. His island sanctuary is a complete
reversal of society's prejudices. There homosexuals will be in
the majority and, at first, heterosexuality will not be legal:
"there'd be too much of an outcry. One'll have to let at least
twenty years go by, until all the resentment has died down" (V
100). Meanwhile, Ambrose promises, heterosexuality will be
winked at, and even a "few bars will be opened for people with
those unfortunate tendencies, in certain quarters of the larger
cities" (V 100):

> We'll have a psychologist on hand to explain . . . that people like
> that do exist, through no fault of their own, and that we must

feel sympathy for them and try to find scientific ways of recondi-
tioning them. . . .

Women, according to Ambrose, will be far better off in his
homosexual utopia. They'll be cared for on breeding farms
and "surely, most of them would greatly prefer artificial insem-
ination, anyway?" In the final analysis, Ambrose concludes,
"women are all Lesbians, really—they take naturally to all the
ineffectual feminine messing about—cuddling and petting—
the kind of thing Ingres shows so brilliantly in that Turkish
bath painting . . . (V 100–1).

But the world cannot be evaded. Once the prostitute Maria
Constantinescu assaults Ambrose's fortress, his fantasy is pil-
laged. She usurps his power, establishes herself as absolute
ruler of the island (V 119), stays as long as she likes, then
departs. But the point has been made. For Ambrose, absolute
severance from society must be more than merely physical. A
few days later, when Christopher unwillingly wishes him farewell, Ambrose has already receded into utter nihilism. Christopher's departure fails to breach his comatose lethargy:

> His indifference shocked me out of my self-control for a
> moment. "But Ambrose," I began in dismay, "don't you—?" I
> stopped myself in time. I'd been about to say, "Don't you *care* if I
> stay or not?" Now I changed it to, "Don't you mind being alone
> here—with nobody but the boys?"
> Ambrose looked at me as if reproaching me for the stupidity
> of the question. "But one's always alone, ducky. Surely you
> know that."                                               (V 134)

The loneliness that consumes Ambrose also devours George
in *A Single Man*, Isherwood's study in forlornness. George, a
university English teacher and British expatriate, is a most
pathetic figure who, nevertheless, rises to heroism "without any
of the Sturm and Drang that pervades most homosexual fic-

tion."[7] In George, Isherwood recapitulates all of his homosexual motifs. Like the Baron, like Ambrose, George dwells on an island: his California house is sequestered from the Others by an uninviting rickety bridge. More important, George lives on a psychological island. His lover, Jim, is now dead, and he can share his grief with no one. George is Isherwood's portrait of the most lonely human being imaginable: the bereaved, middle-aged homosexual. As Dr. Kennedy feared, now that his lover has departed, George's life slowly disintegrates.

To the neighborhood kids, George "is the mean old storybook monster" (SM 20-21), his house "shaggy with ivy and dark and secret-looking." To his bourgeois neighbors, he is a homosexual, the "fiend that won't fit into their statistics" (SM 27), the hideous Gorgon, the blood-slurping, uncultured vampire, "the bad-smelling beast that doesn't use their deodorants," the unspeakable that insists, "despite all their shushing, on speaking its name" (SM 27).

In his fantasies, George, with all the hostility of Bob Wood, retaliates against his unjust treatment. Driving to San Tomas State College where he teaches, George is a Jeremiah, cursing America's insolent high-rises and puritanical campaigns against sexual deviates. He conjures bitter *recherché* schemes from Mortmere. How amusing it would be, he thinks, to spray a new high-rise with an odorant which would eventually reek like rotting corpses and drive its occupants mad; or inject a virus in the steel which would turn the metal into soft, spaghetti-like strands. How amusing to kidnap the newspaper editor responsible for the sex-deviate articles, take him to a sensational underground movie, torture him with hot pokers and pincers, and force him to "perform every possible sexual act . . . with a display of the utmost enjoyment" (SM 38).

Throughout the day, George assumes countless personae. Walking to class, he is the homosexual ogling the lithe bodies of two tennis players. At lunch with a colleague, he acts the part of the expatriate British professor, this time defending American culture against the chic slurs of a faculty wife. In class, he plays the role of the professor whose lecture on Huxley's *After Many a Summer* reveals more about his own life than about the novel:

> "So let's face it, minorities are people who probably look and act and think differently from us and have faults we don't have. We may dislike the way they look and act, and we may hate their faults. And it's *better* if we admit to disliking and hating them than if we try to smear our feelings over with pseudo-liberal sentimentality. If we're frank about our feelings, we have a safety valve; and if we have a safety valve, we're actually less likely to start persecuting. I know that theory is unfashionable nowadays. We all keep trying to believe that if we ignore something long enough it'll just vanish. . . ."          (SM 71)

As evening approaches, as well as death, and as George's loneliness intensifies, he begins to discard his masks, to confront his isolation, his tendency to despair, his fate. After class, George visits Doris, Jim's wife, who is dying of cancer in the hospital. At the sight of death, George recoils:

> This is the gate, George says to himself.
> Must I pass through here, too?
> Ah, how the poor body recoils with its every nerve from the sight, the smell, the feel of this place! Blindly it shies, rears, struggles to escape.          (SM 94–95)

Although Doris represents woman, the Enemy who once robbed George of his beloved Jim, he would not wish death even on her. Staring at her rotting body, George indulges in a Huxleyesque meditation on the flesh:

> And wouldn't you be twice as disgusted, Jim, if you could see her now? Wouldn't you feel a crawling horror to think that maybe, even then, her body you fondled and kissed hungrily and entered with your aroused flesh held seeds of this rottenness?          (SM 96)

George reads her dying as a *memento mori: "We are on the same road, I shall follow you soon"* (SM 98).

Later, George has dinner with Charlotte, whom he calls "Charley." Again woman is the homosexual's Enemy, though now, in this later book, Isherwood is neither stinging nor recriminating. In fact, Charlotte is George's feminine counterpart. Like him, an English expatriate, she has lost her husband and is alone:

> She is a lot younger than George—forty-five next birthday— but, already, like him, she is a survivor. She has the survivor's typical battered doggedness . . . she hasn't given up. (SM 120–21)

There is even a place in George's life for Charlotte. She had often served as a buffer when he and Jim had quarreled:

> How many times, when Jim and I had been quarreling and came to visit you—sulking, avoiding each other's eyes, talking to each other only through you—did you somehow bring us together again by the sheer power of your unawareness that anything was wrong?                (SM 123)

With her, for the first time in the novel, he begins to feel

> this utterly mysterious unsensational thing—not bliss, not ecstasy, not joy—just plain happiness. *Das Glueck, le bonheur, la felicidad—* they have given it all three genders, but one has to admit, however grudgingly, that the Spanish are right; it is usually feminine, that's to say, woman-created.        (SM 123)

After dinner and too many drinks, George prepares to leave; Charlotte wishes him good-by:

> "Goodnight, Geo, my love—" As they embrace, she kisses him full on the mouth. And suddenly sticks her tongue right in. She has done this before, often. It's one of those drunken long shots which just might, at least theoretically, once in ten thousand tries, throw a relationship right out of its orbit and send it

whizzing off on another. Do women ever stop trying? No. (SM 145)

Nor does George stop trying. He does not find happiness in life—he dies before he has a chance. But in George's midnight swim, his conversation with Kenny, his musings before death, Isherwood unveils the truth about George's life. His obstinate, inspired refusal to accept his loneliness, to succumb to his fate; his determination to find another Jim; his yearning for something more—all these give him kinship with Isherwood's saint, as pointed out in the preceding chapter.

In George, Isherwood has drawn a portrait not only of a saint, but also of a homosexual with whom the reader, heterosexual or homosexual, can identify. George's human struggles with loneliness, aging, and death are shared by all. Unlike many of Isherwood's very early homosexuals, creatures in a depraved fantasy, and unlike Isherwood's later homosexual abstractions, George is composed of flesh and blood. Indeed in *A Single Man* Isherwood transcends the confines of "gayness" and in doing so speaks to and for all readers. Claude J. Summers in an excellent article, "Christopher Isherwood and the Need for Community," underscores the relationship of *A Single Man* to modern fiction:

> This book, Isherwood's finest, confronts the most vital issues of contemporary fiction and of modern life. *A Single Man* offers in resolution to the problems of alienation and isolation a vision of community, of self-transcendence through universal consciousness and through involvement in the lives of others. In making concrete this resolution, the novel presents a sustained and moving portrait of male homosexual love—perhaps the most honest of such portraits in contemporary literature—and plumbs insightfully and revealingly the homosexual plight.[8]

Is *A Single Man* autobiographical? Isherwood replies: "Yes, it's a very autobiographical novel, in a way; it's true. But I must

say that if I lived the life of the principal character I would be a very unhappy person, which I'm not."[9]
Isherwood's later frankness about his personal life also accounts for a change in his style. In the last four novels, Isherwood's writing is, as always, a perfect instrument for his perceptions; but, lacking the distant I-Christopher narrator, the books contain less posturing, fewer rhetorical gestures. In *A Single Man,* the style is plain, at times even bare. The only metaphoric passages are religious—George's midnight swim and the rock-pool description. In both passages, because Isherwood is trying to communicate the mystical, he is forced to speak in imagery and parable, for, as he has written, the mystical experience can only be hinted at.

A comparison of similar scenes—one from *Goodbye to Berlin* and one from *A Single Man*—demonstrates the difference in style and tone between the early and later fiction. In *Goodbye to Berlin,* the narrator, Christopher, begins by describing his utter solitude. Here Isherwood relies heavily on triads of adjective and adverb modifiers (italicized below), usually following the word or phrase modified.

> From my window, the *deep solemn massive* streets. Cellar shops where the lamps burn all day, under the shadow of *top-heavy balconied* façades, *dirty plaster* frontages embossed with scroll-work and heraldic devices . . . soon the whistling will begin. . . . Their signals echo down the *deep hollow* street, *lascivious* and *private* and *sad.* Because of the whistling, I do not care to stay here in the evening. It reminds me that I am in a *foreign* city, *alone, far from home.* Sometimes I determine not to listen to it, pick up a book, try to read. But soon a call is sure to sound, *so piercing, so insistent, so despairingly human,* that at last I have to get up and peep through the slats of the venetian blind to make *quite* sure that it is not—as I know very well it could not possibly be—for me.     (GB 1–2)

The three groups of triple modifiers, the hint that the whistles are not for the narrator, and the pervasive melancholy of the

passage do open Isherwood to the charge of "posturing," of
not revealing but concealing. Why are the calls not for the
narrator? The reader has no idea.

In *Christopher and His Kind*, Isherwood comments that once
again he "is playing to the gallery":

> As little Mr. Lonelyheart, with nobody to whistle for him, he
> invites the sympathy of the motherly or fatherly reader. In real
> life, the whistling would only have worried Christopher on some
> occasion when a boy *was* whistling for him and he was afraid
> that Otto, who had a key, might show up unexpectedly and find
> them together and make a scene.                    (CK 58)

In the following selection from *A Single Man*, discussed in
the preceding chapter, Isherwood again describes loneliness,
but here—the I-camera device discarded—there is the use of
the second person pronoun in addressing the reader, the
vigorous participles which contrast with George's emptiness,
and the setting of the passage in the interior of the house.
These, along with the very rhythm of the sentences, communicate much more subtly and less melodramatically the "despair-
ingly human" quality of George's bereavement:

> Think of two people, living together day after day, year after
> year, in this small space, standing elbow to elbow cooking at the
> same small stove, squeezing past each other on the narrow stairs,
> shaving in front of the same bathroom mirror, constantly jog-
> ging, jostling, bumping against each other's bodies by mistake or
> on purpose, sensually, aggressively, awkwardly, impatiently, in
> rage or in love—think what deep though invisible tracks they
> must leave, everywhere, behind them!                    (SM 12)

These passages represent the two poles of Isherwood's treatment of the homosexual in his anti-myth. The one from *Goodbye to Berlin* is arch and melodramatic. George, Isherwood's
own character, might say that its enormous tragedy is that it is
all flirtation. He might address the young writer as follows: "All
. . . you ever do is flirt, and wear your blankets off one shoul-

der, and complain about motels. And miss the one thing that
might really . . . *transform your entire life —*" (SM 176). The one
from *A Single Man* is direct and honest. Here the writer has
explored more deeply both the character and himself. George
might well apply his own description to his creator: formidable
. . . inquisitorial, oracular, a man "who may shortly begin to
speak with tongues" (SM 173).

## Conclusion

# Chiefly for
# Christopher

In 1973 the London Museum held an exhibition entitled "London in the Thirties." The exhibition, which attempted "to reconstitute not only the physical appearance of London in the thirties, but the complex aspirations and attitudes of mind of Londoners of all classes and from all walks of life,"[1] featured historic photographs and posters of the period: the Jarrow Marchers ending their exhaustive trek to London; Sir Oswald Mosley haranguing crowds of British fascists; Neville Chamberlain returning from Munich with the fateful message, "peace with honour"; and the typically tragic street scenes of depression-scarred London. The exhibition also displayed the style in dress, furniture, and architecture; various mechanical gadgets; and life-sized models of the typical room in the average British house. One such room was a study containing a small sampling of the books of the time: of the sixteen books on the shelf, four were written or co-written by Christopher Isherwood.

In 1976 the National Portrait Gallery of London hosted an exhibition entitled "Young Writers of the Thirties"—a show similar in format to the earlier one, but far more specific. The program featured letters, diaries, photographs, published and unpublished manuscripts of "five writers . . . four of them poets, and all of them men who had the most profound effect on their contemporaries: Auden, Day Lewis, Isherwood, MacNeice, and Spender."[2]

"London in the Thirties" and "Young Writers of the Thirties" only confirm what most already realize: that Isherwood is an important writer of that period. But that Isherwood has not remained merely a major author of the thirties has been more slowly, cautiously, even grudgingly conceded. Most readers, whose interest in Isherwood is "partly a function of the Berlin books,"[3] press Isherwood's continuing artistic and personal development as a case against him: "After the Inferno and the Purgatorio, in fact, the Paradiso comes both as a fulfillment and as a disappointment."[4] Bruce Cook, writing for *The Critic*, discusses this unsympathetic, at times hostile, state of affairs:

> For most of us, of course, these three [*The Last of Mr. Norris, Goodbye to Berlin* and *Prater Violet*] comprise the "essential Isher-wood." Knowing them—and them alone—we can comfortably isolate him as one person of that trinity of the English Thirties, Auden-Isherwood-Spender (in alphabetical order, I suppose). That of course is what most have done; and in this they have created a sort of convenient English Lit. identity for him. . . .[5]

But Isherwood, as his career so amply demonstrates, is not so easy to grasp or to isolate. Indeed there are several Isher-woods: the Cambridge-Mortmere Isherwood, the English Isherwood of *All the Conspirators* and *The Memorial*, the Berlin Herr Issyvoo, the American Vedantist Isherwood, the recent homosexual Isherwood. To speak of him only as a member of the Auden group or only as the creator of Norris and Sally or only as a burnt-out Hindu writer turned homosexual spokesman is to miss the whole thrust of his career, of which the thirties is only a beginning and Vedanta and his recent candor its proper and rightful completion. The brash undergraduate, who fled the stuccoed suburbs and the elitist schools and journeyed through the Mortmeresque woods of his own loneliness and confusion, has emerged, neither innocent nor insolent, but remarkably sane and saving.

The charge brought against a character in Rex Warner's *The Wild Goose Chase,* a detailed rendering of the cloak-and-dagger mythology of the early Auden clique, cannot be leveled against Isherwood: "He too had aspired to cross the frontier but had been deterred by the dangers and difficulties of the enterprise."[6] Isherwood has lived in the center, or on the border, of the dangers and difficulties, the terrible Tests of our time: the Great War and its lacerating effects, from which one critic writes the world has not yet recovered;[7] its shattering aftermath; Freudianism; Marxism; pacifism; the Spanish Civil War; the Sino-Japanese War; Germany just before Hitler; the Second Great War; the religious crises of the times; the human rights movement of the seventies. One might also look at Isherwood's career from a psychological perspective, as Auden does in his comments on *Kathleen and Frank.* Auden sees Isherwood, or "Beesh" as Auden claims he was known in his public school days, as having successfully met the crises of identity, of conscience, and of integrity.[8] Yet, through all the cultural and psychological shocks, Isherwood was neither carried to political extremism, as were many others, nor to despair, which in his case would have been the option of the Truly Weak Man. Rather, as David Pryce-Jones writes, Isherwood was able to distill and communicate something an involved writer like George Orwell was apt to overlook,

that the human personality needs self-expression in other ways than purely material terms. Even if the outbreak of war sealed the disillusion of an anti-fascist writer like Isherwood by driving him off to America, at least it can be said of him that he believed in the necessity of self-realization at a time when such an ideal seemed to be discredited for good.[9]

As David Pryce-Jones reminds us, Isherwood has always focused on the personal aspects of the historical drama through which he has lived and has made the crisis of his own identity into the central stuff of his art. His was never the easy solution that these lines from Auden's "Another Time" portray:

> So many try to say Not Now,
> So many have forgotten how
> To say I Am, and would be
> Lost, if they could, in history.[10]

Isherwood has always asserted and maintained his identity in a world that operated from diverse, chiefly antagonistic values. His nine novels are nine autobiographical glimpses—blurred, darkened, partial—into a mirror. Taken together, these nine glimpses coalesce to form a reflected image of what might be called the "essential Isherwood," always investing his life with epic proportions, always creating his ironic anti-myth, the subject of which is, always, the anti-son of Kathleen and Frank. Each new frontier crossed, each new shock survived, each new revelation declared, entails a further probing and fresh articulation of the counter-myth. Though Isherwood could not revise whole novels, once published, as Auden boldly amended lines and entire poems in light of his Christianity, Isherwood, one might say, has rewritten all of his early books. In fact, one might go further and say that Isherwood wrote one novel which he constantly amended, incorporating new, original insights so that the final copy is a palimpsest recording the results of his modified interpretation of the anti-myth; or that he actually wrote a Proustian remembrance of things past with nine books, as well as three autobiographies, which organically expand and change as Isherwood matures, recalling and reliving his past.

In *The World in the Evening* and *A Meeting by the River*, Isherwood takes a second, vastly different look at the protagonist of *All the Conspiraors* and *The Memorial*, enthralled in the clutches of the evil mother and his own dull mother-ridden existence. In *Prater Violet, Down There on a Visit*, and *A Single Man*, he refocuses his camera on the isolation of the lonely observer who first appears in *The Berlin Stories*, and finds new hope and fulfillment—even if, as in the case of George *(A Single Man)*, the protagonist is not conscious of his salvation. In the light of his new maturity and insight, Isherwood curbs, softens, in some cases annuls, his repudiation of Kathleen and of the heroic father; faces and bests his neurotic fear of war; follows to the breaking point the surrealist world of Mortmere; quickens and enriches his early concepts of character and conflict; and reinvestigates the place of the homosexual in a homophobic culture. In *Christopher and His Kind*, Isherwood freely discusses his homosexuality and, thus again, offers another version of his life and anti-myth.

As the man and the myth change, so does the style. As always, Isherwood is a master, his writing exact and unclichéd, a superb medium for his observations. In the books since his conversion, the style is still masterly, but different, simpler, at times more lyrical, and, in the seventies, certainly more honest and straightforward. Isherwood's last three books—*A Meeting by the River, Kathleen and Frank*, and *Christopher and His Kind*—are based on letters and diaries. Intent on telling the truth, Isherwood seems to regard the manner of his early work as a hindrance to revelation. The writing is energetic, subtle, but compared to that of his early works, austere and unembellished. The style here is nonstyle. In these books one meets the strict and adult pen of which Auden wrote,[11] and sees realized the hope expressed in 1949 by a critic in the *Times Literary Supplement:* "What could he do if he really tried."[12]

Isherwood himself summarizes the thrust of his career in a lecture in 1963 entitled "Influences."[13] The lecture is an informal, relaxed, after-dinner affair, composed of readings from a commonplace book Isherwood has kept throughout the years, which, he says, "contains all kinds of little bits and pieces that have struck me for all kinds of various reasons and which I have copied out, and since these bits and pieces all present, directly or indirectly, 'influences' which have been exerted upon me as a writer and as a human being, I'm going to read some of these things and comment on them." Isherwood's readings and commentary graph, in bold lines, his entire career.

In this lecture, his readings from T. E. Lawrence's *Seven Pillars of Wisdom*[14] and his recollection of E. M. Forster clarify his rebellion against what he calls the classical hero and his espousal of the anti-heroic civilian virtues of E. M. Forster. In particular, Isherwood reminisces that on the day before he was to return to Germany, he and E. M. Forster spent the afternoon "talking and laughing, and even going out into the country for an expedition." Ten days later, Isherwood learned that on the day following his departure for Germany, Forster had undergone an operation about which he was told that "his chances for survival were less than twenty per-cent." Writing to Forster from Germany to ask why in the world he hadn't told him, Isherwood received this reply: "I didn't want you to be worried."

Isherwood then moves on to quote a letter from Henry James.[15] James's effect on him "was in the nature of the influence you feel from a person enormously dedicated to your craft, profession, art, what have you." Katherine Mansfield's influence was that of a truly heroic person who fought "throughout all the latter part of her life against tuberculosis." Her journal, the model for Elizabeth Rydal's letters (*The World in the Evening*), consists of "messages being sent from a sinking ship by the radio operator who never deserted it"—a metaphor

Isherwood uses in his "Waldemar" diary to describe his own doomed state of mind *(Down There on a Visit)*. Isherwood says he desired very much to suffer like Mansfield, for suffering meant experience and experience meant material about which to write. In a vocation, or *dharma* in Vedantist terms, which consists of the attempt to be aware (of which James is certainly an examplar), adversity such as Mansfield endured is a necessity, for it is "extraordinarily difficult to be aware when you're happy."

Continuing in his rambling, stream-of-consciousness, often humorous manner, Isherwood then turns to Tolstoy's "My Confession."[16] Tolstoy, Isherwood says, toward the end of his life "loved tearing down what he had built up. . . . He turned around on much that he had done, turned around on the life that he had led and held forth with passion on the virtues of the simplicity of the peasant and a kind of primitive Christianity which he preached." Though Isherwood's own conversion has not meant a tearing down of the past (at times, however, in discussing the uninvolved Berlin narrator he does seem to be "tearing down"), Isherwood has certainly looked back and even relived and passed judgment on his previous life and work. Yet, as George Woodcock writes about Aldous Huxley, conversion is not a break from the past, but a redirection of it.[17]

Using Tolstoy as a transition, Isherwood proceeds from art and artistic concerns to spiritual realities. He begins this final part of his speech by quoting a long passage from an essay by Robert Louis Stevenson, "The Lantern Bearers," drawing special attention to these lines:

> . . . And the true realism, always and everywhere, is that of the poets: to find out where joy resides, and give it a voice far beyond singing.
> For to miss the joy is to miss all.[18]

Isherwood adopts this phrase as a mantra, a kind of touchstone for his own life and writings—a far cry from the phrase

Christopher in *Prater Violet* repeats: "I am a traveler. I have no home" (PV 122). Isherwood reminds his audience that great art transcends the categories of comedy and tragedy. *The Brothers Karamazov, Moby Dick,* the plays of Tennessee Williams and of Samuel Beckett, vibrate with "a sense of extraordinary exhilaration ... a sense of vitality." This observation is repeated in an interview, four years later, in which Isherwood, when asked how he appraised himself as a writer, replied that he believed "in being a serious comic writer.... Not in the terms of the unredeemably tragic view of life, but at the same time, not in terms of screwballism. ... I think the full horror of life must be depicted, but in the end there should be a comedy which is beyond both comedy and tragedy. The thing Gerald Heard calls 'metacomedy.'"[19]

Although such a leisurely lecture would not seem to warrant a climax, Isherwood nonetheless concludes with a rousing, informal peroration. The final passage he reads is from his own scribbled notes of an unpublished conversation with Aldous Huxley. The passage is extraordinarily apt as a description of the search by Isherwood and his generation and, Isherwood would agree, of the search by every generation, for the place where joy resides:

> I came to this thing [an interest in mystical religion] in a rather curious way as a *reductio ad absurdum.* I have mainly lived in the world of intellectual life and art. But the world of knowing about things is unsatisfactory. It's no good knowing about the taste of strawberries out of a book.
>
> The more I think of art I realize that though artists do establish some contact with spiritual reality, they establish it unconsciously.
>
> Beauty is imprisoned, as it were, within the white spaces between the lines of a poem, between the notes of music, in the apertures between groups of sculpture. This function of talent is unconscious; they throw a net and catch something, though the net is trivial.

But one wants to go further; one wants to have a conscious taste of those holes between the strings of the net.

And now obviously one could never possibly give it up.

Having read this passage, Isherwood abruptly stops, permitting the final quotation to achieve its own impact. The passage seems to catch a highly-charged moment like that at the end of *Kathleen and Frank* when Isherwood, looking over his life and over the influence of Kathleen and Frank on his life, suddenly, with Prospero-like vision, glimpses the perfect harmony he has attained with his parents—or in Huxleyesque terms, detects the spaces between the many-patterned fabric of Bradshaw-Isherwood history. Though Isherwood borrows the words from Huxley, the sentiments are very much his own, for Huxley's remarks not only conclude Isherwood's lecture on literary and metaliterary influences, but also stand as a miniature apologia for his own myth and anti-myth.

Having read the passage, Isherwood steps down from the podium. For a few seconds the audience, as if consciously trying to catch the unspoken reality imprisoned within Isherwood's silence, sits hushed, even meditative, before breaking into generous applause.

# ⚞Notes⚟

## Introduction: Chiefly about Christopher

1. Isherwood's full name is Christopher William Bradshaw-Isherwood. The Bradshaw family began to call itself Bradshaw-Isherwood in 1761, when Marple Hall passed on to Nathaniel Isherwood, husband of Mary Bradshaw. Isherwood was given the
   second name "William" at his baptism, after Captain William
   Bradshaw, one of Frank's few friends, killed in the Boer War.
   Captain William Bradshaw was not a relative.
2. Wyberslegh is in the village of Disley, from which one can
   "follow the high ground up north into Yorkshire and reach
   Haworth without crossing any urban area; so Disley may claim to
   belong geographically to the land of the Brontës, although it is
   nearly forty miles from their home" (KF 255).
3. Kathleen's diary for May 9, 1911, reads: "Read Christopher
   Lamb's version of Midsummer Night's Dream, he had seen
   pictures of the play in the illustrated papers and anything to do
   with plays he is wild about" (KF 352).
4. Christopher Isherwood, Foreword to "The Railway Accident,"
   by Allen Chalmers (Edward Upward) in *New Directions in Prose*

*and Poetry,* ed. James Laughlin, XI (New York: James Laughlin, 1949), 84.

5. C. Day Lewis, "Letter to a Young Revolutionary," in *New Country,* ed. Michael Roberts (London: Hogarth Press, 1933), p. 25.

6. C. Day Lewis, *The Buried Day* (London: Chatto and Windus, 1960), p. 85.

7. G. H. Bantock, "The Novels of Christopher Isherwood," in *The Novelist as Thinker,* ed. B. Rajan (London: D. Dobson, 1947), p. 47.

8. David Pryce-Jones, "Isherwood Reassessed," *Time and Tide,* XLI (October 1, 1960), 1162.

9. Cyril Connolly, Introduction to *All the Conspirators,* by Christopher Isherwood (London: Traveller's Library, 1939).

10. Cyril Connolly, *Enemies of Promise and Other Essays* (1938; rpt. New York: Macmillan Company, 1948), p. 74.

11. Cyril Connolly, *The Modern Movement* (London: Andre Deutsch and Hamish Hamilton, 1965), p. 80.

12. John Lehmann, *New Writing in Europe* (Harmondsworth, Middlesex, England: Penguin Books, 1940), pp. 46–56.

13. David Garnett, "Books in General," *The New Statesman and Nation,* XVII (March 11, 1939), 362.

14. "Isherwood and I met on the doorstep. He is a slip of a wild boy: with quicksilver eyes: nipped: jockeylike. That young man [sic], said S. Maugham, 'holds the future of the English novel in his hands.'" (Virginia Woolf, *A Writer's Diary,* ed. Leonard Woolf [London: Hogarth Press, 1972], pp. 306–7.)

15. Cyril Connolly, "Comment," *Horizon,* I (February 1940), 69.

16. John Lehmann, *In My Own Time* (Boston: Little, Brown and Company, 1969), pp. 284–85.

17. Ibid., p. 241.

18. Stephen Spender, *World Within World* (New York: Harcourt, Brace and Company, 1951), p. 269.

19. John Lehmann, *In My Own Time,* p. 233.

20. G. H. Bantock, "The Novels of Christopher Isherwood," p. 46.

21. Jacob Isaacs' six lectures were delivered on the Third Programme of the BBC in September and October, 1950, and printed as spoken in *An Assessment of Twentieth Century Literature* (London: Secker and Warburg, 1951). Isaacs' statement that Isherwood's talent may have burned itself out can be found on p. 173 (lecture VI).

22. V. S. Pritchett, "Books in General," *The New Statesman and Nation*, XLVII (June 19, 1954), 803.

23. Kingsley Amis, "Book Notes," *Twentieth Century*, CLVI (July 1954), 87–89. Amis concludes his review on this note: "And that dazzling carrer which was going to justify on its own the whole of the contemporary English novel—all that reminds us of that is a couple of blazing descriptions of the feeling of being in love, a 'Starnese' fantasy or so, a few jokes: the last sparks of the rocket-burst which tells us that all that is left is the stick."

24. Thom Gunn, "Book Reviews," *The London Mazazine*, I (October 1954), 81–85.

25. "Behind the Film," *Times Literary Supplement*, June 1, 1946, p. 257.

26. Richard Mayne, "The Novel and Mr. Norris," *Cambridge Journal*, VI (June 1953), 561–70.

27. Jean Weisgerber, "Les Romans et Récits de Christopher Isherwood," *Revue de l'Université de Bruxelles*, X (July–September 1958), 371.

28. Hena Maes-Jelinek, "The Knowledge of Man in the Works of Christopher Isherwood," *Revue des Langues Vivantes*, XXVI (1960), 360.

29. Hena Maes-Jelinek, *Criticism of Society in the English Novel Between the Wars* (Paris: Société d'Éditions, 1970), pp. 449–71.

30. Julian Symons, *The Thirties: A Dream Revolved* (London: Cresset Press, 1960), p. 25.

31. Justin Replogle, "The Gang Myth in Auden's Early Poetry," *Journal of English and German Philology*, LXI (1962), 481–95.

32. Dilys Powell, *Descent from Parnassus* (London: Cresset Press, 1934), p. 179.

33. Cyril Connolly, *Enemies of Promise*, p. 70.

34. Christopher Isherwood, ed., *Great English Short Stories* (New York: Dell Publishing Company, 1957), p. 9.

## Chapter 1: Mothers and Sons

1. G. W. Stonier, a contemporary reviewer, charges that "the mother is the one unfocused point of the play." (*The New Statesman and Nation*, XVIII [July 1, 1939], 35.) The *Times* reporter,

reviewing the production in which Alec Guinness plays Ransom, asserts that the symbolism of the mother "fails to declare itself . . ." and that generally the play lacks unity "for the plain reason that its implications have not been fully thought out, selected and assembled." (The *Times,* June 28, 1939, p. 12.)

2. Alan Wilde views the book as "the angriest of Christopher Isherwood's novels, a gesture of defiance on the part of its younger characters and its author . . ." (*Christopher Isherwood* [New York: Twayne Publishers, Inc., 1971], p. 27). Wilde stresses the author's youthful rebellion to the point, I think, of underplaying Isherwood's basically balanced attack against all that is spurious in *both* generations.

3. Christopher Isherwood, trans., *The Intimate Journals of Charles Baudelaire* (1930; rpt. Hollywood: Marcel Rodd, 1947), p. 81.

4. Christopher Isherwood, "Translator's Preface," *Baudelaire,* p. 7.

5. Cyril Connolly, Introduction to *All the Conspirators* by Christopher Isherwood (1928; rpt. Traveller's Library, London: Jonathan Cape, 1939).

6. "Books," *The Sphere,* July 21, 1928, p. 138.

7. The reviewer for the *Times Literary Supplement,* June 14, 1928, writes of it: "The little there is is done fastidiously, neatly, charmingly, and with a sense sharpened by what appears to be the influence of Mr. E. M. Forster, of what can be done without underlining and over emphasis" (p. 452). To quote another review, twenty-six years after the *Times* review, Angus Wilson refers to *All the Conspirators* as "a slight but admirable first novel *à la Forster.*" ("The New and the Old Isherwood," *Encounter,* III [August 1954], 67.) In *Lions and Shadows* Isherwood himself writes that his "'thought-stream' passages in the fashionable neo-Joyce manner . . . yielded nothing, in obscurity, to the work of the master himself" (LS 258). And in his introduction to the New Directions edition of *All the Conspirators,* he again acknowledges his youthful aping of the Joycean interior monologue.

8. The reviewer continues: "Mr. Isherwood has collected various parts of a machine but he has not succeeded in putting them together." (The *Times Literary Supplement,* June 14, 1928, p. 452.) This use of mechanical imagery certainly resonates with Isherwood's own idea of the novel at that time: "I imagined a novel as a contraption—like a motor bicycle, whose action depends upon the exactly co-ordinated working of all its interrelated parts . . ." (LS 259).

9. John Lehmann, *New Writing in Europe* (Harmondsworth, Middlesex, England: Penguin Books, 1940), p. 48.

10. Philip Larkin, "Poetry of Departures," 11. 7–8, in *The Less Deceived* (New York: St. Martin's Press, 1965), p. 34.

11. W. H. Auden, "XXII," 11. 27–28, in *Poems* (London: Faber and Faber, 1930), p. 68.

12. Colin Wilson, "An Integrity Born of Hope: Notes on Christopher Isherwood," in *Twentieth Century Literature*, XXII (October 1976), 317.

13. Louis MacNeice, "Happy Families," 11. 1–6, in *The Collected Poems of Louis MacNeice*, ed. E. R. Dodds (London: Faber and Faber, 1966), p. 8.

14. John Lehmann, *New Writing in Europe*, p. 48.

15. "Books," *The Sphere*, p. 138.

16. Horace Walpole, "Books I Have Liked Best Since the War—A Symposium," *The Sunday Times*, November 12, 1933, p. iii.

17. Cyril Connolly, Introduction to *All the Conspirators*.

18. Christopher Isherwood, rev. of "Janet Fergus," *Perilous Privilege*, *The Listener*, XIV (October 9, 1935), 629.

19. Cyril Connolly, *Enemies of Promise and Other Essays* (New York: Macmillan Company, 1948), pp. 12 and 18.

20. William Makepeace Thackeray, *Vanity Fair* (New York: Random House, 1955), p. 431.

21. James Joyce, *Dubliners* (New York: Viking Press, 1972), p. 36.

22. Emily Dickinson, "No. 712," in *The Poems of Emily Dickinson*, ed. Thomas H. Johnson (Cambridge: Belknap Press, 1951), II, 546.

23. Jean Weisgerber praises Mary as *"une femme 'saine,' lucide et énergique qui se réalise dans le présent, librement et pleinement. . . . C'est un être au 'coeur pur,' donce heureux."* ("Les romans et récits de Christopher Isherwood," *Revue de l'Université de Bruxelles*, X [juillet-sept. 1958], 366.) Hena Maes-Jelinek concurs with Weisgerber: "Mary is above social conventions of any kind. Hardship and experience have made her tolerant and understanding. She lives in the present, free from the burden of tradition and beyond the needs of new conventions. . . . She stands on her own firm ground. She takes people for what they are and her relationships with them are strictly personal. That is why she is accepted and even appealed to by everyone." ("The Knowledge of Man in the Works of Christopher Isherwood," *Revue des Langues Vivantes*, XXVI [1960], 345.) Ten years later Maes-Jelinek reiterates this positive support of Mary: "She is truly

'pure in heart' and has always acted according to her nature."
(*Criticism of Society in the English Novel Between the Wars* [Paris:
Société d'Éditions, 1970], p. 457.) Alan Wilde summarizes the
case *against* Mary: "Certain things about Mary immediately
strike the wrong note, if one regards her as the ideal: the failure
of her marriage, her resentment against men, the oversophistica-
tion that Eric notices, the ironic manner that both her daughter
Anne and Lily comment upon, the air of contrivance about the
almost chaotic freedom of her life. There . . . is . . . a quality of
overreaction in Mary, which leads more easily to the subversion
of Vernon ideals than to genuine involvement in life." (*Christopher Isherwood*, p. 42.)

24.    E. M. Forster, *Howards End* (New York: Random House Inc.,
Vintage Books, 1921).

25.    W. H. Auden, "Paid on Both Sides," in *Poems* (London: Faber
and Faber, 1930), p. 25.

26.    Some critics receive Eric's efforts in a kinder light. Lloyd Morris
writes: "Eric Vernon is a solitary exception to the general spectacle of frustration and futility." ("Englishman in a Dissolving
World," *New York Herald Tribune Weekly Book Review*, January 5,
1947, p. 6.) David Pryce-Jones interprets Eric as generally successful in "loosening the ties that go with the Elizabethan country
houses . . . even to the length of shocking his mother with his
communist views." ("Isherwood Reassessed," *Time and Tide*, XLI
[October 1, 1960], 1162.) Hena Maes-Jelinek summarizes the
optimistic views of Eric's conversion: "His conversion to Catholicism gives him the feeling of security he has always craved for: it
illustrates the longing for stability and order characteristic of the
men of Isherwood's generation." (*Criticism of Society in the English
Novel Between the Wars*, p. 458.) In opposition to their views is
Alan Wilde's: "The irony is overwhelming: Eric is in full flight
back to authority, to exactly the force, now in intensified form,
from which he has been fleeing and against which he has been
revolting." (*Christopher Isherwood*, p. 48.)

27.    Thom Gunn, "Book Reviews," *The London Magazine*, I (October
1954), 83.

28.    Ibid.

29.    Kingsley Amis, "Book Notes," *The Twentieth Century*, CLVI (July
1954), 88.

30.    Angus Wilson, "The New and the Old Isherwood," *Encounter*,
III (August 1954), 64-65.

31. Katherine Mansfield, *Journals of Katherine Mansfield*, ed. J. Middleton Murry (New York: Alfred A. Knopf, 1941), pp. 135–36.
32. V. S. Pritchett, "Books in General," *The New Statesman and Nation*, XLVII (June 19, 1954), 803.
33. Thom Gunn, "Book Reviews," 85.
34. Edwin Muir, "The Natural Man and the Political Man," *New Writing and Daylight*, I (Summer 1945), 7–15.
35. John Lehmann, *In My Own Time* (Boston: Little, Brown and Company, 1969), p. 325.
36. Edwin Muir, "The Natural Man and the Political Man," p. 7.
37. Ibid. 38. Ibid., p. 14. 39. Ibid.
40. Katherine Mansfield, *Journals of Katherine Mansfield*, p. 248.

## Chapter 2: Fathers and Sons

1. Jacob Isaacs, *An Assessment of Twentieth Century Literature* (London: Secker and Warburg, 1951), pp. 169–70.
2. Christopher Isherwood, *An Approach to Vedanta* (Hollywood: Vedanta Press, 1963), p. 7.
3. Daniel Halpern, "A Conversation with Christopher Isherwood," *Antaeus*, XIII–XIV (Spring-Summer 1974), 370.
4. Christopher Isherwood, ed., *Great English Short Stories* (New York: Dell Publishing Company, 1957), p. 185.
5. Henry Green, *Pack My Bag* (London: Hogarth Press, 1940), p. 33.
6. Because he was less than four years old when his father was reported missing, Richard Isherwood, unlike his brother, had no memory of Frank to embroider. Frank had not told him stories and "drawn drawings for him and taught him the magic of make-believe" (KF 503). Isherwood writes that "in 1968 Richard read some of Frank's letters which Christopher had just copied. They astonished him, he said; they made Frank seem like somebody quite different—a human being, in fact. Richard was glad to have Frank and the Hero-Father finally disentangled from each other in his mind; but he couldn't be expected to feel strongly about him as a person" (KF 503).
7. Christopher Isherwood, "What Vendanta Means to Me," in *What Vedanta Means to Me, a Symposium*, ed. John Yale (New

York: Doubleday and Company, 1960), pp. 44–58. Isherwood's essay was first published in *Vedanta and the West*, XIV (September-October 1951), 152–60. Later, Isherwood expanded the article into a pamphlet of seventy-two pages, *An Approach to Vedanta*. This pamphlet was also first published in *Vedanta and the West*, CLXI (May–June 1963), 5–72. To avoid a plethora of footnote references, when quoting from Isherwood's chapter in John Yale's symposium, I will place the page number in parentheses following the quotation.

8. Contrasting himself to Huxley, Isherwood says: "I think we're the most dissimilar creatures alive. I'm very fond of Huxley personally and we've been friends now for about twenty years. But Aldous, in the first place, is an intellect, and I'm a purely intuitive person." ("A Conversation on Tape," *The London Magazine*, I [June 1961], 54.) In the same interview, when asked if pacifism is a difficult position to maintain, Isherwood responds by stressing his intuitive nature: "I don't feel that it is a difficult position, as far as I'm concerned, to maintain, because I don't bother about justifying it with a tremendous lot of intellectual reasoning: I just *know* that I personally ought to do this." ("A Conversation on Tape," *The London Magazine*, 57.)

9. Foreseeing that many critics might scoff at his conversion as a drowning man's desperate grasping at the nearest straw, Isherwood retorts, "Can one keep afloat for twenty-three years on a straw?" (*An Approach to Vedanta*, p. 72.)

10. Gerard Manley Hopkins, "No. 64" ("Carrion Comfort"), ll. 1–2, in *The Poems of Gerard Manley Hopkins*, eds. W. H. Gardner and N. H. MacKenzie (New York: Oxford University Press, 1967), p. 99.

11. Carolyn G. Heilbrun, "Christopher Isherwood: An Interview," *Twentieth Century Literature*, XXII (October 1976), 262.

12. Romain Rolland, *The Life of Vivekananda and the Universal Gospel*, trans. E. F. Malcolm-Smith (Mayavati, Almora, Himalayas: Adraita ashrama, 1947), p. 3.

13. In his essay, Isherwood also mentions three "more or less incidental considerations which, nevertheless, played an important part in my acceptance of Vedanta" (58). Vedanta's contemporaneity: "Its latest exemplars . . . had lived so recently"; its small, non-political nature; and its language: "I liked Vedanta because it talked Sanskrit. I do not mean that I am a lover of the obscure

and exotic; quite the reverse. But I was suffering, at the period of my first acquaintance with Vedanta, from a semantic block against the words which were associated with my Christian upbringing: God, savior, comforter, soul, heaven, redemption, love, salvation, etc., etc. To some of these, indeed, my reaction was so violent that I would wince and clench my fists whenever they were uttered. I could only approach the subject of mystical religion with the aid of a brand-new vocabulary. Sanskrit supplied it. Here were a lot of new words, exact, antiseptic, uncontaminated by use in bishops' sermons, schoolmasters' lectures, politicians' speeches. To have gone back along the old tracks, to have picked up the old phrases and scraped them clean of their associations—that job would have been too disgusting for a beginner. But now it wasn't necessary. Every idea could be made over, restated in the new language" (56–57). In the same collection, John van Druten, a friend of Isherwood who cast *The Berlin Stories* into a Broadway play, *I Am a Camera*, has no such language blockage. In fact, van Druten first felt deterred by Sanskrit: "It had, for me, the scars of being a ritualistic Oriental religion, full of Sanskrit words. These deterred me as a kind of exotic mumbo jumbo, as they seem to have attracted Mr. Isherwood by the lack of empty Christian pious phraseology" (62). Van Druten had no Christian upbringing and therefore no prejudice against traditional Christian words and symbols.

14. Reminiscing on his relationship with Isherwood, Berthold Viertel writes that he is indeed the model for Bergmann and that Isherwood sent him "the completed manuscript asking if I had any objections to its publication. I raised none. It was too good a book not to be printed." (Berthold Viertel, "Christopher Isherwood and Dr. Friedrich Bergmann," *Theatre Arts*, XXX [May 1946], 295.)

15. Diana Trilling, "Fiction in Review," *Nation*, CLXI (November 17, 1945), 530–31.

16. James T. Farrell, *Literature and Morality* (New York: Vanguard Press, Inc., 1947), p. 125. David Dempsey's view is similar to Farrell's: "If I were asked to define, in a sentence, what *Prater Violet* is about, I think my answer would be that it concerns the inability of the moral man to live truthfully in relation to this time." ("Connolly, Orwell and Others: An English Miscellany," *The Antioch Review*, VII [Spring 1947], 148.)

17. Richard Mayne, "The Novel and Mr. Norris," *Cambridge Journal,* VI (June 1953), 563.

18. In actual fact, Viertel has the highest praise for Isherwood's talent as a script writer: "I had the good luck to find," he writes, "in Christopher Isherwood, a so-called highbrow, a dialogue writer of unusual finesse and tenderness." ("Christopher Isherwood and Dr. Friedrich Bergmann," *Theatre Arts,* 295.)

19. Virginia Woolf argues that the writers of the thirties were no longer in an ivory tower, but, nonetheless, because of superior education and talent, were still not part of the masses: hence, they were in a tower, but a leaning one. ("The Leaning Tower," in *The Moment and Other Essays* [London: Hogarth Press, 1952], pp. 128–54.)

20. Diana Trilling, "Fiction in Review," 530.

21. Swami Aseshananda, "Meditation According to the Upanishads," in *Vedanta for Modern Man,* p. 292.

22. Walter Bernstein, "A Novelist's Search for Truth in the Malaise of the Thirties," *New York Times Book Review,* October 28, 1945, p. 3.

23. Quoted by F. O. Matthiessen, *The Achievement of T. S. Eliot* (New York: Oxford University Press, 1958), pp. 89–90.

24. Eliot, as quoted by F. O. Matthiessen in *The Achievement of T. S. Eliot,* defines the "auditory imagination": "the feeling for syllable and rhythm, penetrating far below the conscious levels of thought and feeling, invigorating every word; sinking to the most primitive and forgotten, returning to the origin and bringing something back, seeking the beginning and the end. It works through meanings, certainly, or not without meanings in the ordinary sense, and fuses the old and obliterated and the trite, the current, and the new and surprisingly, the most ancient and the most civilized mentality. Arnold's notion of 'life,' in his account of poetry, does not perhaps go deep enough" (p. 81).

25. Christopher Isherwood and Swami Prabhavananda, trans., *The Song of God: Bhagavad-Gita* (New York: New American Library, a Mentor Religious Classic, 1954), p. 63.

26. Diana Trilling, "Fiction in Review," pp. 531–32.

27. "Behind the Film," the *Times Literary Supplement,* June 1, 1946, p. 257. The writer goes on to say that this new promise of Isherwood "may not be fulfilled within the field of fiction."

28. Christopher Isherwood, lecture, "The Autobiography of My Books," Part III, delivered at the University of California at Berkeley, May 8, 1963.

29. In *Christopher and His Kind*, Isherwood analyzes his relationship with Viertel in terms of sexuality. Viertel, he says, needed a victim, "a willing victim and a victim who could thrive on victimization. My theory is that Viertel's ideal victim could only have been a male homosexual—and not just any male homosexual but one who, like Christopher, was able to enjoy both the *yang* and the *yin* role in sex" (CK 153).

30. Clifford Solway, "An Interview with Christopher Isherwood," *The Tamarack Review*, X (Spring 1966), 30.

31. Oliver's description of the swami is similar to Isherwood's in *An Approach to Vedanta*: "The Swami, also, I found to be small and impressive. Not formidable. Not in the least severe or hypnotic or dignified. But very definitely and unobtrusively one who had the authority of personal experience. Outwardly he was a Bengali in his middle forties who looked at least fifteen years younger, charming and boyish in manner, with bold straight eyebrows and dark wide-set eyes. He talked in a gentle, persuasive voice. His smile was extraordinary—so open, so brilliant with joy that it had a strange kind of poignancy which could make your eyes fill suddenly with tears" (pp. 26–27).

## Chapter 3: The Idea of War

1. "Journey to a War," *The Times*, March 17, 1939, p. 10.

2. Evelyn Waugh, "Mr. Isherwood and Friend," *The Spectator*, CLXII (March 24, 1939), 496–98.

3. Concerning his trip to China, Isherwood writes in another place: "As a matter of fact, our visit to wartime China did me a great deal of good. First, it reduced my neurotic fear of War in the abstract. True, our journey through the combat zone wasn't really very dangerous. I think there were only three or four occasions on which we were at all likely to have been killed by bombs or bullets. But a very little danger will go a long way,

psychologically. Several times I was afraid, but only healthily afraid. I now no longer dreaded some unknown horror, or feared that I should behave much worse than other people in the same circumstances.

"Secondly, the visit to China brought me back from a world of political principles to a world of human values which I had temporarily lost. In China I saw boys in their early teens who had been conscripted to serve in the front-line trenches. I saw corpses of old men and women killed in an air raid. I smelled the rotting bodies of wounded soldiers dying of gas gangrene. War starts with principles but it ends with people—people who have usually little or no interest in the principles. This was an obvious fact which I had been overlooking; and nothing hits you harder than the obvious, when you suddenly become aware of it."(*An Approach to Vedanta* [Hollywood, California: Vedanta Press, 1963], p. 9.)

4. D. H. Lawrence, *Kangaroo* (New York: Viking Press, 1968), p. 221.

5. E. M. Forster, *The Development of English Prose Between 1918 and 1939* (Glasgow: Jackson, Son and Company, 1945), p. 6.

6. George A. Panichas, ed., Introduction to *Promise of Greatness* (New York: John Day Company, 1968), p. XXV.

7. Robin Skelton, ed., Introduction to *Poetry of the Thirties* (Harmondsworth, Middlesex, England: Penguin Books Ltd., 1971), p. 17.

8. Richard Aldington, *Death of a Hero* (New York: Covici-Friede, Inc., 1929), p. 28.

9. Robert Graves and Alan Hodge, *The Long Week-end* (1940; rpt. Harmondsworth, Middlesex, England: Penquin Books Ltd., 1971), p. 26. Graves and Hodge describe this "Memorial Craze" in more detail: "The war had now to be solidly commemorated by public subscription. Plans were made for the organization of vast war cemeteries in France, and in every village in England the problem of the local war memorial was raging—where should it be placed? What form should it take—statue, obelisk, or cross? Could the names of all the dead be inscribed on it? Or would it not be more sensible to use the money collected for a recreation ground and engrave the names on an inexpensive plaque in the church? So great was the demand for war-memorial designs and so puzzled were committees as to where they

should go for them that the Medici Society inserted a full-page disclaimer in the weekly journals: 'In view of the daily enquiries for price-lists, catalogues, etc., of Memorials, the Medici Society begs to repeat that it does *not* supply "stock designs," *nor* issue price-lists or catalogues of Memorials." (*The Long Week-end,* p. 26.)

While Isherwood attended Cambridge he could well have read the following copy in *The Cambridge Review*: "That part of the War Memorial of Fitzwilliam Hall . . . which consists in the purchase of the Playing Field by subscriptions, has now been completed. A tablet of Hopton Stone . . . has been placed at the entrance to the field with the inscription: 'To the forty-three from Fitzwilliam Hall who fell in the Great War this field is dedicated by their successors, 1923.' Two War Memorial Exhibitions are still in process of endowment." (*The Cambridge Review,* XLIV [May 18, 1923], 357.)

10. Isherwood was literary editor of *The Reptonian* in 1922, his sixth form year. Victor Gollancz, former master at Repton, remembers *The Reptonian* as "the usual parish affair, with lists of academic and athletic distinctions, an occasional letter from some distinguished O. R., and maybe a potted sermon: printed, you can be sure (though I don't remember), on that smooth shiny paper known as 'imitation art.'" (*More For Timothy* [London: Camelot Press Ltd., 1953], p. 264.)

11. *The Reptonian* sketches the Repton War Memorial as follows: "The Cross stands 17 feet high in the centre of the Garth and is made of Clipsham Stone. It bears on the western panel a representation of the Crucifixion and on the eastern panel a representation of the Resurrection. On the two side niches are figures of St. Guthlac and St. Wystan. Round the base in very beautiful lettering is the following inscription:

AD LAUDEM DEI / ET IN HONOREM / FRATRUM QUI / MORTE OBITA

SALUTEM NOBIS / SIBI GLORIAM / COMPARAVERE / MCMXIV—XVIII.

The tablet bearing the names is of Hopton Wood Stone; the panes are polished with the names cut in and painted: round the panels is a carved border, and at the top the words: These Died for England 1914–1918. To the left and right are coloured reproductions of the School Arms and the Seal of the Priory." ("The Memorial," *The Reptonian,* XLVI [December 1922], 8–9.)

12. Giles and Esmond Romilly view the public school man from another point of view: "Thus, in criticizing the public schools, it is essential to bear in mind the part they play in relation to capitalist society, to see how all their teaching, the emphasis on games, for instance, is conditioned by the economic motives of the middle class. The aim is to produce a being so indoctrinated as to be fitted to maintain their ascendancy. Within these limits it is possible to produce, on occasions, a very fine man, the best type of English civil servant, for instance. But people who no longer think British imperialism, with its attendant misery and starvation, worth the price, will agree that a disastrous lot is left out. The English public school man is famous for his Philistinism all over Europe." (*Out of Bounds. The Education of Giles Romilly and Esmond Romilly* [London: Hamish Hamilton Ltd., 1935], pp. 96–97.) To such youthful observers from within the system, it is loyalty to Philistinism that obelisks and memorials commemorate.

13. "The Memorial Service," *The Reptonian*, XLVI (December 1922), 6–8.

14. "The Dedication of the War Memorial," *The Reptonian*, XLVI (December 1922), 2–5.

15. "Editorial," *The Reptonian*, XLIV (March 1920), 297–98.

16. D. H. Lawrence, *Kangaroo*, p. 226.

17. Isherwood remembers medical school as a nightmare: "At the beginning of October, 1928, I began my career as a medical student—not without the darkest misgivings. It was like starting school all over again, not as the prize scholar, the scholarship candidate, but as the backward, overgrown boy who finds himself left behind in the infants' class. Nearly all my fellow students had just passed out of their public schools; I was five or six years older than any of them—amidst those pink unfinished faces I felt like a man of forty. Nor was it any good my trying to imagine myself their superior on account of my advanced years; in the one essential subject I knew far less than they did. At school, I had done little or no science, my mathematics were disgraceful, chemistry I had never even touched. The hospital authorities had assured us that no preliminary knowledge was necessary; the courses would all start from the letter A. But the fact remained that my fellow students were merely covering familiar ground, while I was setting out, alone, into an unknown country" (LS 284).

18. In *Before the Deluge,* a portrait of Berlin in the twenties, Otto Friedrich describes *Die goldenen zwanziger Jahre,* the golden twenties: "the magic names keep recurring—Marlene Dietrich, Greta Garbo, Josephine Baker, the grandiose productions of Max Reinhardt's 'Theatre of the 5,000,' three opera companies running simultaneously under Bruno Walter, Otto Klemperer, and Erich Kleiber, the opening night of *Wozzeck,* and *The Threepenny Opera.* . . . Almost overnight, the somewhat staid capital of Kaiser Wilhelm had become the center of Europe, attracting scientists like Einstein and von Neumann, writers like Auden and Isherwood, the builders and designers of the Bauhaus School, and a turbulent colony of more than fifty thousand Russian refugees. Vladimir Nabokov gave tennis lessons here, and young daredevils forced their cars to more than a hundred miles an hour on the new Avus speedway, and ladies in evening dress would proceed directly from the theatre to the pandemonium of the six-day bicycle races. Berlin's nightclubs were the most uninhibited in Europe; its booted and umbrella-waving streetwalkers the most bizarre. Above all, Berlin in the 1920's represented a state of mind, a sense of freedom and exhilaration. And because it was so utterly destroyed after a flowering of less than fifteen years, it has become a kind of mythical city, a lost paradise." (*Before the Deluge* [New York: Harper and Row, 1972], pp. 19–20.) Friedrich does, however, qualify his hymn to Berlin: "The twenties were not golden for everyone, of course, for these were the years of the great inflation, of strikes and riots, unemployment and bankruptcy, and Nazis and Communists battling in the streets" (p. 19).

19. As a flagrant example of the older generation's hatred of Germans and Germany, *The Left Review* writes "Kipling deserves fame for the following: 'There are only two divisions in the world to-day—human beings and Germans. And the German knows it. Human beings have long ago sickened of him and everything connected with him, of all he does, says, thinks and believes.'" ("Speech at Southport, June 22, 1915," in *The Left Review,* I [October 1935], 13.)

20. Christopher Isherwood, "German Literature in English," *The New Republic,* LXXXXVIII (April 5, 1939), 254–55.

21. Interestingly enough, *The Political Imagination in Literature. A Reader,* eds. Philip Green and Michael Walzer (New York: Free Press, 1969) and *Politics Through Literature,* ed. Henry M. Hol-

land, Jr. (Englewood Cliffs, New Jersey: Prentice Hall, Inc., 1968), two recently published political science readers, include selections from "The Landauers." Green and Walzer's book keys on the persecution of Bernhard Landauer, Isherwood's "docile conformist," while Holland's work centers on the effects of Nazi policies on the Landauer family.

22. "Isherwood was one of the first prose artists of his generation to receive the full impact of Europe as the Fascist tidal wave began to roll over it, and one of the very few who neither turned their backs on the catastrophe to write of other subjects nor were deflected by it—and one must remember the enormous pressure of political persuasion that was at work at the time—into more obviously propagandist and party activities. Instead, he absorbed the whole scene into his imagination, without a single hiccup of indigestion that one can detect." (John Lehmann, *New Writing in Europe* [Harmondsworth, Middlesex, England: Penguin Books, 1940], pp. 50–51.)

23. André Chamson, "My Enemy," *New Writing,* I (Spring 1936), 73-86.

24. John Lehmann, *In My Own Time* (Boston: Little, Brown and Company, 1969), p. 157.

25. Hena Maes-Jelinek, *Criticism of Society in the English Novel Between the Wars* (Paris: Société d'Éditions, 1970), p. 463. In another section of the chapter, Maes-Jelinek states that "Isherwood never deals directly with important issues; he interprets them in concrete and personal terms" (p. 462). David Dempsey sees this interest in people and not politics as the reason for the endurance of *The Berlin Stories*: "Almost all of Isherwood's characters inhabit the same world and, roughly, the same little era.... They are part of the politics, as well as the immorality, of evil. The Communist-Nazi struggle for power, in *The Berlin Stories,* is the cross-ruff in a game which only the opportunists can win, and in which everyone, sooner or later, seeks to be an opportunist. Isherwood does not moralize this, he demonstrates it. Perhaps that is why his lost people have outlived their moral betters through fifteen years of revolution and war and remain, even after their defeat, our own spiritual contemporaries." ("Books: Connolly, Orwell and Others: An English Miscellany," *The Antioch Review,* VII [Spring 1947], 149–50). The *Times Literary Supplement* sums up Isherwood's *ars politica* as follows: "Mr. Isher-

wood expresses no opinions; he is too clever for that." ("The Huge Northern Circuit," *Times Literary Supplement,* May 23, 1952, p. 344.)

26.  W. H. Auden, "The Model," 11.21–27, in *The Collected Poetry of W. H. Auden* (New York: Random House, 1945), pp. 45–46.

27.  John Lehmann, *New Writing in Europe,* p. 47.

28.  Three prominent critics emphasize Norris' comedic side by placing him in the mainstream of renowned comic characters. For instance, G. H. Bantock calls Norris "Falstaffian" ("The Novels of Christopher Isherwood," in *The Novelist as Thinker,* ed. B. Rajan [London: D. Dobson, 1947], p. 53); Walter Allen calls him "Firbankian" (*The Modern Novel* [New York: E. P. Dutton and Company, Inc., 1964], p. 237); and Frank Kermode labels him "Dickensian" (*Puzzles and Epiphanies* [London: Routledge and K. Paul, 1962], p. 121).

29.  Otto Friedrich, *Before the Deluge,* p. 372. Concerning the few who escaped the Nazis, Friedrich writes, "The Berliners who left early were the lucky ones, or the wise ones, or simply the accidental survivors" (410).

30.  Alfred Kazin, "Leaves From Under the Lindens," *New York Times Herald Tribune Books,* March 12, 1939, p. 10.

31.  W. H. Auden, "Lullaby," 11.21–28, in *Selected Poetry of W. H. Auden* (New York: Modern Library, 1958), pp. 27–28.

32.  John Lehmann, *In My Own Time,* p. 137.

33.  Ibid.

34.  Ibid., pp. 137–38.

35.  Claud Cockburn, ed., *The Week,* CCLXXVI (August 10, 1938), 2.

36.  W. H. Auden, "A New Age," 1. 3, in *The Selected Poetry of W. H. Auden,* p. 45.

37.  T. S. Eliot, "Last Words," *The Criterion,* XVIII (January 1939), 274–75.

38.  Cyril Connolly, "Comment," *Horizon,* I (January 1940), 5.

39.  Concerning the "Waldemar" diary, Isherwood says: "That is an absolutely authentic diary—I mean the basis of it. On the other hand, you'd be astounded at how much of this is invented. If I can only have one little fact, then I start inventing." (George Wickes, "An Interview with Christopher Isherwood," *Shenandoah,* XVI [Spring 1965], 23.) Elaborating on the Munich crisis, Isherwood writes: "The autumn of 1938 was a period of confusion for all of us. There was the climax and anticlimax of

Munich. There was the tragedy of the crumbling of the Spanish Government, destroyed from within quite as much as from without; allies accusing each other of treason and the clear-seeming lines of political integrity becoming more and more distorted. There was the emerging possibility of almost indefinite Nazi expansion without general war. Clear thinking was impossible during the Munich crisis." (*An Approach to Vedanta*, [Hollywood, California: Vedanta Press, 1963], p. 9.)

40.    F. L. Lucas, *Journal Under the Terror, 1938* (Edinburgh: T. and A. Constable Ltd., 1939), p. 12.

41.    Ibid.

42.    Ibid., p. 245.

43.    W. H. Auden, "In Legend," 11.11–14, *Selected Poems*, pp. 17-18.

44.    Cyril Connolly, "Comment," *Horizon*, I (February 1940), 68.

45.    Stephen Spender, "How Shall We be Saved," *Horizon*, I (January 1940), 52–53.

46.    Cyril Connolly, "Comment," *Horizon*, I (February 1940), 69.

47.    John Lehmann, *In My Own Time*, p. 222.

48.    Ibid., p. 223.

49.    Ibid.

50.    W. H. Auden, "XVI," 11. 34–35, in *Poems* (London: Faber and Faber, 1930), p. 56.

51.    John Lehmann, *In My Own Time*, p. 223.


## Chapter 4: Mortmere

1.    Harrison Smith writes, "It would be hard to conceive of a better observation post for an inquiring and humanitarian mind than shabby, violent and morally corrupt Berlin in those days." ("Disintegrating World," *The Saturday Review of Literature*, XXIX [March 9, 1944], 11.) In a far less flattering light, G. H. Bantock states: "It is clear that the Berlin of the early 'thirties answers to much in Isherwood's termperament. The chaos of values, the tension of opposing parties, the particular moral relaxation brought about among many of its habitués through the years of uncertainty and strain that had been the lot of post-war Germany, the feeling of disillusionment which meant more a burden

lifted than a load imposed, were bound to appeal to the peculiar quality of weakness that Isherwood both consciously and subconsciously reveals." ("The Novels of Christopher Isherwood," in *The Novelist as Thinker,* ed. B. Rajan [London: D. Dobson, 1947], pp. 52–53.

2. Christopher Isherwood, Foreword to "The Railway Accident," by Allen Chalmers (Edward Upward) in *New Directions in Prose and Poetry,* ed. James Laughlin, XI (New York: James Laughlin, 1949), 85. In an excellent essay, "Laily, Mortmere and All That," Brian Finney, consulting unpublished Mortmere stories by both Isherwood and Upward, traces the development of this exotic, gloomy land of perpetual midnight (*Twentieth Century Literature,* XXII [October 1976], 286–302).

3. G. H. Bantock, "The Novels of Christopher Isherwood," in *The Novelist as Thinker,* ed. B. Rajan, pp. 47–48.

4. D. H. Lawrence, "A Letter from Germany," in *Phoenix, the Posthumous Papers of D. H. Lawrence,* ed. Edward D. MacDonald (1936; rpt. London: William Heinemann Ltd., 1961), pp. 107–8. There is some dispute about the date of Lawrence's letter. *The New Statesman and Nation,* XII (October 13, 1934), 150–54, states that the letter was written in 1928 and "shows a remarkable sensitiveness·to the trend of events in Germany at a time when Hitlerism, as we know it now, hardly existed. . . ." Edward D. McDonald, however, asserts that the letter was definitely written in 1924 and thus is all the more remarkable (p. xv).

5. Ibid., pp. 109–10. (Those whom God wishes to destroy, he first drives mad.)

6. Stephen Spender, *World Within World* (New York: Harcourt, Brace and Company, 1948), p. 43.

7. John Lehmann, *In My Own Time* (Boston: Little, Brown and Company, 1969), p. 136.

8. John Whitehead, "Christophananda: Isherwood at Sixty," *The London Magazine,* V (July 1965), 92.

9. H. H. Wollenberg, *Fifty Years of German Film* (1948; rpt. London: Falcon Press Limited, 1972), p. 16. After France comes Great Britain with 44 feature films and Poland with 17.

10. Ibid., p. 20.     11. Ibid., p. 19.

12. Paul Rotha, *The Film Till Now,* with an additional section by Richard Griffith (1949; rpt. New York: Twayne Publishers, Inc., 1963), pp. 254–56, 257, and 709.

13. Contrasting Graham Greene and Isherwood, G. S. Fraser writes: "The actual writing in Isherwood's novels is much more interesting and distinctive than that in Greene's. Greene's clipped, vivid sentences make us see what he wants us to see, but they do not convey the deeper resonances of judgment or personality. Isherwood, on the other hand, has style; any competent writer could get hold of Greene's techniques (and, in fact, many have) but the special and inimitable note of Isherwood's writing springs from his personality. The style is the man. It looks easy and simple, it is exactly like somebody talking to us, and Isherwood never seems to be taking any special pains with his writing, but at the same time there is no waste; the deceptively casual-looking sentences create the impression, convey the idea, hit the exact tone that Isherwood is aiming at." (*The Modern Writer and His World* [New York: Criterion Books, 1964], pp. 104-5.)

14. John Lehmann, *In My Own Time*, p. 201.

15. Stephen Spender defines the "terrifying mystery of cities" as follows: "This is that a great city is a kind of labyrinth within which at every moment of the day the most hidden wishes of every human being are performed by people who devote their whole existences to doing this and nothing else." (*World Within World*, p. 109.)

16. Concerning Bradshaw's discovery of his false nose, V. S. Pritchett writes: "It is a considerable moment in the history of first person narrations when Chris [*sic*] arrives at the drunken party and does not recognize his own state until he sees in a mirror that he has just walked through the streets wearing a false nose." ("Books in General," *The New Statesman and Nation*, XLIV [August 23, 1952], 213.)

17. Joseph Conrad, Preface to *The Nigger of the Narcissus* (New York: Doubleday and Company, Inc., 1947), p. xiv.

18. Naomi Bliven, "The Rueful Cameraman," *The New Yorker*, XXXVIII (September 1, 1962), 77.

19. Herbert Mitgang, "Books of the Times," *The New York Times*, March 23, 1962, p. 31.

20. William Peden, "Odyssey to Inner Being," *The Saturday Review of Literature*, XLV (March 24, 1962), 25.

21. C. Day Lewis, *The Buried Day* (London: Chatto and Windus, 1960), p. 87.

## Chapter 5: The Hero

1. C. Day Lewis, "#32," *The Magnetic Mountain,* in *Poetry of the Thirties,* ed. Robin Skelton (Harmondsworth, Middlesex, England: Penguin Books, 1971), p. 50. Lewis' poem begins, "You that love England, who have an ear for music,/ . . . Can you not hear the entrance of a new theme?" (11. 1 and 8).
2. W. H. Auden, "To a Writer on His Birthday," in *Poetry of the Thirties,* ed. Robin Skelton, pp. 167–70.
3. Isherwood was not the only undergraduate to own a motorcycle. *The Granta,* a Cambridge magazine of humor, dedicated an entire number in 1922 to motorcyclists, a group it dubbed "The Suicide Club." A year later it carried the following burlesque: "Very shortly the University will have to make a choice between two alternatives. . . . Either it will have to dynamite Cambridge . . . and then rebuild it on more generous lines with broad streets and subways . . . or it will have to decrease the number of motorcycle fiends. . . . The aim of the average motor cyclist seems to be to travel through life, causing the maximum of noise and annoyance." (*The Granta,* XXXII [May 25, 1923], 453.)
4. Christopher Isherwood, lecture, "The Autobiography of My Books," Part I, delivered at the University of California at Berkeley, April 23, 1963.
5. Hena Maes-Jelinek, *Criticism of Society in the English Novel Between the Wars* (Paris: Société d'Éditions, 1970), p. 450.
6. Christopher Isherwood, "The Hero," *Oxford Outlook,* VII (June 1925), 153–69.
7. T. S. Eliot, *The Wasteland,* 1. 18, in *Collected Poems* (New York: Harcourt, Brace and World, Inc., 1963), p. 53.
8. W. H. Auden, "Atlantis," 11. 44–48, in *Selected Poetry of W. H. Auden* (New York: Random House, 1958), p. 73.
9. Christopher Isherwood, lecture, "The Autobiography of My Books," Part II, delivered April 30, 1963.
10. "Mr. Isherwood Changes Trains," *Times Literary Supplement,* November 11, 1949, p. 727.
11. Christopher Isherwood, lecture, "The Autobiography of My Books," Part II.
12. Daniel Halpern, "A Conversation," *Antaeus* XIII–XIV (Spring–Summer 1974), 368.

13. Isherwood, "The Autobiography of My Books," Part II.

14. Christopher Isherwood, lecture, "Report on Work in Progress," delivered at the University of California at Berkeley, December 9, 1960.

15. Personal communication received by Leon Surmelian from Christopher Isherwood. Printed in *Techniques of Fiction Writing: Measure and Madness* (New York: Anchor Books, 1968), p. 81.

16. "Apologia for a Myth," *Times Literary Supplement,* March 9, 1962, p. 151.

17. Ibid.

18. "The Problem of the Religious Novel" was first published in *Vedanta and the West,* IX (March–April 1946), 61–64. Citations in the text are from *Vedanta for Modern Man,* ed. Christopher Isherwood (New York: New American Library, Inc., A Mentor Book, 1972), pp. 273–77.

19. Ibid., p. 273.   20. Ibid., p. 274.   21. Ibid.   22. Ibid.   23. Ibid., p. 275.   24. Ibid.   25. Ibid.   26. Ibid.   27. Ibid., pp. 275–76.   28. Ibid.   29. Ibid.

30. Concerning the narrative technique in *A Single Man,* Isherwood writes: "The story is told in the present tense by a non-personal seemingly disembodied narrator who never says 'I' and addresses the reader with the air of a surgeon lecturing to medical students during an operation. The 'patient' is the chief character, George. The narrator knows everything that George feels and thinks and is present with him at all times. But he is not a part of George. Indeed it will be possible for George to die while the narrator looks on and describes his death to the reader." (Leon Surmelian, *Techniques of Fiction Writing,* p. 80.) As the novel progresses, however, I think Isherwood's medical lecturer goes far beyond the bounds of case history—in fact, the surgeon reveals extensive knowledge of the spirit, and for this reason I have preferred to call him a kind of guru.

31. *The Reptonian,* XLV (March 1922).

32. George Greene, "Crying for Help," *The Commonwealth,* LXXXI (October 2, 1964), 53.

33. Cyril Connolly, *The Rock Pool* (1936; rpt. New York: Atheneum, 1968), p. 4.

34. Leon Surmelian, *Techniques of Fiction Writing,* p. 80.

35. E. M. Forster, *A Passage to India* (New York: Harcourt, Brace and World, Inc., a Harvest Book, 1952), p. 289.

36. Christopher Isherwood, rev. of Edward Upward, *"In the Thirties," Time and Tide*, XLIII (August 16, 1962), 28.

## Chapter 6: The Homosexual as Hero

1. W. I. Scobie, "Christopher Isherwood," *The Advocate*, December 17, 1975, p. 6.
2. Arthur Bell, "Christopher Isherwood: No Parades," *The New York Times Book Review*, March 25, 1973, p. 10–12. In this same interview, Isherwood continues: "But I never felt that I was concealing it [his homosexuality] as far as my own life and my own relations with other people were concerned. In the first place, over a great period of my life I lived in a domestic relationship with some other man, and we've always gone around everywhere together, and there's never been any question about that, so there's never been any question of covering up in any sort of way. That makes a difference" (p. 12).
3. Dennis Altman, *Homosexual: Oppression and Liberation* (New York: Dutton, 1971), p. 41.
4. Basil Davenport, "Atmosphere of Decay," *The Saturday Review*, XIX (April 15, 1939), 14.
5. Richard Stanley, "Isherwood," *In Touch*, XXIV (July–August 1976), 28.
6. Dennis Altman, *Homosexual: Oppression and Liberation*, p. 41.
7. Ibid., p. 40.
8. Claude J. Summers, "Christopher Isherwood and the Need for Community," to be published in *Perspectives on Contemporary Literature*.
9. Roy Newquist, *Conversations* (Chicago: Rand McNally and Company, 1976), p. 181.

## Conclusion: Chiefly for Christopher

1. John Hayes, Preface to *London in the Thirties*, by Alice Prochaska (London: Her Majesty's Stationery Office, 1973), p. 3.

2.  John Hayes, Forward to *Young Writers of the Thirties,* by Alice Prochaska (London: National Portrait Gallery), p. 4.
3.  Richard Mayne, "Herr Issyvoo Changes Trains," *New Statesman and Nation,* LXII (March 9, 1962), 338.
4.  Ibid. Asked in an interview how he felt about being "plagued" by his Berlin writings, Isherwood responded: "Everybody is plagued by something they wrote, or did, earlier. I mustn't complain about that because after all it's a great thing to be plagued by anything, to have something to be plagued by." (Clifford Solway, "An Interview with Christopher Isherwood," *The Tamarack Review,* X [Spring 1966], 29.)
5.  Bruce Cook, "The Trouble with George," *The Critic,* XXIII (October–November 1964), 65.
6.  Rex Warner, *The Wild Goose Chase* (London: Boriswood, 1937), p. 43.
7.  Benjamin Ifor Evans, *English Literature Between the Wars* (London: Methuen, 1949), p. 102.
8.  W. H. Auden, "The Diary of a Diary," *New York Review of Books,* January 27, 1972, pp. 19–20.
9.  David Pryce-Jones, "Isherwood Reassessed," *Time and Tide,* XLI (October 1, 1960), 1967.
10.  W. H. Auden, "Another Time," 11. 5–8, in *The Collected Poetry of W. H. Auden* (New York: Random House, 1945), p. 41.
11.  W. H. Auden, "To a Writer on His Birthday," 1. 82, in *Poetry of the Thirties,* ed. Robin Skelton (Harmondsworth, Middlesex, England: Penguin Books, 1971), p. 169.
12.  "Mr. Isherwood Changes Trains," *Times Literary Supplement,* November 11, 1949, p. 727.
13.  Christopher Isherwood, lecture, "Influences," delivered at the San Francisco Public Library, April 23, 1963.
14.  T. E. Lawrence, *Seven Pillars of Wisdom* (New York: Doubleday and Company, Inc., 1966), pp. 462, 469–70.
15.  Henry James, *The Letters of Henry James,* ed. Percy Lubbock (New York: Charles Scribner's Sons, 1920), I, pp. xx-xxi.
16.  Count Lev. N. Tolstoy, "My Confession," in *The Complete Works of Count Tolstoy,* trans. and ed. Leon Wiener (New York: Ams Press, 1968), XIII, 8–10 and 13–14.
17.  George Woodcock, *Dawn and the Darkest Hour* (New York: Viking Press, 1972), p. 24.

18. Robert Louis Stevenson, "The Lantern Bearers," in *Essays by Robert Louis Stevenson*, ed. William Lyon Phelps (New York: Charles Scribner's Sons, 1918), p. 314.

19. Roy Newquist, *Conversations* (Chicago: Rand McNally and Company, 1967), pp. 179-80.

# Selected

# Bibliography

## I. Works by Christopher Isherwood

*All the Conspirators.* 1928; rpt. New York: New Directions, 1958.

"The Autobiography of My Books." Lectures delivered at the University of California at Berkeley, April 23, April 30, and May 8, 1963.

*The Berlin Stories* [*The Last of Mr. Norris and Goodbye to Berlin*]. New York: New Directions, 1954.

*Christopher and His Kind, 1929–1939.* New York: Farrar, Straus and Giroux, 1976.

*The Condor and the Cows; A South American Travel Diary.* New York: Random House, 1949.

*Down There on a Visit.* New York: Simon and Schuster, 1962.

*Exhumations: Stories, Articles, Verses.* New York: Simon and Schuster, 1966.

"German Literature in English." *New Republic,* LXXXXVIII (April 5, 1939), 254–55.

*Great English Short Stories.* Ed. by Isherwood. New York: Dell Publishing Company, 1957.

"The Hero." *Oxford Outlook,* VII (June 1925), 153–69.

*How to Know God: The Yoga Aphorisms of Patanjali.* Trans., with Swami

Prabhavananda. 1953; rpt. Hollywood, California: Vedanta Press, 1962.

"Influences." Lecture delivered at the San Francisco Public Library, April 23, 1963.

*Journey to a War.* With W. H. Auden. New York: Random House, 1939.

*Lions and Shadows.* 1938; rpt. Norfolk, Connecticut: New Directions, 1947.

*A Meeting by the River.* New York: Simon and Schuster, 1967.

*The Memorial: Portrait of a Family.* 1932; rpt. Norfolk, Connecticut: New Directions, 1946.

Introduction to *Mr. Norris and I,* by Gerald Hamilton. London: Allan Wingate, 1956.

*On the Frontier.* With W. H. Auden. New York: Random House, 1939.

*Prater Violet.* New York: Random House, 1945.

Foreword to "The Railway Accident," by Allen Chalmers (Edward Upward), in *New Directions in Prose and Poetry, Number Eleven.* New York: James Laughlin, 1949.

*Ramakrishna and His Disciples.* New York: Simon and Schuster, 1965.

*Shankara's Crest-Jewel of Discrimination.* Trans., with Swami Prabhavananda. Hollywood: Vedanta Press, 1947.

*A Single Man.* New York: Simon and Schuster, 1964.

*The Song of God: Bhagavad-Gita.* Trans., with Swami Prabhavananda. 1944; rpt. New York: New American Library, 1954.

*Two Great Plays by W. H. Auden and Christopher Isherwood.* With W. H. Auden. New York: Random House, 1959.

*Vedanta for Modern Man.* Ed. by Isherwood. New York: New American Library, Inc., A Mentor Book, 1972.

"What Vedanta Means to Me," in *What Vedanta Means to Me, a Symposium,* ed. John Yale. New York: Doubleday and Company, 1960.

*The World in the Evening.* New York: Random House, 1954.

## II. Works about Christopher Isherwood

Allen, Walter. *The Modern Novel in Britain and the United States.* New York: Dutton, 1964.

"All the Conspirators." *Times Literary Supplement,* June 14, 1928, p. 452.

Amis, Kingsley. "Book Notes." *The Twentieth Century,* CLVI (July 1954), 87–89.

—— "A Bit Glassy." *The Spectator,* CVIII (March 9, 1962), 309.

Annan, Gabriele. "The Issyvoo Years." *Times Literary Supplement,* April 1, 1977, p. 401–2.

"Apologia for a Myth." *Times Literary Supplement,* March 9, 1962, p. 151.

Auden, W. H. "The Diary of a Diary." *New York Review of Books,* XVII (January 27, 1972), 17–20.

Bantock, G. H. "The Novels of Christopher Isherwood," in *The Novelist as Thinker,* ed. B. Rajan. London: D. Dobson, 1947.

"Behind the Film." *Times Literary Supplement,* September 10, 1964, p. 837.

Bell, Arthur. "Christopher Isherwood: No Parades." *New York Times Book Review,* March 25, 1973, pp. 10–14.

Bliven, Naomi. "The Rueful Cameraman." *The New Yorker,* XXXVIII (September 1, 1962), 77–80.

Connolly, Cyril. Introduction to *All the Conspirators,* by Christopher Isherwood. London: Traveller's Library, 1939.

—— *Enemies of Promise and Other Essays.* 1938; rpt. New York: Macmillan Company, 1948.

Cook, Bruce. "The Trouble with George." *The Critic,* XXIII (October–November 1964), 65–66.

Dewsnap, Terence. "Isherwood Couchant." *Critique,* XIII (1971), 31–47.

Dolbier, Maurice. "Out of a Certain Foreignness." *New York Herald Tribune Books,* March 11, 1962, p. 5.

Farrell, James T. *Literature and Morality.* New York: Vanguard Press, Inc., 1947.

Garnett, David. "Books in General." *The New Statesman and Nation,* XVII (March 11, 1939), 362.

"George and Jim." *Times Literary Supplement,* September 10, 1964, p. 837.

Greene, George. "Crying for Help." *Commonweal,* LXXXI (October 2, 1964), 51–53.

Gunn, Thom. "Book Reviews." *London Magazine,* I (October 1954), 81–85.

Halpern, Daniel. "A Conversation." *Antaeus,* XIII-XIV (Spring-Summer 1974), 366–88.

Heilbrun, Carolyn G. *Christopher Isherwood.* New York: Columbia University Press, 1970.

Heilbrun, Carolyn G., ed. "Christopher Isherwood Issue." *Twentieth Century Literature, XXII (October 1976).*

"The Huge Northern Circuit." *Times Literary Supplement,* May 23, 1952, p. 344.

"Mr. Isherwood Changes Trains." *Times Literary Supplement,* November 11, 1949, p. 727.

Kazin, Alfred. "Leaves From Under the Lindens." *New York Herald Tribune Books,* March 12, 1939, p. 10.

Kermode, Frank. *Puzzles and Epiphanies.* London: Routledge and K. Paul, 1962.

Lehmann, John. *New Writing in England.* New York: Critics Group Press, 1939.

—— *New Writing in Europe.* Harmondsworth, Middlesex, England: Penguin Books, 1940.

Maes-Jelinek, Hena. "The Knowledge of Man in the Works of Christopher Isherwood." *Revue des Langues Vivantes,* XXVI (1960), 341–60.

—— *Criticism of Society in the English Novel Between the Wars.* Paris: Société d'Éditions, 1970.

Mayne, Richard. "The Novel and Mr. Norris." *Cambridge Journal,* VI (June 1953), 561–70.

—— "Herr Issyvoo Changes Trains." *New Statesman and Nation,* LXIII (March 9, 1962), 337–38.

Nagarajan, S. "Christopher Isherwood and the Vedantic Novel, a Study of *A Single Man.*" *Ariel,* III (July 1972), 63–71.

"Naked, Not Unashamed." *Times Literary Supplement,* June 15, 1967, p. 525.

Newquist, Roy. *Conversations.* Chicago: Rand McNally and Company, 1967.

Piazza, Paul. "Isherwood: A Remembrance of Things Past." *The Washington Post,* November 25, 1976, p. C 2.

—— "So Many Isherwoods." *The Chronicle of Higher Education,* XIII (December 20, 1976), 9.

Pritchett, V. S. "Books in General." *New Statesman and Nation,* XLIV (August 23, 1952), 213–14.

—— "Books in General." *New Statesman and Nation,* XLVII (June 19, 1954), 803.

Pryce-Jones, David. "Isherwood Reassessed." *Time and Tide,* XLI (October 1, 1960), 1162–63.

Raban, Jonathan. *The Technique of Modern Fiction.* Notre Dame, Indiana: University of Notre Dame Press, 1969.

Raymond, John. "Isherwood and Powell." *Listener,* LII (December 16, 1954), 1067.

"Record of Experience." *Times Literary Supplement*, June 18, 1954, p. 389.

Scobie, W. I. "Art of Fiction: Interview." *Paris Review*, XIV (Spring 1974), 138–82.

—— "Isherwood." *The Advocate*, December 17, 1975, pp. 6–8.

Solway, Clifford. "An Interview with Christopher Isherwood." *The Tamarack Review*, X (Spring 1966), 22–35.

Spender, Stephen. "Isherwood's Heroes." *The New Republic*, CXLVI (April 16, 1962), 24–25.

Stansky, Peter. *"Christopher and His Kind." New York Times Book Review*, November 28, 1976, pp. 31–34.

Summers, Claude J. "Christopher Isherwood and the Need for Community." To be published in *Perspectives on Contemporary Literature*.

Surmelian, Leon. *Techniques of Fiction Writing: Measure and Madness*. New York: Doubleday and Company, Inc., 1969.

Thomas, David P. *"Goodbye to Berlin:* Refocusing Isherwood's Camera." *Contemporary Literature, XIII (Winter 1972)*, 44–52.

Trilling, Diana. "Fiction in Review." *Nation*, CLXI (November 17, 1945), 530–32.

Vidal, Gore. "Art, Sex and Isherwood." *New York Review of Books*, XXIII (December 9, 1976), 10–18.

Viertel, Berthold. "Christopher Isherwood and Dr. Friedrich Bergmann." *Theatre Arts*, XXX (May 1946), 295–98.

Wain, John. "Bergmann's Masterpiece." *Spectator*, CXCII (June 18, 1954), 742–43.

Waugh, Evelyn. "Mr. Isherwood and Friend." *Spectator*, CLXII (March 24, 1939), 496–98.

Weisgerber, Jean. "Les romans et récits de Christopher Isherwood." *Revue de l'Université de Bruxelles*, X (1958), 360–79.

Westby, Selmer, and Clayton M. Brown. *Christopher Isherwood: a Bibliography, 1923–1967*. Los Angeles: California State College at Los Angeles Foundation, 1968.

Whitehead, John. "Christophananda: Isherwood at Sixty." *London Magazine*, V (July 1965), 90–100.

Wickes, George. "An Interview with Christopher Isherwood." *Shenandoah*, XVI (Spring 1965), 23–52.

Wilde, Alan. *Christopher Isherwood*. New York: Twayne Publishers, Inc., 1971.

Wilson, Angus. "The New and the Old Isherwood." *Encounter*, III (August 1954), 62–68.

### III. Other Works

Altman, Dennis. *Homosexual: Oppression and Liberation.* New York: Dutton, 1971.

Auden, W. H. *The Orators.* 1932; 2d ed. New York: Random House, 1967.

—— *Poems.* Oxford: Holywell Press, 1928.

Crew, Louie, and Rictor Norton. "The Homosexual Imagination." *College English,* XXXVI (November 1974).

Evans, Benjamin Ifor. *English Literature Between the Wars.* London: Methuen and Company, 1949.

Forster, E. M. *The Development of Prose Between 1918 and 1939.* Glasgow: Jackson, Son and Company, 1945.

Fraser, G. S. *The Modern Writer and His World.* New York: Criterion Books, 1964.

Friedman, Norman. "Point of View in Fiction: the Development of a Critical Concept." *PMLA,* LXX (December 1955), 1160–84.

Fussell, Paul. *The Great War and Modern Memory.* New York: Oxford University Press, 1975.

Graves, Robert, and Alan Hodge. *The Long Week-End.* 1940; 2d ed. Harmondsworth, Middlesex, England: Penguin Books, 1971.

Green, Martin. *Children of the Sun.* New York: Basic Books, Inc., 1976.

Isaacs, Jacob. *An Assessment of Twentieth Century Literature.* London: Secker and Warburg, 1951.

Lehmann, John. *In My Own Time.* Boston: Little, Brown and Company, 1969.

Liddell, Robert. *A Treatise on the Novel.* London: Jonathan Cape, 1947.

MacNeice, Louis. *Autumn Journal.* London: Faber and Faber, 1939.

Muggeridge, Malcolm. *The Thirties.* London: H. Hamilton, 1940.

Muir, Edwin. "The Natural Man and the Political Man." *New Writing and Daylight,* I (Summer 1942), 7–15.

Panichas, George A., ed. *Promise of Greatness.* New York: John Day Company, 1968.

Replogle, Justin. "The Gang Myth in Auden's Early Poetry." *Journal of English and Germanic Philology,* LXI (July 1962), 481–95.

Roberts, Michael, ed. *The Faber Book of Modern Verse.* London: Faber and Faber, 1936.

—— *New Country.* London: Hogarth Press, 1933.

—— *New Signatures.* London: Hogarth Press, 1932.

Skelton, Robin, ed. *Poetry of the Thirties.* Harmondsworth, Middlesex, England: Penguin Books, 1971.

Spender, Stephen. *World Within World.* New York: Harcourt, Brace and Company, 1951.

Symons, Julian. *The Thirties: A Dream Revolved.* London: Cresset Press, 1960.

Woolf, Virginia. "The Leaning Tower," in *The Moment and Other Essays.* London: Hogarth Press, 1952.

# INDEX